Dimensions of Constructive Art in Brazil

Dimensions of Constructive Art in Brazil

WITH TEXTS BY
Mari Carmen Ramírez
Adolpho Leirner

The Adolpho Leirner Collection

THE MUSEUM OF FINE ARTS, HOUSTON

This catalogue was published to coincide with the exhibition *Dimensions of Constructive Art in Brazil: The Adolpho Leirner Collection,* organized by The Museum of Fine Arts, Houston, and presented May 20–September 23, 2007.

GENEROUS SUPPORT WAS PROVIDED BY:
Mr. Samuel F. Gorman
Macy's

ISBN 978-0-89090-155-7

COVER
Waldemar Cordeiro, *Idéia visível* [*Visible Idea*] (detail), 1956, wood plastered with paint, The Adolpho Leirner Collection of Brazilian Constructive Art, museum purchase with funds provided by the Caroline Wiess Law Accessions Endowment Fund, 2007.15.
PHOTO: Tom Jenkins.

WORTHAM CURATOR OF LATIN AMERICAN ART AND DIRECTOR, THE INTERNATIONAL CENTER FOR THE ARTS OF THE AMERICAS
Mari Carmen Ramírez

PUBLICATIONS DIRECTOR
Diane Lovejoy

EDITOR
Heather Brand

ICAA PUBLICATIONS AND TRANSLATIONS EDITOR
Héctor Olea

COPYRIGHT PERMISSIONS
Sonia Montoya
Joel Hernandez

DESIGN
HvADesign, New York
Henk van Assen, Amanda Bowers

PRINTING
Chas P. Young, Houston, Texas

Printed in the United States of America

Contents

View of the Caroline Wiess Law Building, designed by Ludwig Mies van der Rohe.

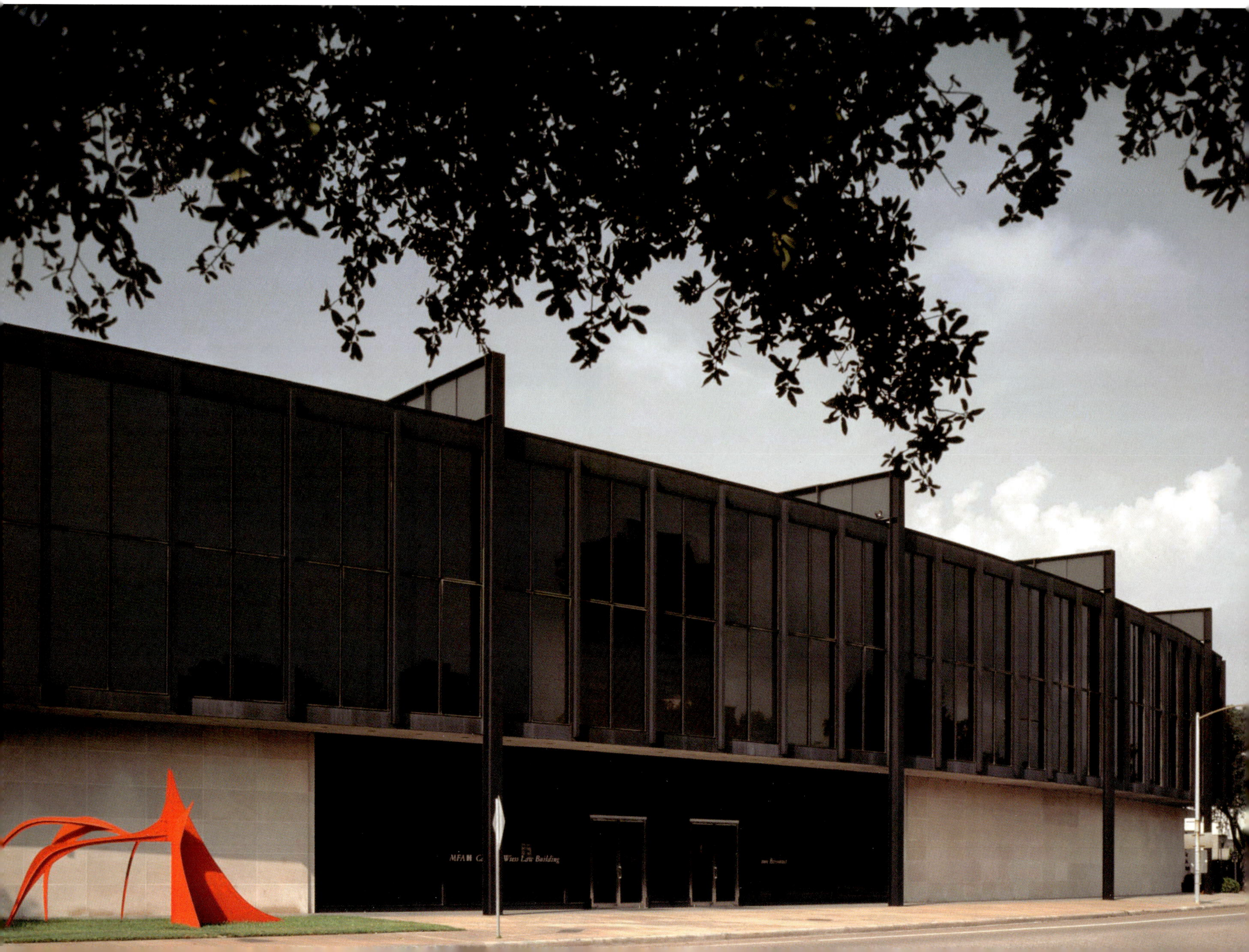

Foreword

The 1950s and 1960s were transformative decades in modern art. Just as Houstonians were embracing the exhilarating spirit that has come to be defined as "midcentury modern," so too were our neighbors in South America.

When we focus on Brazil, we see works of art that were created during periods of relative prosperity. The country's oil industry was expanding, its cities were growing, and, in 1960, its modernist capital, Brasília, was founded. As air travel became more accessible, artists crossed national boundaries to come into contact with their counterparts in New York, Paris, and elsewhere. Art, in the form of organized exhibitions, brought then-contemporary modernist works into Brazil, where they sparked dialogues and fostered new ideas.

At the same time, on the other side of the equator, Houston was also undergoing its own rapid modernization. The oil industry was booming, the city was expanding, and new buildings were constructed, many of which reflected the pure genius of the International Style. The Caroline Wiess Law Building of the Museum of Fine Arts, Houston, designed by the Bauhaus master Ludwig Mies van der Rohe, is one sterling example. This building was completed in 1958, only a few years before Adolpho Leirner had the foresight to buy a brilliant work, *Em vermelho* [*In Red*] (1958), by Milton Dacosta. The then-young textile engineer from São Paolo and the painting by the scarcely known artist from Rio de Janeiro proved to be a perfect fit in sensibility.

Mr. Leirner went on to build the world's leading collection of Brazilian Constructive art. When the opportunity to acquire this collection of more than one hundred artworks was presented to the MFAH, the Trustees recognized the tremendous benefits of being able to exhibit art that speaks to our universal values and shared experiences, especially at a time when Houston is once again growing exponentially, and when boundaries between North and South America are more permeable than ever.

The Caroline Wiess Law Building is now being called upon to serve as a fitting backdrop for this exhibition of the artworks that Adolpho Leirner assembled with such focus and clarity. We thank him for his vision, on so many levels, and for demonstrating that art has the ability to empower each of us.

Peter C. Marzio
Director
The Museum of Fine Arts, Houston

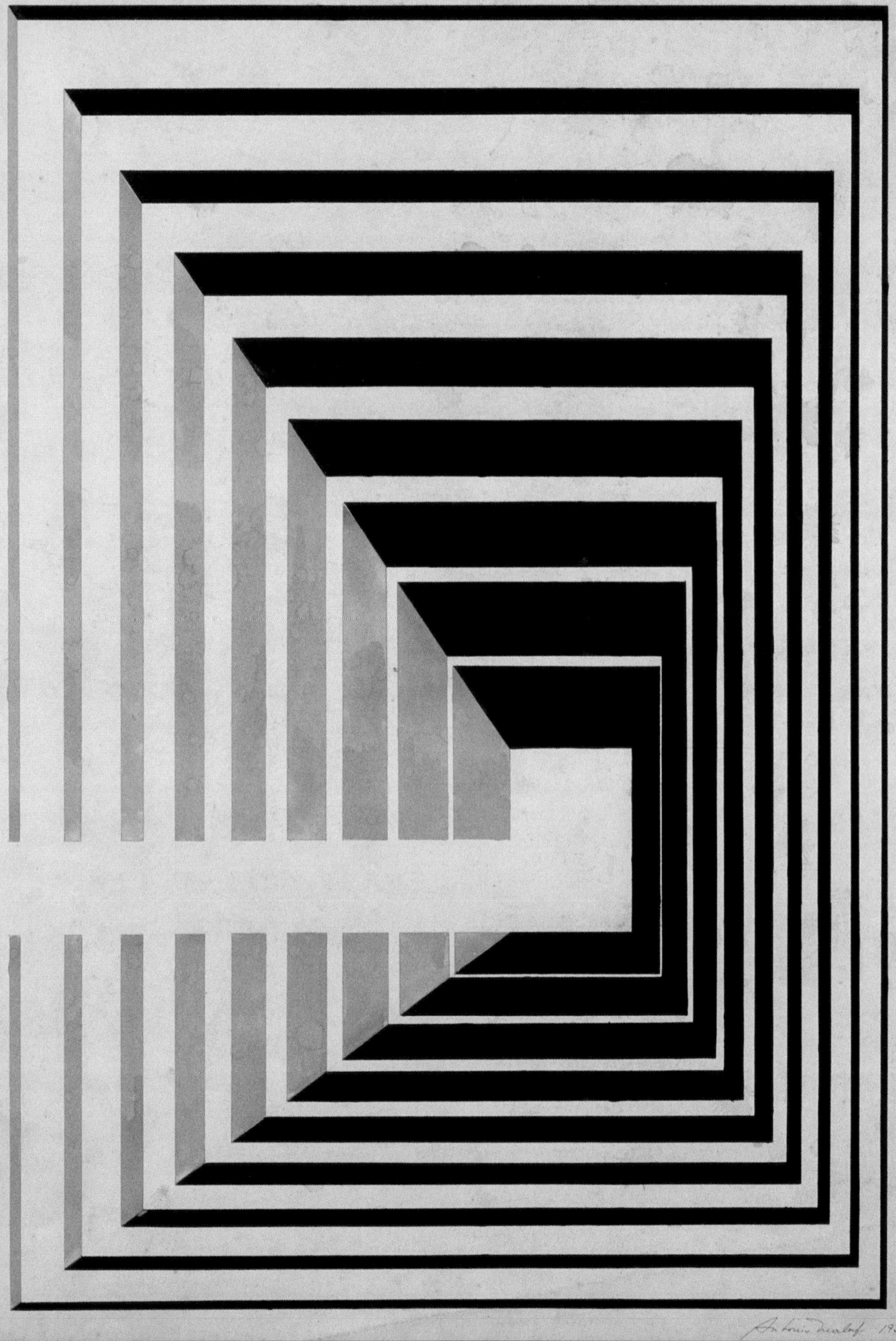

Antônio Maluf
Estudio para cartaz da I Bienal de São Paulo [*Study for Poster for the First São Paulo Biennial*]
1951
Tempera on board
29 x 20 1/16 inches
(73.7 x 51.6 cm)
The Adolpho Leirner Collection of Brazilian Constructive Art, gift of the Caroline Wiess Law Foundation
2005.1016
PHOTO: Rômulo Fialdini

Fitting Pieces Out of Place?

The Adolpho Leirner Collection of Brazilian Constructive Art at the Museum of Fine Arts, Houston

Mari Carmen Ramírez

How often does what first appeared to be an insignificant deed become a rather significant accomplishment in the art world? In 1961, Adolpho Leirner, a young textile engineer from São Paulo, bought *Em vermelho* [*In Red*] (1958) **[PAGE 173]**, by Milton Dacosta (1915–1988), a barely known artist from Rio de Janeiro who worked outside of any group affiliation. Although this painting is related to modes of Constructive art then in vogue in Brazil, it escapes any strict categorization. The contrast between the concrete materiality of the solid red plane and the play of proportionately distributed white rectangles and squares on the lower center of the composition creates a surface that is both static and rhythmic, expanding and meditative. In its strict visual economy, Dacosta's work echoed the more rational approach to nonobjective art that other groups of Brazilian artists favored. In other words, its perceptual sensibility announced the most radical (in the sense of subjective) manifestations of this phenomenon. Unbeknownst to the collector, this *sui generis* work would constitute the first piece of what eventually became known as the Adolpho Leirner Collection of Brazilian Constructive Art, recently acquired by the Museum of Fine Arts, Houston. Indeed, *Em vermelho* anticipated the focus of Leirner's collecting endeavors: more than one hundred exemplary paintings, constructions, works on paper, posters, and graphic materials by fifty-six well-known and under-recognized artists from the Rio de Janeiro and São Paulo artistic milieus. In their combination of economy of means and theoretical rigor, the art pieces and documents that make up this ensemble brilliantly illustrate the radical dimensions achieved by these artists' broad rereading of Constructive art in Brazil during the seminal decade of the 1950s.

Stimulated by the post-World War II economic boom and a surge in modernization that sought to place Brazil at the vanguard of the region's social and cultural development, this decade stands for what was, perhaps, one of the most animated enclaves of innovative activity in the Western Hemisphere. Two paramount events defined the Utopian spirit of this time: the establishment of the São Paulo Biennial in 1951 and the inauguration of Brasília, the futuristic new capital, in 1960. Energized by these unprecedented achievements, artists from the São Paulo-Rio de Janeiro axis thoroughly embraced the legacies of Russian Constructivism, Dutch Neo-Plasticism, and, above all, the School of Ulm. Moreover, despite the thirty-year lag that separated them from these movements, they proceeded to transform their tenets into unprecedented proposals that centered first on quite different approaches to Constructivist rules and later on the potential of non-objective art to mediate an individual's relationship to his/her environment. The Brazilian artists' contributions in this area launched a highly original chapter in the history of international Modernism that has achieved its due recognition only in the last fifteen years. It is not an exaggeration to state that this long-awaited validation owes a great debt to the groundbreaking specificities of these movements, as revealed in the cohesive collection assembled by Adolpho Leirner.

In gathering these pieces, the collector was driven by what he himself recognizes as a *deep-seated passion* for Constructive art, as well as by a desire to protect this body of work from falling into oblivion. It must be stressed that the groups and movements that pursued Constructive tendencies in São Paulo and Rio de Janeiro were short-lived and generally lacked both an institutional and an art-market presence. Most of the artists who integrated these tendencies survived by means and trades other than art, a fact that resulted in a fairly reduced body of production, both individually and collectively. In fact, the extremely precarious situation of these movements may be hard to grasp in its due importance today, given both the overriding presence of the market in the art world and its (sometimes overstated) impact on the rising values of commercial works that are not represented in the focused Leirner Collection. Furthermore, by the time that Adolpho Leirner began to acquire these works, art-world fads such as Informalism and Pop Art were on the rise in Brazil. These trends led many of the same artists previously associated with Concrete and Neo-Concrete tendencies to move on to new visual and conceptual territory. And yet, these circumstances proved to be felicitous, making insightful collecting in this field a timely and deeply rewarding—if not urgent—pursuit. The Leirner Collection thus emerged from the impulse to preserve for posterity a singular moment in the history of Brazilian art.

Not surprisingly, the most outstanding features of the collection are its tight focus and its avowed mission to represent a particular period. These two traits distinguish the Leirner Collection from other private collections of Latin American art, particularly those whose criteria for incorporating works into their holdings tend to revolve exclusively around subjective standards of taste. By contrast, the Leirner Collection offers a rare example of a disciplined and rigorous approach and, for this very reason, has emerged as the foremost scholarly reference on this decisive period. As the critic and curator Paulo Sérgio Duarte has observed, "To possess an important portion of Brazilian art collected in an articulate and consistent manner is to seize an entire cross-cultural and interpersonal movement that, at the same time, takes sides with the vision it portrays."[1] Because the works range from the earliest manifestations of geometric abstraction to the programmatic proposals of the experimental São Paulo and Rio de Janeiro Concrete art groups, the Leirner Collection is uniquely positioned to play a key role in disseminating the Brazilian reinterpretation of Constructive art. Since the early 1990s, works from the collection have been shown in more than 130 national and international exhibitions. Additionally, the collection has served to showcase paradigmatic proposals, such as Lygia Clark's *Ovo* [*Egg*] (1959) and Hélio Oiticica's *Vermelho cortando o branco* [*Red Going through White*] (1958), which, in turn, have brought heightened attention and visibility to the individual production of these visionary artists abroad.

To the extent that the history of the Brazilian Constructive movement has yet to be fully written, the Leirner Collection has fulfilled an even more critical function. It has provided a solid foundation from which to simultaneously build and project the very field that it aims to represent. From this point of view, the collection provides a paradigm for how the private eye can bring together and provide a framework for pondering artworks beyond the official purview of either art history or the museum. The Leirner Collection's singular scope supports this observation. Adolpho Leirner did not limit his collecting activity to the artists who constituted the well-known avant-garde groups of this period—Grupo ruptura (1952), Grupo Frente (1954–56), and Neoconcretismo (1959–61). Following his own intuitive responsiveness to art, he chose to expand his field of action and to construct a new stage, one on which a series of unanticipated or controversial actors would perform; in his view, without their participation, the collection would be incomplete. These artists include key harbingers of abstraction in Brazil, such as the Paris-based painter Cícero Dias, as well as the more conservative groups, such as Atelier Abstração (1951), led by Samson Flexor. Leirner also collected pivotal works by independent artists, including Alfredo Volpi, Mira Schendel, Milton Dacosta, and Sérgio Camargo, whose highly iconoclastic approaches to Concrete art further amplified the already complex visual and theoretical parameters of the Brazilian Constructive art project.

Rather than generating a seamless narrative, the act of bringing together this diverse selection of artists in the specific context of a collection necessarily produces incongruities and accidents if the standard accounts of these movements are considered. These unforeseen elements—the result of the collector's shrewd eye—can only serve to underscore an additional visionary asset exemplified by the Leirner Collection. Like an art exhibition, this private repository of visual culture provides opportunities for displacing, redrawing, or even expanding established art-historical platitudes while, in the process, articulating new frameworks for interpreting these tendencies. Moreover, in an unevenly defined art-historical field, such as that embodied by Brazilian Constructive art, the Leirner Collection should be able to both facilitate the task of documenting and defining the meteoric rise of this artistic trend in the 1950s and revealing unknown, even unexplored, aspects of this phenomenon.

This point becomes abundantly clear when we consider, for instance, the way that these groups functioned. In an attempt to establish a tabula rasa and to declare their independence from the art of the past, groups such as ruptura and Neoconcretismo avoided any reference to local artistic developments and instead proceeded to position themselves as nonderivative proponents of the international Constructive art tendencies initiated, as previously stated, by Constructivism, Neo-Plasticism, Max Bill, and the Hochschule für Gestaltung. The insistence with which they and their supporters stressed this point has led art historians to trace the beginnings of Constructive art to the presentation of Bill's prize-winning sculpture *Dreiteilig Einheit* [*Tripartite Unity*] (1949) at the First São Paulo Biennial in 1951. However, as Aracy Amaral has argued, despite the presence of a strong figurative and social-realist tradition, abstraction had found a rather fertile ground in Brazil as early as the late 1930s and the 1940s.[2] Hence, the presence of Cícero Dias in the Leirner Collection serves to counter the official narrative by reinserting the debate over Constructive art into the context of the evolution of geometric abstraction in Brazil. In a similar vein, the inclusion of Paris-oriented

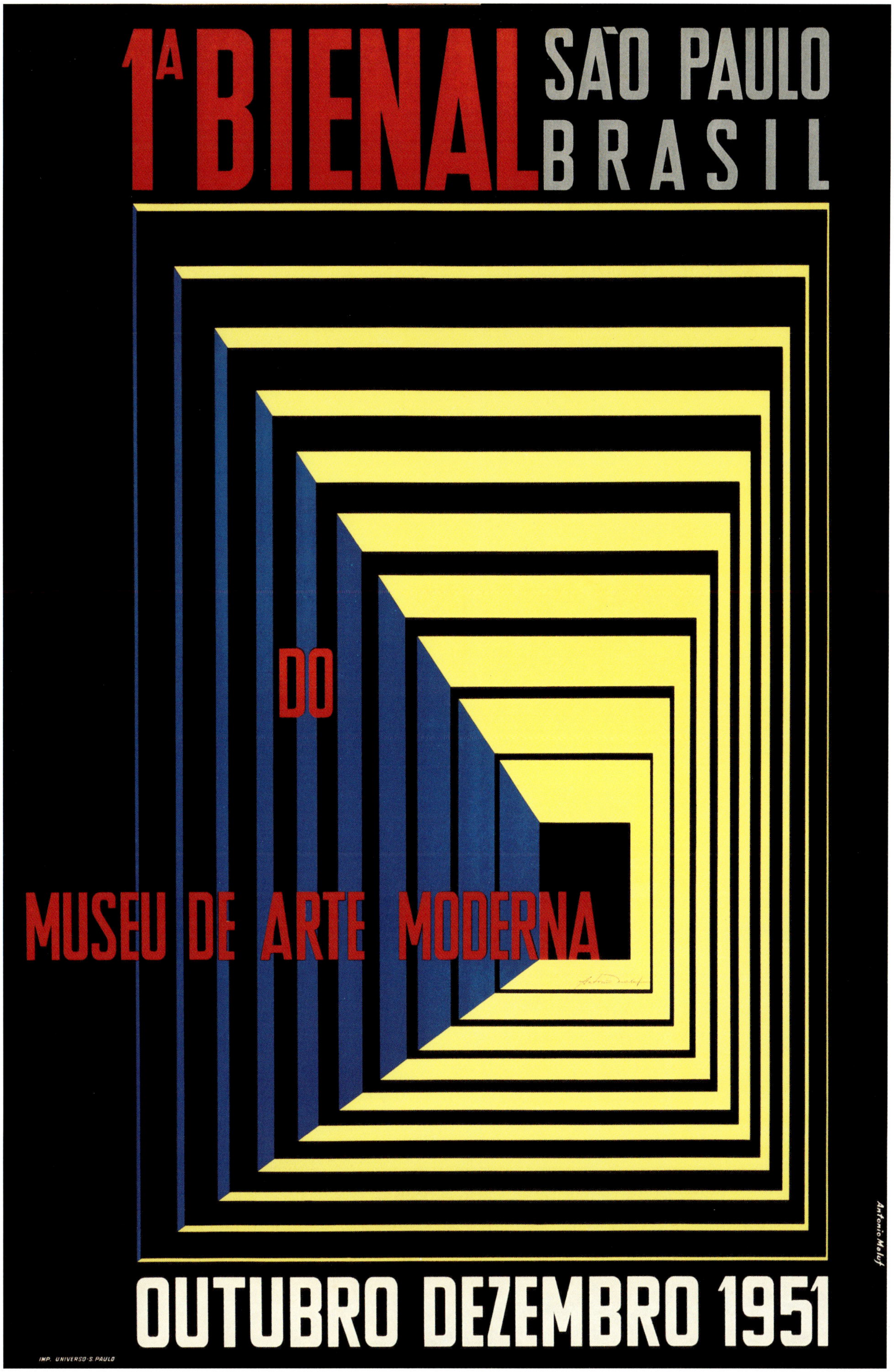

Antônio Maluf
Cartaz da I Bienal de São Paulo
[*Poster for the First São Paulo Biennial*], 1951
Screenprint
37 3/8 x 25 5/8 inches
(95 x 65 cm)
The Adolpho Leirner Collection of Brazilian Constructive Art, museum purchase with funds provided by the Caroline Wiess Law Accessions Endowment Fund
2007.18
PHOTO: Rômulo Fialdini

ruptura

charroux — cordeiro — de barros — fejer — haar — sacilotto — wladyslaw

a arte antiga foi grande, quando foi inteligente.
contudo, a nossa inteligência não pode ser a de Leonardo.
a história deu um salto qualitativo:

não há mais continuidade!

então nós distinguimos

- os que criam formas novas de principios velhos.
- os que criam formas novas de principios novos.

por que?

o naturalismo científico da renascença — o método para representar o mundo exterior (três dimensões) sôbre um plano (duas dimensões) – esgotou a sua tarefa histórica.

foi a crise

foi a renovação

hoje o novo pode ser diferenciado precisamente do velho. nós rompemos com o velho por isto afirmamos:

é o velho

- tôdas as variedades e hibridações do naturalismo;
- a mera negação do naturalismo, isto é, o naturalismo "errado" das crianças, dos loucos, dos "primitivos" dos expressionistas, dos surrealistas, etc. . . . ;
- o não-figurativismo hedonista, produto do gôsto gratuito, que busca a mera excitação do prazer ou do desprazer.

é o novo

- **as expressões baseadas nos novos princípios artísticos;**
- **tôdas as experiências que tendem à renovação dos valores essenciais da arte visual (espaço-tempo, movimento, e matéria);**
- **a intuição artística dotada de princípios claros e inteligentes e de grandes possibilidades de desenvolvimento prático;**
- **conferir à arte um lugar definido no quadro do trabalho espiritual contemporâneo, considerando-a um meio de conhecimento deduzivel de conceitos, situando-a acima da opinião, exigindo para o seu juizo conhecimento prévio.**

arte moderna não é ignorância, nós somos contra a ignorância.

Waldemar Cordeiro, Lothar Charoux, Geraldo de Barros, Luís Sacilotto, Anatol Wladyslaw, et al.
Manifesto Grupo ruptura [*The ruptura Group Manifesto*], 1952
Offset lithograph
13 x 8 5/8 inches (33 x 22 cm)
The Adolpho Leirner Collection of Brazilian Constructive Art, museum purchase with funds provided by the Caroline Wiess Law Accessions Endowment Fund
2007.16
PHOTO: Arquivo Luís Sacilotto, Santo André

Flexor and the Atelier Abstração artists opens up another productive line of investigation, one that quietly sidesteps the overarching influence of the School of Ulm in favor of the geometric-abstract offshoots of the School of Paris. Although active during the same period as the ruptura and Concrete art groups, the members of Atelier Abstração adhered to a different brand of geometric abstraction that ruptura leader Waldemar Cordeiro contentiously labeled "hedonistic." To further stir things up, the six outstanding works by Alfredo Volpi in the Leirner Collection present us with a paradox. That is, in the context of the collection, a painter who consistently and deliberately refused the "Concrete" classification emerges as the silent towering presence and unquestionable point of reference for the vastly diverse Concrete art vocabularies practiced by both the São Paulo and Rio de Janeiro groups. In this way, the array of artworks gathered by Leirner functions to gauge the history of the phenomenon it seeks to recover from all possible angles.

From a curatorial point of view, even the sheer juxtaposition of pieces in a gallery space calls these interactions into play. Depending on how the works dialogue with each other, the collection can illustrate either the established history of Brazilian Constructivism or previously unforeseen lines of inquiry that may inspire fruitful interpretations. For instance, in its play of transparent planes and virtual volumes, an early painting such as *Composição ortogonal no. 2* [*Orthogonal Composition no. 2*] (1952) **[PAGE 59]**, by the ruptura artist Anatol Wladyslaw, appears much closer to works by Flexor and the Atelier Abstração artists than to group leader Cordeiro's rational aesthetic proposals. Hence, the richness contextualized by the Leirner Collection brings to the fore many possibilities for displacing received accounts that are free to be accessed but also potentially exploited at any given time.

• • •

Ultimately, the importance accorded to a collection that aims to represent a particular art-historical moment can only stem from the careful balance between the selective choices made and the quality of the pieces gathered, and from the general vision of this historic moment that it is able to display. In the case of the Leirner Collection, a large number of the artists and works included in its holdings are emblematic of developments that helped to critically consolidate the diverse manifestations of Brazilian Constructivism. As previously emphasized, this representative ensemble encompasses well-known avant-garde leaders whose reputations have soared in recent years—such as the already cited cases of Lygia Clark and Hélio Oiticica—as well as under-recognized creators for whom consistent exposure and dedicated research will eventually bring the prominent worldwide recognition they deserve.

Cícero Dias (1907–2003)—considered to be the first Brazilian artist to embrace geometric abstraction—is one of the cases in point. Dias was a self-taught figurative painter who worked initially in a Surrealist mode and shifted to abstract art only in the 1940s during an extended stay in Paris, where he was an active participant in avant-garde circles. His four outstanding paintings in the Leirner Collection were first exhibited at the Galerie Denise René in Paris in the mid-1950s. Dias was, indeed, one of the artist-participants in the new constructive and kinetic wave promoted by this legendary dealer. In their refined and lyrical play of geometric shapes, his paintings exemplify the facile approach to geometry rejected by the more orthodox proponents of Concrete art. Samson Flexor (1907–1971)—the leader of the already cited São Paulo-based (*Paulista*) workshop school and artists' organization known as Atelier Abstração (1951), where he also taught—was a Romanian-born artist who relocated from Paris to São Paulo in 1948. Shortly afterward, he too embraced geometric abstraction. His dynamic compositions, based on virtual volumes generated by sequences of finely modulated color, set the standard for many other abstract artists of the period.

In addition to featuring these exponents of abstract art in Brazil, the collection excels in showcasing major works by the most cutting-edge avant-garde artists and groups active in the 1950s. The remarkable São Paulo-based Grupo ruptura (1952)—responsible for effecting "the qualitative leap"[3] from geometric to rational modes of abstraction—is represented by emblematic works produced by its leading members Cordeiro (1925–1973) and Maurício Nogueira Lima (1930), as well as by other key members: Geraldo de Barros (1923–1998), Luís Sacilotto (1924–2003), and Alexandre Wollner (1928). Nogueira Lima's *Objeto rítmico no. 2 (segunda versão)* [*Rhythmic Object no. 2 (second version)*] (1970s; first version, 1952) [PAGE 81]—a spiraling yellow and black square composition in which the repetition of geometric elements appears to generate movement—and Cordeiro's *Idéia visível* [*Visible Idea*] (1956) [PAGE 73]—a visual ideogram featuring a progressive repetition of vanishing lines that plays with the viewer's perception of how to organize space—emblematize the group's use of industrial materials, modular elements, and an objective, rational approach toward the Constructive idea of structure. Luís Sacilotto is a lesser-known artist who nevertheless deserves serious attention for his highly original, mathematically based formal progressions rendered in aluminum or on canvas. His *Concreção 5942* [*Concretion 5942*] (1959) [PAGE 83] is an example of the type of handmade unfolded aluminum constructions that has come to identify the Grupo ruptura's impersonal brand of Constructivism. The short-lived Grupo ruptura was survived by both the Poesia Concreta and the Arte Concreta movements inaugurated by the 1a Exposição de Arte Concreta [First Exhibition of Concrete Art] at the Museu da Arte Moderna de São Paulo in 1956, which brought together artists and poets from Rio de Janeiro and São Paulo.

Through its emphasis on intuition, empiricism, and individualism, the Rio de Janeiro-based Grupo Frente (1954–56) acted as the counterpoint to the orthodox stance of the ruptura and Arte Concreto artists. The group's avowed preference for color—a feature broadly highlighted in the recent exhibition *Hélio Oiticica: The Body of Color,* organized by and presented at the Museum of Fine Arts, Houston—becomes evident in *Faixas ritmadas* [*Rhythmic Strips*] (1953) [PAGE 103], an iconic piece made of chromatic progressions by the Grupo Frente's leader and respected mentor, Ivan Serpa (1923–1973). This approach to color in terms of increasing or decreasing modulations of contrasting or related hues is also present in key compositions by the Oiticica brothers César (1939) and Hélio (1937–1980), Abraham Palatnik (1928), and Décio Vieira (1922–1988) [PAGE 113]. Hélio Oiticica's *Vermelho cortando o branco* [*Red Going through White*] (1958)—one of only a handful of the oil-on-canvas works in his celebrated Metaesquemas series—is grounded in his formative experiences with master Ivan Serpa and other artists of Grupo Frente, such as Lygia Pape and Lygia Clark. Palatnik's "machines to make paintings"—of which *Aparelho cinecromático* [*Chromo-Kinetic Set*] (1964) [PAGE 115] provides a prime example—not only won him the jury's special prize at the First São Paulo Biennial but also made him a pioneer of kinetic abstraction in his native country and beyond. In his use of technology to produce color and movement, Palatnik created a groundbreaking proposal that fulfills Moholy-Nagy's visionary pursuit of an art of pure light and movement. His chromo-kinetic achievements thus challenge the limits of Constructive art, taking it into uncharted dimensions.

Some of the Rio de Janeiro artists who made up this loose artistic association went on to establish Neoconcretismo, a tendency that came together in March 1959 as a reaction to the excessive rationalism of Concrete art that was practiced by the São Paulo groups. Contrary to the notion of a "new concretism" suggested by its title, Neoconcretismo sought to "deconcretize" the presumed objectivity of the modes of Constructive art practiced by the ruptura and Arte Concreto groups. In recent years, Neoconcretismo has gained recognition for its radical theoretical propositions and advanced artistic manifestations. Its emphasis on the reincorporation of the subjective dimension (*expressão*), as well as on the elements of real time and space in the experience of the viewer-as-participant in the work (*vivência*), resulted in daring innovations (*não-objetos*), some of which are extremely well represented in the Leirner Collection. Among its holdings by leading Neo-Concrete artists are six major constructions by Lygia Clark that progressively map this artist's radical investigations of painting in relation to unexplored parameters of time and space. These include two of the best-known examples of her series titled Planes on Modulated Surfaces—*Planos em superfície modulada no. 1* and *Planos em superfície modulada no. 5* (both 1957)—as well as *Espaço modulado no. 2* [*Modulated Space no. 2*] (1958). Additionally, the collection features the outstanding *Ovo* [*Egg*] (1959), an enigmatic work that straddles the border between painting and the conception of space introduced by Clark. The artist's *Bicho* (*Máquina*) [*Critter* (*Machine*)] (1962)—part of the landmark series she produced during the Neo-Concrete period—reveals her pioneering work with hinged aluminum structures. This series stimulates the viewer to become an active participant or even a cocreator of the work in order to complete one of the many possible configurations embodied in its pliant structure. The Leirner Collection also includes a first-rate example from the series by Willys de Castro (1926–1988) titled Active Objects (c. 1960)—narrow laths mounted on the wall and that

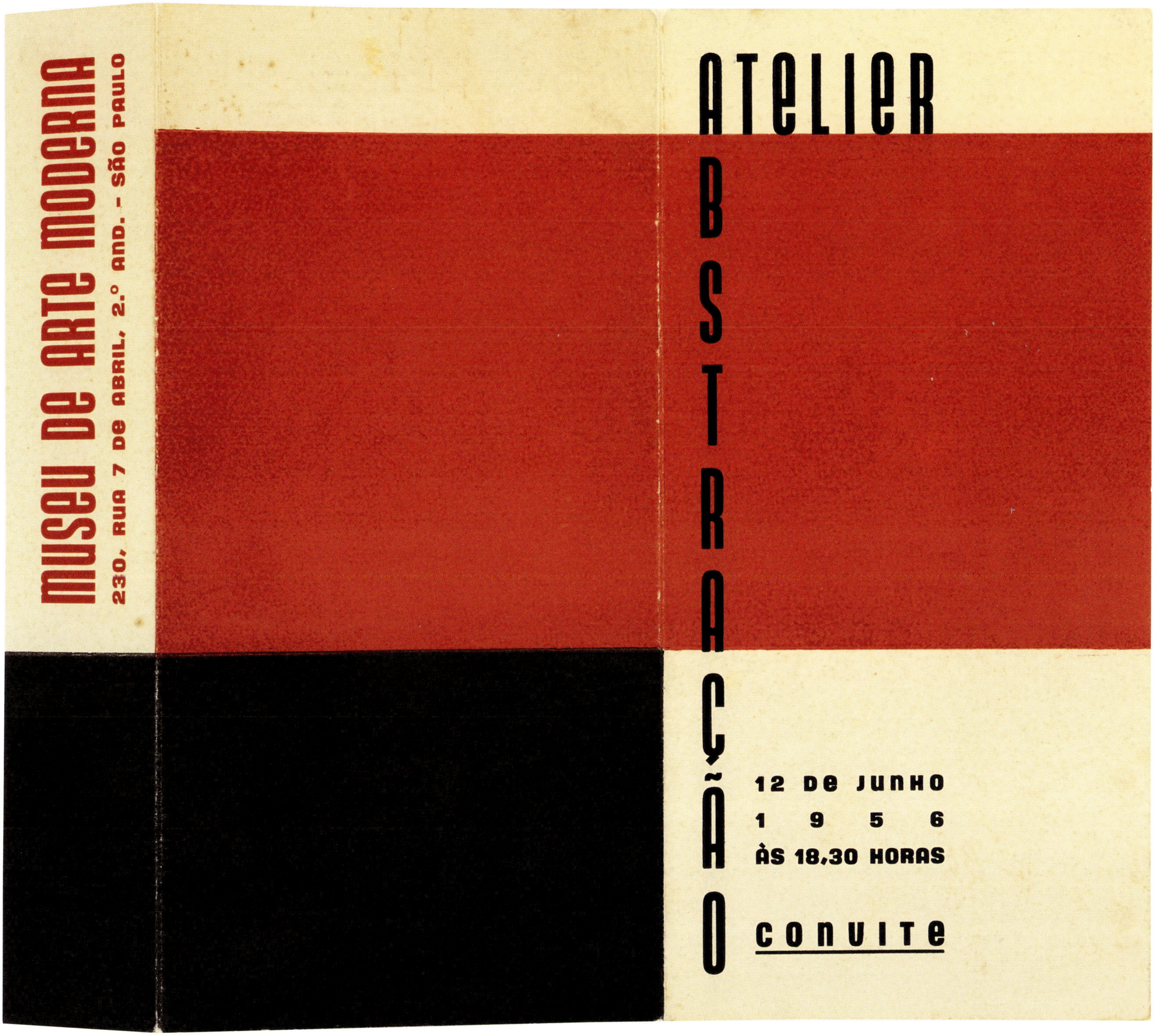

Norberto Nicola
Convite de exposição do Atelier Abstração no MAM-SP *e o manifesto redigido por Flexor no seu verso* [*Invitation for the Exhibition of Atelier Abstração at Museu de Arte Moderna de São Paulo and Manifesto Signed by Flexor on its Back*], 1956

Screenprint
9 7/8 x 11 1/16 inches
(25.1 x 28.1 cm)
The Adolpho Leirner Collection of Brazilian Constructive Art, museum purchase with funds provided by the Caroline Wiess Law Accessions Endowment Fund
2005.1064, 2005.1005
PHOTO: Tom Jenkins

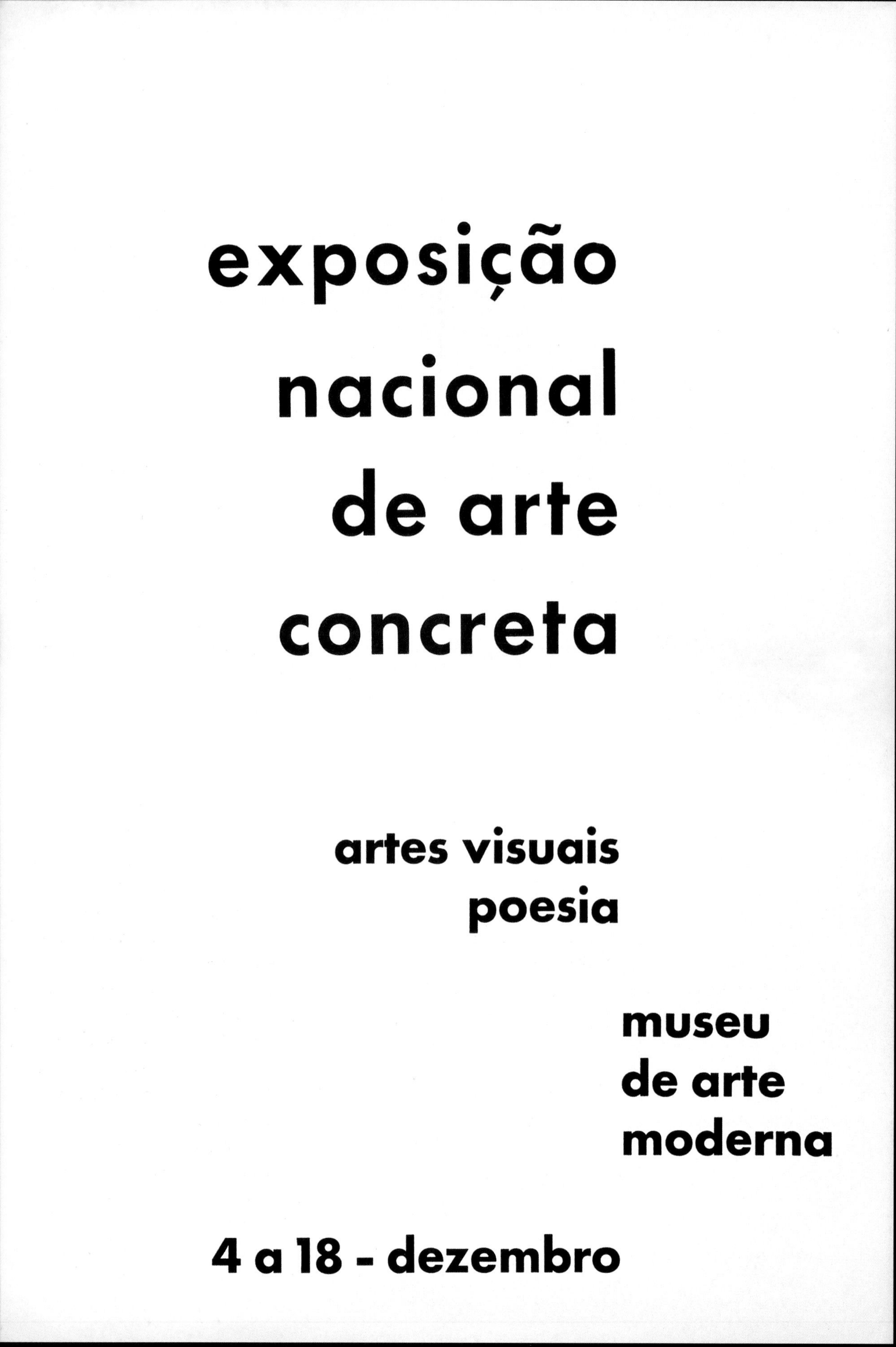

Waldemar Cordeiro, Lothar Charoux, Geraldo de Barros, Luiz Sacilotto, Anatol Wladyslaw, et al.
Primeira Exposição Nacional de Arte Concreta [*Poster for the First National Exhibition of Concrete Art*], 1956
Offset lithograph
19 1/4 x 12 3/4 inches
(48 x 32.5 cm)
The Adolpho Leirner Collection of Brazilian Constructive Art, museum purchase with funds provided by the Caroline Wiess Law Accessions Endowment Fund
2007.17

collapse the distinction between painting and sculpture **[PAGE 123]**—as well as examples of Hércules Barsotti's White/Black series (1959–61) **[PAGE 119]**. The Neo-Concrete sculptors Amílcar de Castro (1920–2002) and Franz Weissmann (1914–2006)—proponents of the new type of sensory space introduced by the Neo-Concretes—are also well represented in the collection. Weissmann's *Ponte* [*Bridge*] (1958) **[PAGES 130–31]**—a model for a larger public project that never materialized—was shown at the 1a Exposição de Arte Neoconcreta [First Exhibition of Neo-Concrete Art]. It exemplifies a series of modular studies in metal trimming and in the folding of squares that generate a dynamic interplay of virtual volumes suspended in space. De Castro, by contrast, bends sheets of raw, rusted cast iron to achieve three-dimensional volumes suggesting notions of positive and negative spaces.

In addition to showcasing these well-documented groups, the Leirner Collection features a number of major artists who, although they embraced Constructive modes, worked independently of the already cited historical movements. The most outstanding of these artists is the Italian-born *Paulista* Alfredo Volpi (1896–1988), whose intuitive poetics of Concrete color and space, combined with an extraordinarily sensitive treatment of the pictorial surface and the use of the ancient tempera technique, informed works such as *Concreto* [*Concrete*] (1950s) and *Bandeiras verdes sobre rosa* [*Green Flags on Pink*] (c. 1957). The latter was inspired by the decorative paper flags that hang in the streets of Brazilian cities during Saint John's Day celebrations. This fact underscores a singular trait of certain Constructive trends in this country: the incorporation of vernacular elements into what can otherwise be considered highly intellectualized art forms. Other paintings by Volpi, such as the spatially rigorous *Composição* [*Composition*] (c. 1958), have been hailed by some as antecedents to the works of Minimalist artists like Richard Serra. The Swiss-born Mira Schendel (1919–1988) is another major artist who worked for decades in isolation, producing contained and intense paintings and works on paper that employ the Concrete language in vogue in São Paulo to explore the existential and unfathomable Zen philosophical concept: the "void of the world." Coincidentally, this notion also lay at the core of the research undertaken by Lygia Clark and other Neo-Concrete artists. *Sem título* [*Untitled*] (1954) **[PAGE 175]**—one of Schendel's best-known early works—combines both painting and sculpture to create a poetic and enigmatic construction that has elicited multiple interpretations ever since it first came to light. The artist further developed the Constructive potential of this work in a well-known series titled Sarrafos [Laths] (1980s), which she undertook toward the end of her life. Sérgio Camargo, the Rio de Janeiro artist who began his career in Buenos Aires in the late 1940s as a student of Emilio Pettorutti and Lucio Fontana, turned to light and the color white as the basis for his unique and extensive wood Reliefs series **[PAGE 169]**. Unfortunately, other outstanding examples worthy of mention lie outside of the scope of this introduction.

• • •

As suggested by the question posed in the title of this essay—fitting pieces out of place?—one could argue that the acquisition of the Leirner Collection by the Museum of Fine Arts, Houston, has removed this extremely valuable artistic resource from its most immediate cultural context, Brazil. In this sense, the transfer has endowed the works with a "misplaced"[4] quality. What specific role can the Adolpho Leirner Collection play in its new context? To answer this question, we must first describe the characteristics of the museum that now houses the Leirner Collection. The Museum of Fine Arts, Houston, is a large, encyclopedic institution committed to a long-term research, collection, and exhibition program focused on Latin American art. Furthermore, this museum is strategically located in a metropolitan city that thrives within the increasingly permeable border between North and South. In this culturally diverse environment, the Leirner Collection takes its place as the centerpiece of a broad and ambitious scholarly undertaking led by the museum's International Center for the Arts of the Americas. The center's unprecedented initiative is supported by in-depth research, multilingual dialogue, professional exchange, a globally accessible digital archive, and a publication series. The geographic distance afforded by this "out-of-place" perspective should substantially increase the Leirner Collection's potential to displace both entrenched views about Brazilian art in general and postwar Constructivism in particular.

Within such a frame of reference, we must keep in mind that the longing for universal communion/communication lay at the core of Constructivism since its inception. In Brazil, the very notion of Constructive art—via Max Bill or not—was still undeniably an idea *out of place*: imported, adopted, and subject to manifold readjustments and adaptations. For this reason, as critic Duarte observes, the artworks that form the Leirner Collection were created in the belief that "local culture could be reinserted in the world environment through a quest for universal values such as art languages that, without eluding the idiosyncrasies of the author and his/her origin, were capable of transcending the particular ground and reaching a communication ideal."[5] Therefore, the repositioning of the Leirner Collection's ensemble of key pieces in the Museum of Fine Arts, Houston, and the resulting confrontation/comparison with similar manifestations from around the world, should enable these works to fully manifest the universal values they represent.

Furthermore, the museum's acquisition of the Leirner Collection will pave the way for thoroughly assessing this critical chapter of Brazilian and international Modernism. In this context, the museum has the ability to display the works of the Leirner Collection in close proximity to those by other European, North American, and Latin American artists who explored similar artistic and intellectual issues—thus challenging historical classifications, abolishing automatic pigeonholing, and annihilating, once and for all, the worn-out commonplaces about the peripheral, derivative, or even "marginal" status previously assigned to this underestimated art. Therefore, what may appear at first glance to be termed a *loss* is, in fact, a significant *gain*. The Leirner Collection thus emerges as both the perfect subject of and catalyst for pioneering research. To that end, the Museum of Fine Arts, Houston, is empowered to put these out-of-place pieces *into* place.

1
Paulo Sérgio Duarte, "Modernos fora dos eixos" [Modernity on the Fringes], in Aracy Amaral, ed., *Arte construtiva no Brasil. Coleção Adolpho Leirner* [Constructive Art in Brazil. Adolpho Leirner Collection] (São Paulo: Companhia Melhoramentos, 1998), 183–221: 184.

2
Aracy Amaral, "Surgimento da abstração geométrica no Brasil" [The Advent of Geometric Abstraction in Brazil], in Aracy Amaral, ed., *Arte construtiva no Brasil. Coleção Adolpho Leirner* [Constructive Art in Brazil. Adolpho Leirner Collection], 30–63.

3
Waldemar Cordeiro, et al., "Manifesto ruptura," São Paulo, 1962. In: Aracy Amaral, ed., *Projeto Construtivo Brasileiro na arte (1950–1962)* (Rio de Janeiro/ São Paulo: 1977), 69. See also page 16 of this catalogue.

4
The notion of a "misplaced" or an "out-of-place" idea is a reference to the by-now classic interpretation of the Brazilian writer Machado de Assis by the foremost literary theorist Roberto Schwartz. I have relied on this idea as a starting point to characterize the development of Constructivism in Latin America. See my essay "Vital Structures: The Constructive Nexus in Latin America," in Mari Carmen Ramírez and Héctor Olea et al., *Inverted Utopias: Avant-Garde Art in Latin America* (New Haven and London: Yale University Press in association with The Museum of Fine Arts, Houston, 2004), 191–201.

5
Paulo Sérgio Duarte, "Modernos fora dos eixos" [Modernity on the Fringes], 183–221: 184.

Adolpho Leirner at his home
in São Paulo.

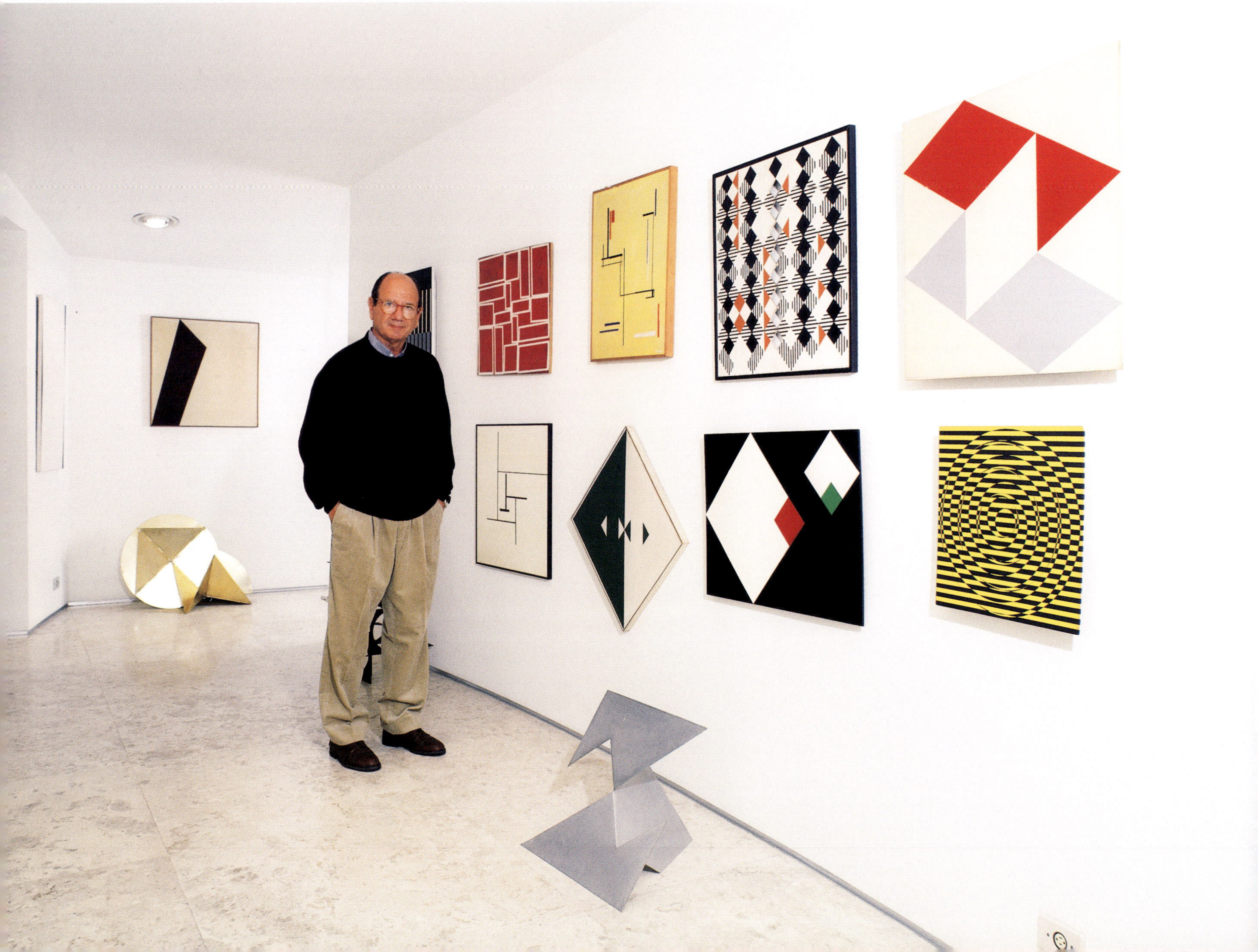

Collecting Is Searching

Adolpho Leirner

Collectors are regarded as mad, manic, paranoid. For me, collecting is love, passion, a discovery, and a search. To collect is a feeling, an experience that comes from the inside. It may be a profession. You don't know when it starts or when it ends; it's like life.

It's very important to maintain a collection preserved as a whole, not dispersed by other generations or in pages of auction catalogues. Collectors have not only made the link between artists and institutions, but also have fostered art markets, criticism, and exhibitions.

This collection shows a path of the early days of Constructive art in Brazil, a time of rupture with figurative art. As starting point, it spans from the roots of Brazilian Constructivism, planted in the 1930s; São Paulo's Concrete Ruptura Group; Atelier Abstração, headed by Samson Flexor; and Rio de Janeiro's Frente Group; to Neo-Concrete and geometric-abstract artists who worked independently in the 1950s and 1960s and their influence on visual design.

The art produced during this period has had a definitive influence on Brazilian contemporary art. No doubt, most of our contemporary artists, particularly Conceptual and Minimal artists of the 1970s, have a Constructive background, for example, Waltércio Caldas, Cildo Meireles, Antonio Dias, and José Resende.

I am lucky to be surrounded by these works and to watch them with respect. Putting together this collection became my way of life. I think my collection is the expression of my personality, which sometimes transports me to moments of silence and reflection. I take great pleasure in showing and publishing my collection, because this means sharing with viewers and readers something that I have always held as very private to me.

When I first started collecting, I felt a bit lonely. Few understood my craziness, especially those who thought of a collection as an investment. I fielded questions like this: "Are these little lines and dots worth something?" When I bought Alfredo Volpi's *Composition,* c. 1958, I didn't care about what people said, but about what satisfied my taste.

Each collector has his own personal way of collecting. My family arrived in Brazil from Poland in the beginning of the 1930s. They were always involved in Brazilian culture. This involvement led me into collecting as a young man, and provided marvelous contacts for the development of my ideas.

My professional studies as a textile engineer decisively contributed to and informed my way of looking and my perceptions. During my studies I couldn't help but be constantly in contact with the pieces of graph paper on my desk. Design was made manually; we didn't have computers at that time.

With great interest in architecture and design, I directed my attention to the Russian Constructivists, to the Dutch movement De Stijl, to the German Bauhaus, to the French Art Deco, to the schools of Vienna and Glasgow. This interest propelled me into this world of lines, forms, colors, planes, and tensions—the dominance of order over disorder—, bringing me closer to rational thought.

At age twenty-two, I was still a child when I got married. I felt the need to fill the emptiness of the white that surrounded me in my house. I wanted to replace it with something geometric that would really touch me. In the beginning of my professional practice I didn't have the resources required to buy works of art; however, during a working trip to Rio de Janeiro in the beginning of the 1960s I came across a painting that really attracted me: Milton Dacosta's *Em vermelho* [*In Red*], 1958; it looked to me like a house project on a red background, with two rooms and a living room. I purchased this work as the first Constructive painting of my collection. Later this image became the cover of the book *Constructive Art in Brazil. Adolpho Leirner Collection,* published in 1998. I think it was a lucky choice.

In 1974, together with Fúlvia Leirner, I organized the exhibition *Tempo dos Modernistas* [*Times of the Modernists*] at MASP – Museu de Arte de São Paulo, commissioned by Pietro Maria Bardi. This event served as a counterpoint to the great Bauhaus exhibition brought from Germany. Furthermore, it was the first time that international Art Deco and, mainly, Brazilian Art Deco were displayed in this country. The show featured tapestries, furniture, and objects by Regina and John Graz, works by Antonio Gomide, vases, objects, and sculptures of Constructive connotation.

Although I was familiar with top-quality artworks by artists such as Jose Pancetti, Alberto da Veiga Guignard, Tarsila do Amaral, Emiliano Di Cavalcanti, Ismael Nery, Cândido Portinari, and other deceased artists acknowledged by both critics and the market, I could not establish direct contact with these creators. Therefore, when I first started my collection, the number-one criterion was to gather works by contemporary artists, which I found to be a more difficult as well as a more stimulating activity. I was out to take risks, which entailed the possibility of making mistakes. It never occurred to me to acquire a painting for speculative purposes.

In the early 1960s, when lyrical and informal abstraction was the focus of public attention, I noticed a certain indifference toward artists who had participated in abstract-geometric movements and who were then "outmoded." Right away I realized that these artists appreciated my initiative, not only because of the purchase in itself (given the depreciated value of their works on the market), but because a new personage was entering the scene: a collector of art of the 1950s. After having witnessed the manner in which these artists were rejected in the 1960s, today I take pleasure in witnessing the acknowledgment of their quality.

Historically, the relations between collectors and artists have always been difficult for a number of reasons that include a difference in intellectual viewpoints, distinct backgrounds, distinct visions of the world, low amounts offered as pay (which artists regard as highly insulting), or yet a great lack of concern for their work. In turn, however, mutual interests have always generated considerable satisfaction. I have been involved in situations in which artists at times felt jealous, possessive, or merely stunned by the "loss" of their artworks, as if these works were their own children. To me, their attitudes seem perfectly natural, because only very seldom and in strict circumstances would I agree to let go of works from my collection of Constructive art.

In the 1950s, art production was somewhat limited by the fact that most artists could not afford to live off their work. There were graphic artists, landscape artists, ad people, poets, physicians, textile designers, and bank clerks who formed a close-knit group. Given the lack of an art market, so to speak, they exchanged works among themselves, as gifts.

Personal contact with artists not only served to enhance my art knowledge, but allowed me to sense their emotions up close. I remember the first time Willys de Castro came to our house. He saw a painting by Milton Dacosta (*Em vermelho,* 1958) and said that it was the only work, out of a set of seven, that he really liked. When I asked him to show me his work, he answered with a smile. At age twenty-five, I was neither an artist nor an intellectual. At that moment I realized I was not even ready to set my hands on one of his offspring. He was terribly jealous of his works and his "active objects," and his small house on Rua Haddock Lobo was an insurmountable stronghold. I have always been enthusiastic about Willys's thoughts and ideas. He was a leader of our rational movement. Later in life he would become one of my gurus.

One morning, as I was walking down Rua Martins Fontes, in downtown São Paulo, I entered an art gallery and furniture store called Ambiente. On a short column I spotted one of Willys's works (*Objeto ativo* [*Active Object*], c. 1960), which I promptly bought. From that moment on I felt like a winner. After all, I now owned an artwork by Willys, a privilege he himself had denied to me earlier. Willys de Castro has a strong influence on Hércules Barsotti's attitude toward the art market. Like his peer, for many years Barsotti refused to sell his earlier works, which he kept safely tucked away. My dear friend kept me waiting for many years before I acquired his *Branco/Preto* [*White/Black*] (1960) in 1984.

I remember the strong emotion of Alberto Teixeira and Maria Helena Andrés upon learning that their works had been shown at the Bienal Brasil Século XX (Twentieth-century Brazil Biennial). What a privilege to be Norberto "Nicolino"

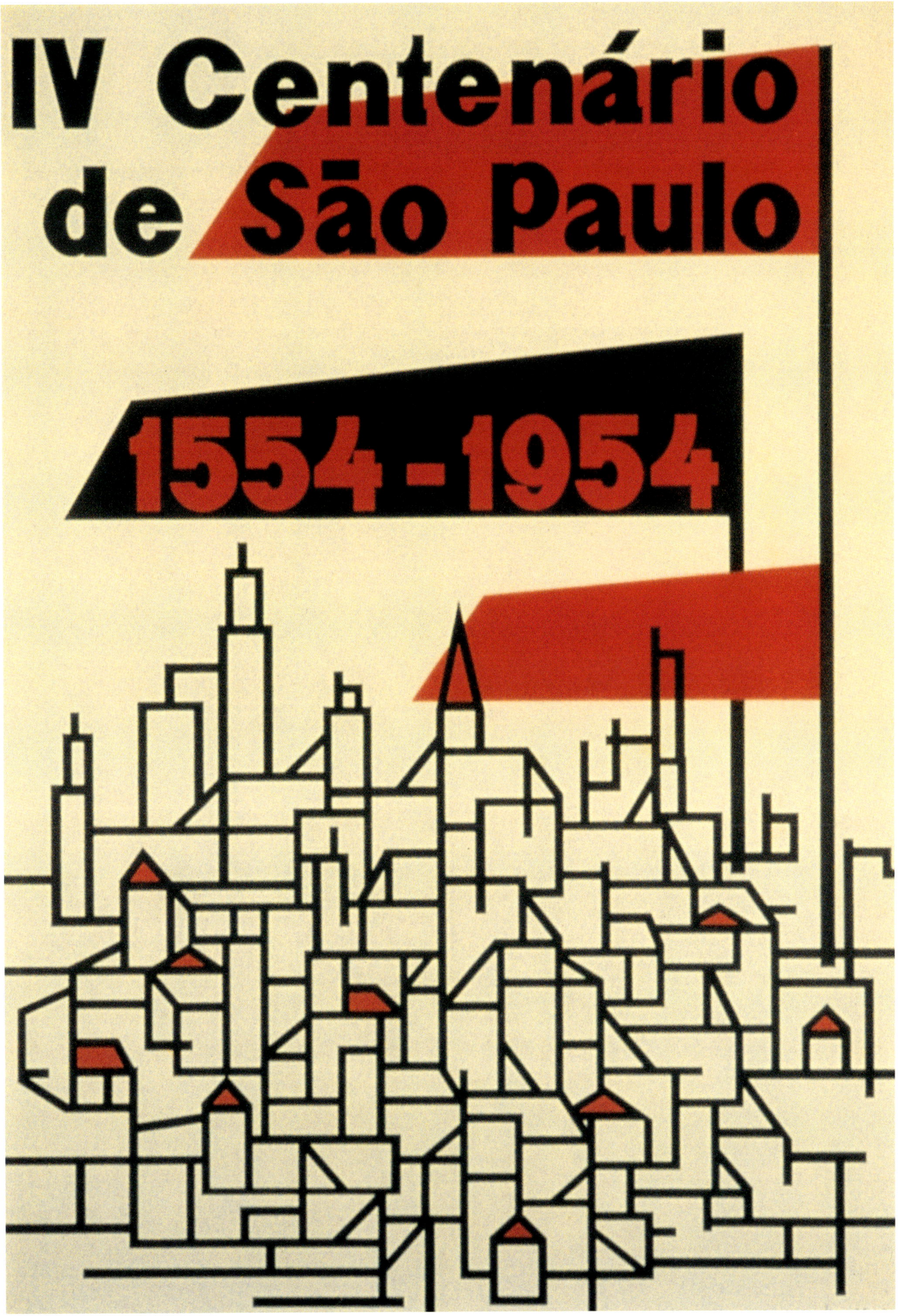

Geraldo de Barros
Cartaz para o IV Centenário de São Paulo [*Poster for the Fourth Centennial of the City of São Paulo*], 1954
Screenprint
41 1/4 x 29 1/4 inches
(104.8 x 74.3 cm)
The Adolpho Leirner Collection of Brazilian Constructive Art, gift of the Caroline Wiess Law Foundation
2005.980

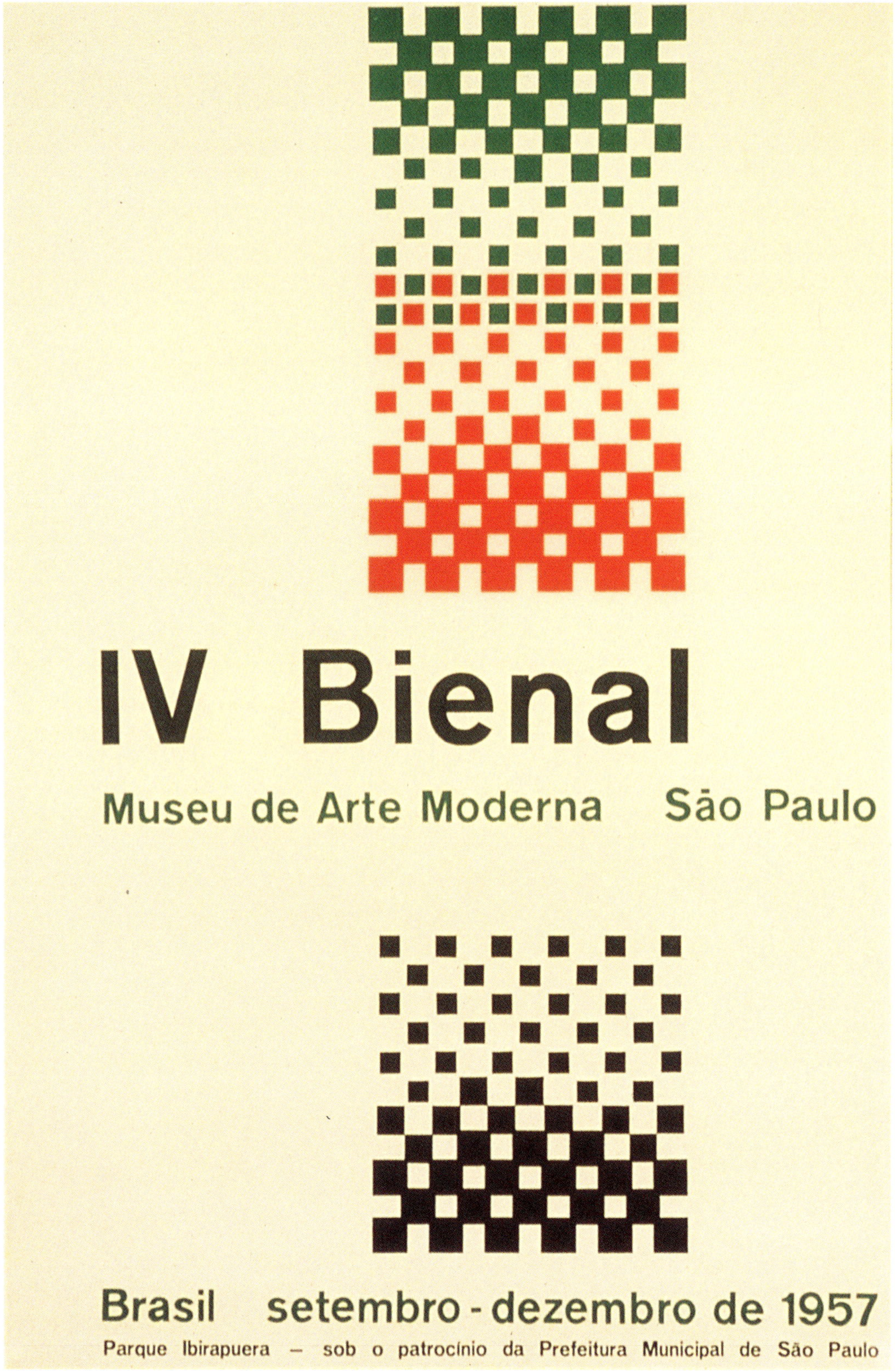

Alexandre Wollner
Cartaz da IV Bienal de São Paulo [*Poster for Fourth São Paulo Biennial*], 1957
Offset lithograph
37 1/2 x 25 1/4 inches
(95.3 x 64.1 cm)
The Adolpho Leirner Collection of Brazilian Constructive Art, museum purchase with funds provided by the Caroline Wiess Law Accessions Endowment Fund
2005.1047

Nicola's friend and receive as a present his fantastic *Trama ativa* [*Active Web*], 1955, a harbinger of his future tapestry production! I remember sharing the emotion shown in Antônio Maluf's teary eyes, himself a man of unique sensibility! I remember Helena, Waldemar Cordeiro's wife, telling stories of my early childhood days when we lived in the same building, in the district of Bom Retiro, and of how she carried me for leisurely strolls in the nearby park. I remember chatting with Anatol Wladyslaw, whose Polish accent touched me, as it reminded me of my father's voice. I remember not only Judith Lauand, a delicate and serious person, but also Lothar Charoux, at whose work desk I sat to see his *Abstrato geométrico* [*Geometric Abstract*] of 1952. I remember discussing music with Luís Sacilotto, at his home in Santo André; drinking beer with Hermalindo Fiaminghi, whose instigating, ironical wit I greatly enjoyed; and Maurício Nogueira Lima's accounts of meetings with Lygia Clark and Sacilotto, at which Clark declared to be capable of making sculptures like Sacilotto's *Concreção 5730* [*Concretion 5730*] of 1957, though hers was to be a moving structure. Her famous *Bichos* [*Critters*] were conceived in those meetings. I remember feeling that we belonged in Geraldo de Barros's family. I remember working in close contact with a perfectionist friend, Alexandre Wollner; spending time with Lygia Pape, a sweet and caring beauty; meeting with Franz Weissmann and his wife, Maria Eugênia Franco, at his Rio de Janeiro studio in my attempts to acquire his sculpture *Ponte* [*Bridge*] of 1958. I remember corresponding with Cícero Dias and my joy at walking in Galerie Denise René, in Paris, and finding four of his canvases painted in the 1950s. I remember my frequent visits to Alfredo Volpi's place, where I was deeply touched both by the environment and by the simple, naive personality of this man whom I view as one of the greatest Brazilian artists of all time. I remember how I felt so privileged for having met Mario Schenberg and Theon Spanudis and for discussing with them a few ceramic works in my collection; and for my close relationship with my parents' friends Margot and Samson Flexor.

I cherish the emotions and reactions I have shared with curators of major foreign institutions who have visited my collection in the last few years. There are those who agreed with my comparison of Volpi's Concrete works of the 1950s with the works of U.S. Minimalist artists, such as Richard Serra and Ellsworth Kelly, of the 1960s, which I hadn't known about when I started collecting Volpi's works. Others recognized that Abraham Palatnik's *Aparelho cinecromático* [*Chromo-Kinetic Set*], 1964, was a forerunner of kinetic art. Still others considered Brazilian geometric-abstract artists to be harbingers of the Neo-Geo movement, thanks to their bright colors, including purple, lime green, and shocking pink, which represent a lively Brazilian coloring featured, for example, in Cícero Dias's works of the 1950s. They discovered Lygia Clark's organic line in her *Bichos* and *Trepantes* [*Creepers*]; Hélio Oiticica's *Relevo espacial* [*Spatial Relief*], and Mira Schendel's works of 1954, which introduced her heavily textured phase and her future *Sarrafos* [*Laths*]. They were surprised by the work of Maurício Nogueira Lima (*Objeto rítmico* [*Rhythmic Object*], 1952), a forerunner of the Op Art movement. They were in awe of Willys de Castro's *Objeto ativo*. They experienced the sensation of seeing Barsotti's painting *Branco/Preto* seem to "move" on the wall. They saw Maluf's original poster drawing for the First São Paulo Biennial, held in 1951.

I take great joy in witnessing the revival and acknowledgment of Lygia Clark's and Hélio Oiticica's works, currently being shown in capital cities in Europe and the United States as major visiting exhibitions curated by international organizations. Unfortunately, these initiatives occurred before Brazil was able to organize any comparable exhibitions of these artists' works.

I have no intention of presenting geometric abstraction as the greatest movement of twentieth-century Brazilian art. My sole intent is to show this trend as being very much alive and current, as well as significantly influential on the development of the country's art milieu. I feel I have partly covered the early path of Brazilian Constructive art, thus blazing a trail for a subsequent, in-depth research on this trend in the 1970s, 1980s, and 1990s.

After years of organizing my archive, I was surprised to discover that selections from my collection have been shown in one hundred exhibitions in Brazil and thirty exhibits abroad, recently in four American museums, and have been published in about six hundred publications.

At this moment, I am satisfied by what I have accomplished during my forty years of collecting, by my role as a participant in the history of Constructive art in Brazil, and by the recognition these artists, who were rejected for more than thirty years, are receiving in Brazil and abroad.

Although this collection is incomplete, for it would be virtually impossible to cover the entire production of this period, it comprises a coherent selection, made with logic and reasoning, by an impassioned amateur.

This statement has been adapted from the text published in *Arte construtiva no Brasil. Coleção Adolpho Leirner* [Constructive Art in Brazil. Adolpho Leirner Collection], ed. Aracy Amaral (São Paulo: Companhia/Melhoramentos, 1998) and from a talk given by Adolpho Leirner at the Museum of Fine Arts, Houston, in November 2004.

Alexandre Wollner
Geraldo de Barros
Cartaz para o Festival Internacional de Cinema do Brasil
[*Poster for the International Festival of Brazilian Cinema*], 1954
Offset lithograph
34 1/4 x 23 1/4 inches
(87 x 59.1 cm)
The Adolpho Leirner Collection of Brazilian Constructive Art, museum purchase with funds provided by the Caroline Wiess Law Accessions Endowment Fund
2005.1008
PHOTO: Tom Jenkins

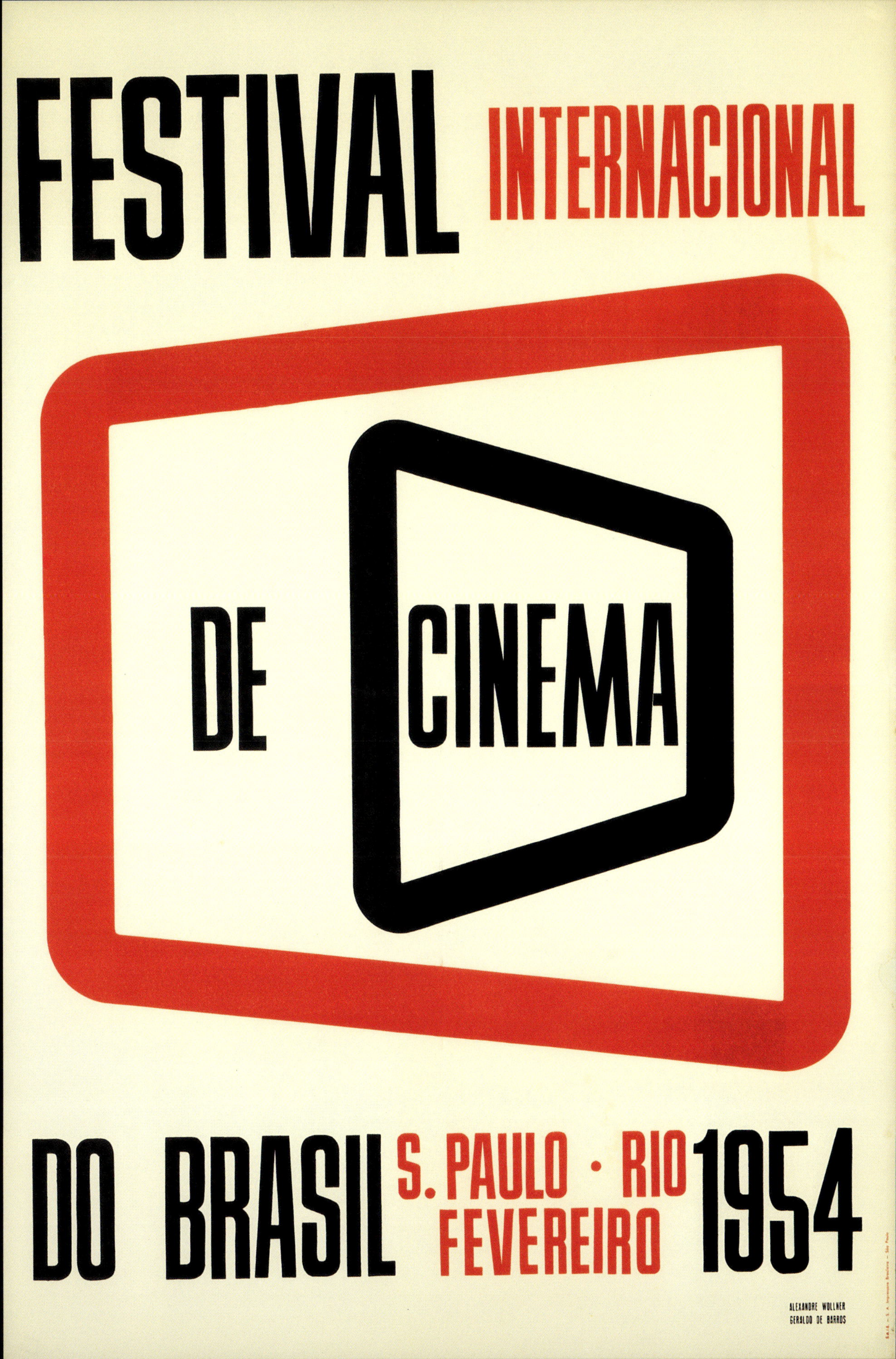

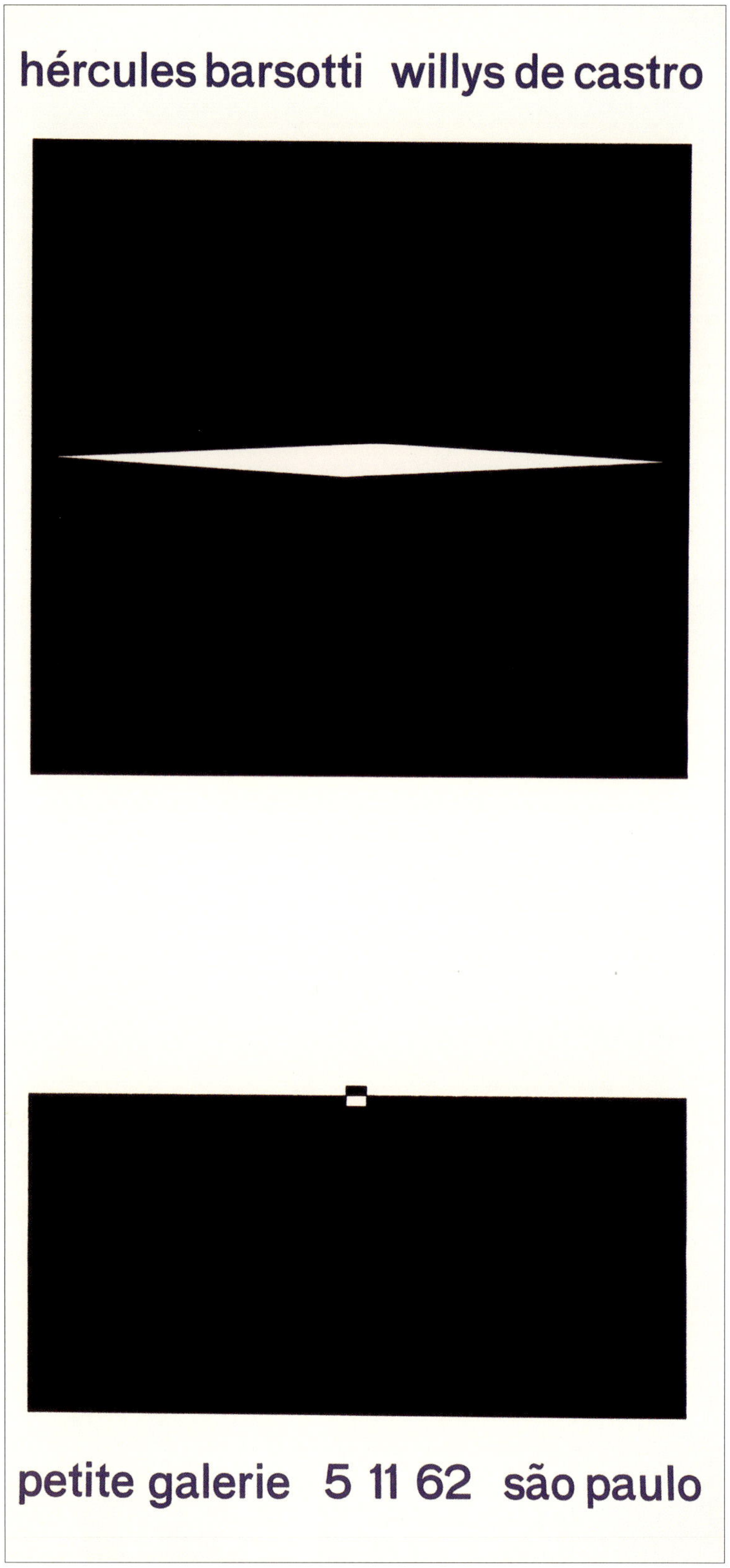

Willys de Castro
Cartaz para exposição de Hércules Barsotti and Willys de Castro at Petite Galerie, Rio de Janeiro [Poster for an Exhibition of Hércules Barsotti and Willys de Castro at Petite Galerie, Rio de Janeiro], 1962
Offset lithograph
29 3/4 x 14 3/8 inches
(75.6 x 36.5 cm)
The Adolpho Leirner Collection of Brazilian Constructive Art, museum purchase with funds provided by the Caroline Wiess Law Accessions Endowment Fund
2007.11
PHOTO: Tom Jenkins

Goebel Weyne
Cartaz da IX Bienal de São Paulo [Poster for Ninth São Paulo Biennial], 1967
Screenprint
37 x 25 1/4 inches (94 x 64.1 cm)
The Adolpho Leirner Collection of Brazilian Constructive Art, museum purchase with funds provided by the Caroline Wiess Law Accessions Endowment Fund
2005.1041
PHOTO: Tom Jenkins

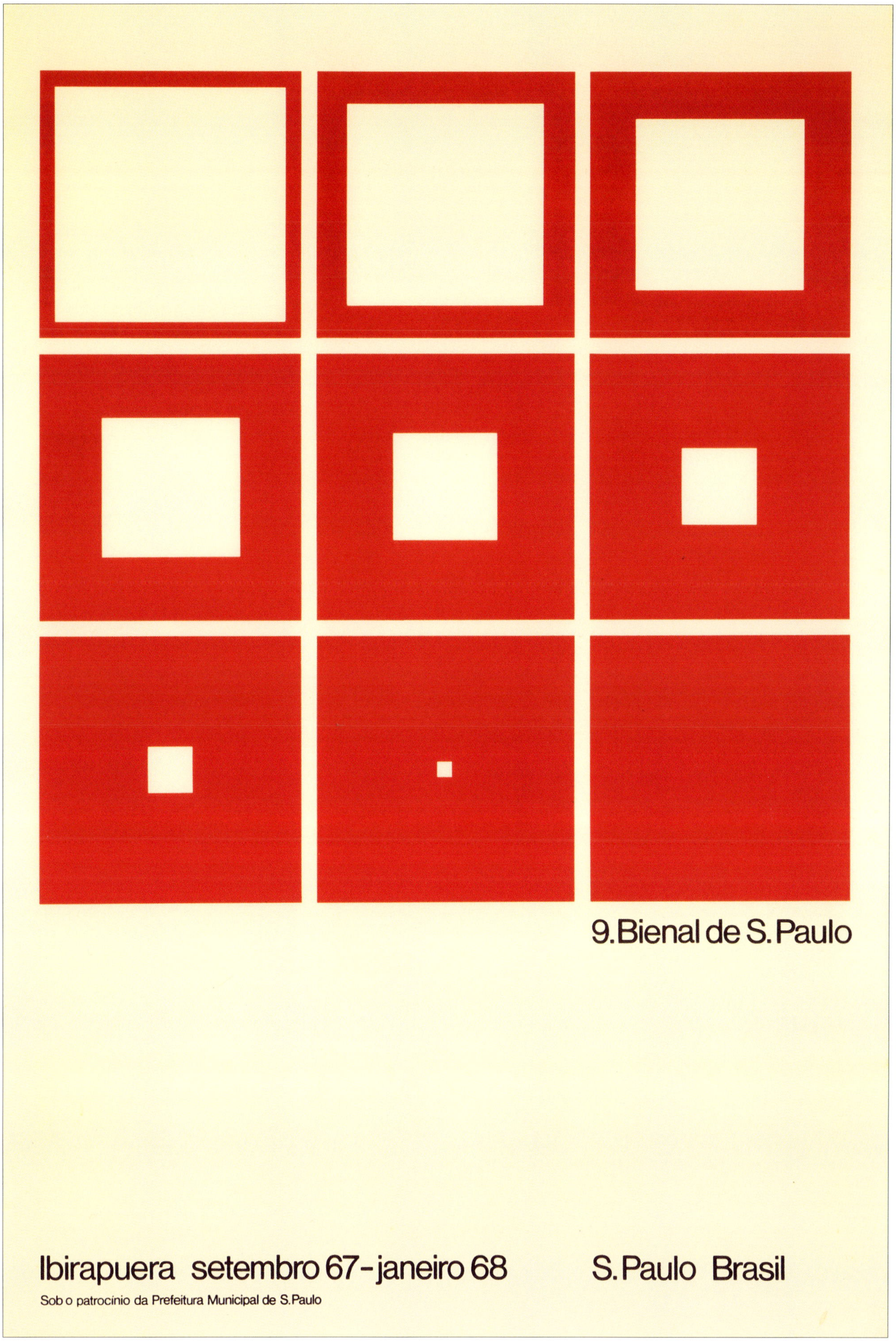
9.Bienal de S.Paulo
Ibirapuera setembro 67-janeiro 68
S.Paulo Brasil
Sob o patrocínio da Prefeitura Municipal de S.Paulo

Plates

Samson Flexor
and
Atelier Abstração

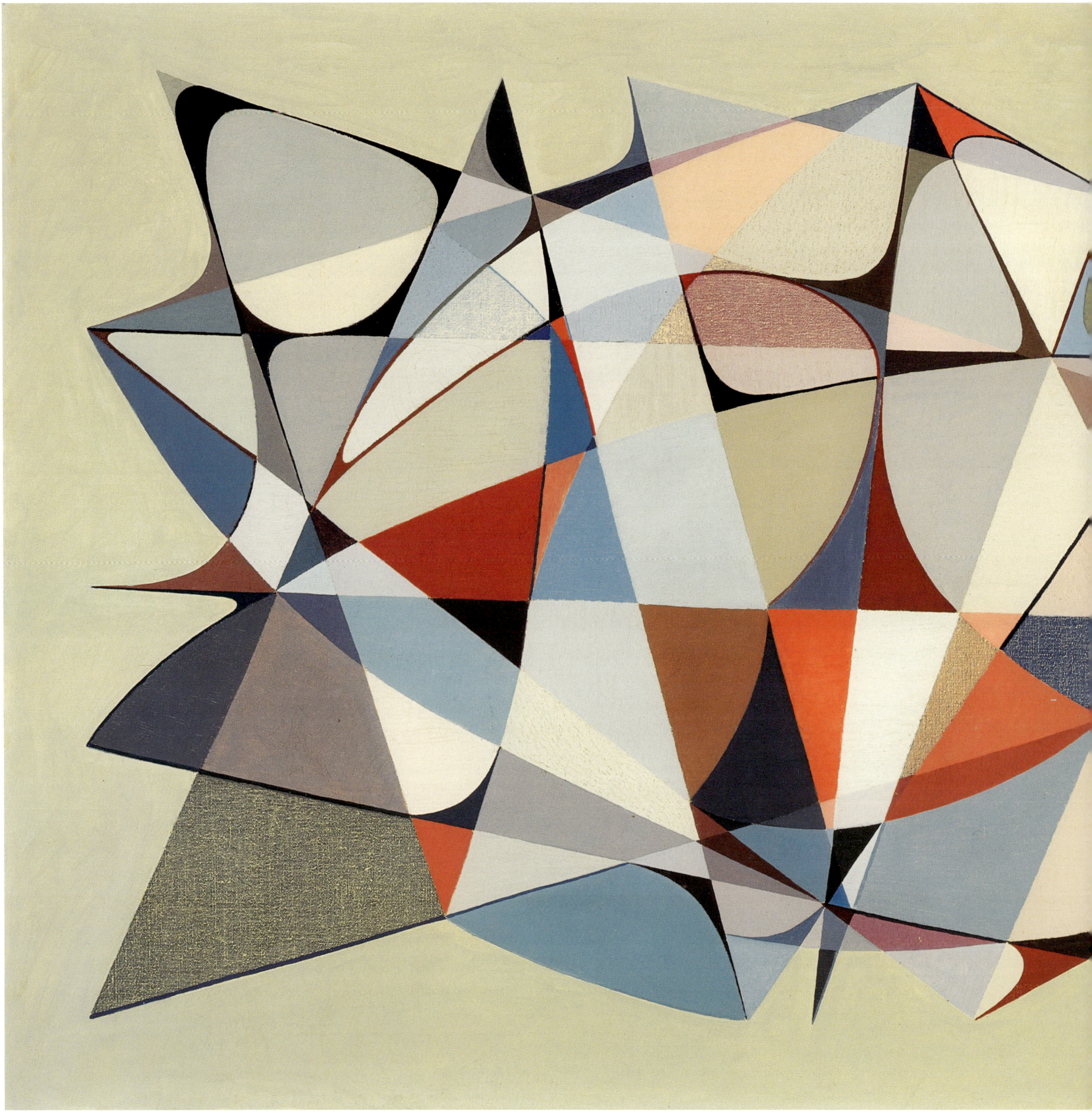

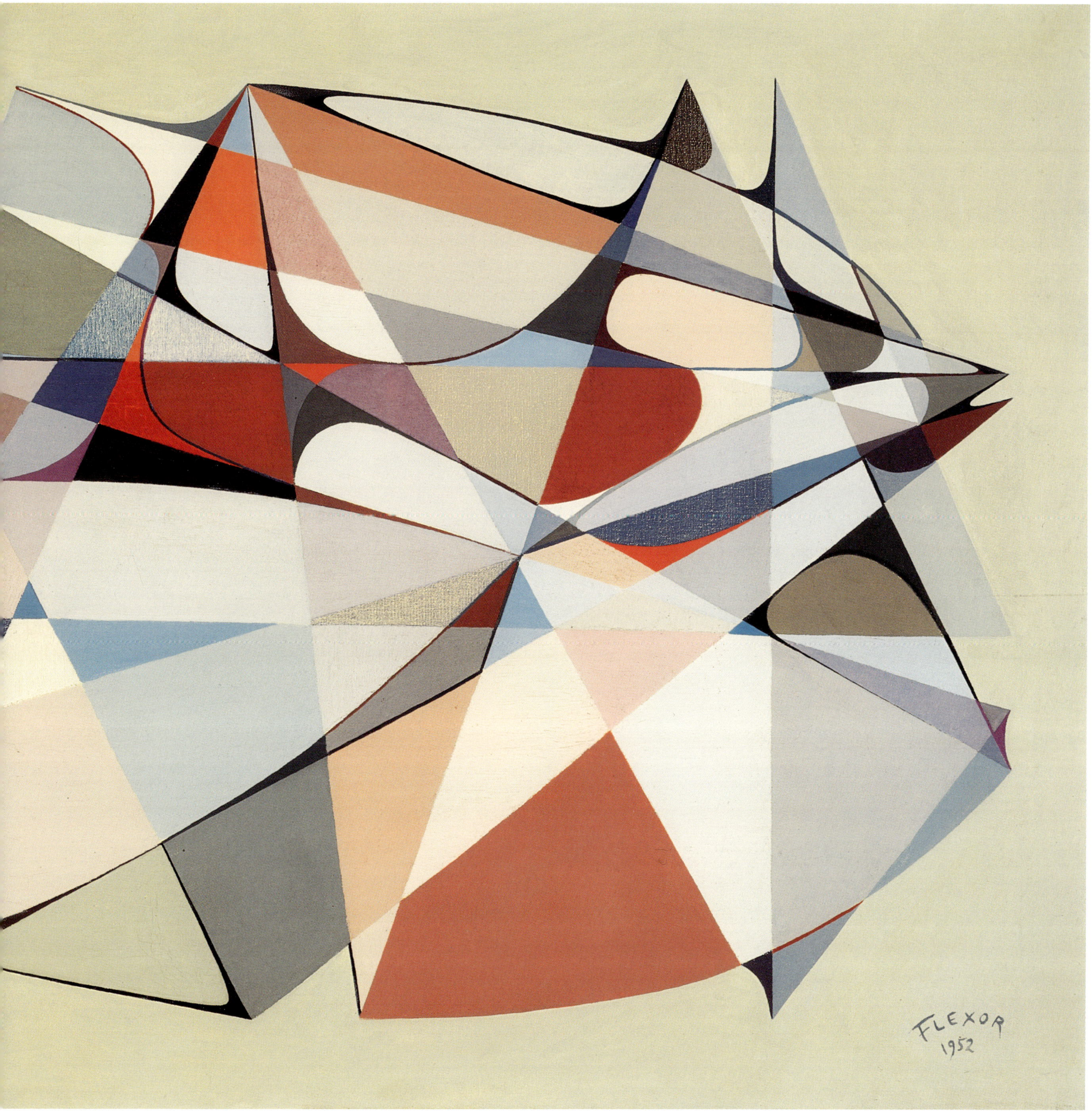
FLEXOR
1952

PREVIOUS PAGES
Samson Flexor
Invenção baiana no. 1
[*Invention from Bahia no. 1*],
1952
Oil on canvas
24 1/4 x 49 3/8 inches
(61.6 x 125.4 cm)
The Adolpho Leirner Collection of Brazilian Constructive Art, gift of the Caroline Wiess Law Foundation
2005.1001
PHOTO: Tom Jenkins

Samson Flexor
Geométrico I [*Geometric no. 1*],
1952
Oil on canvas
13 1/8 x 18 1/4 inches
(33.3 x 46.4 cm)
The Adolpho Leirner Collection of Brazilian Constructive Art, gift of the Caroline Wiess Law Foundation
2005.1002

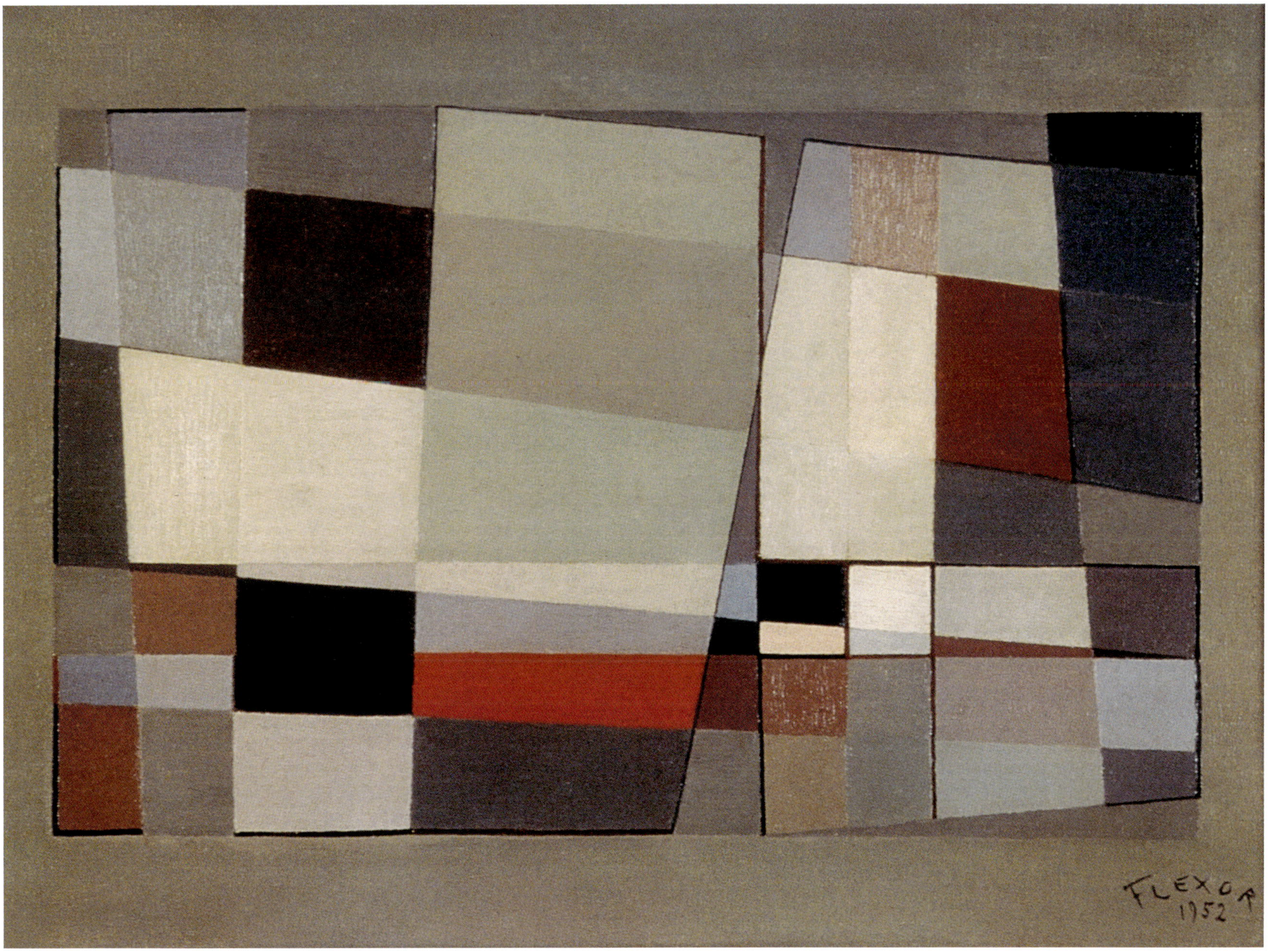
FLEXOR
1952

Samson Flexor
Geométrico II [*Geometric no. 2*],
1952
Oil on canvas
23 5/8 x 32 inches
(59.9 x 81.3 cm)
The Adolpho Leirner Collection
of Brazilian Constructive Art,
gift of the Caroline Wiess Law
Foundation
2005.1003
PHOTO: Rômulo Fialdini

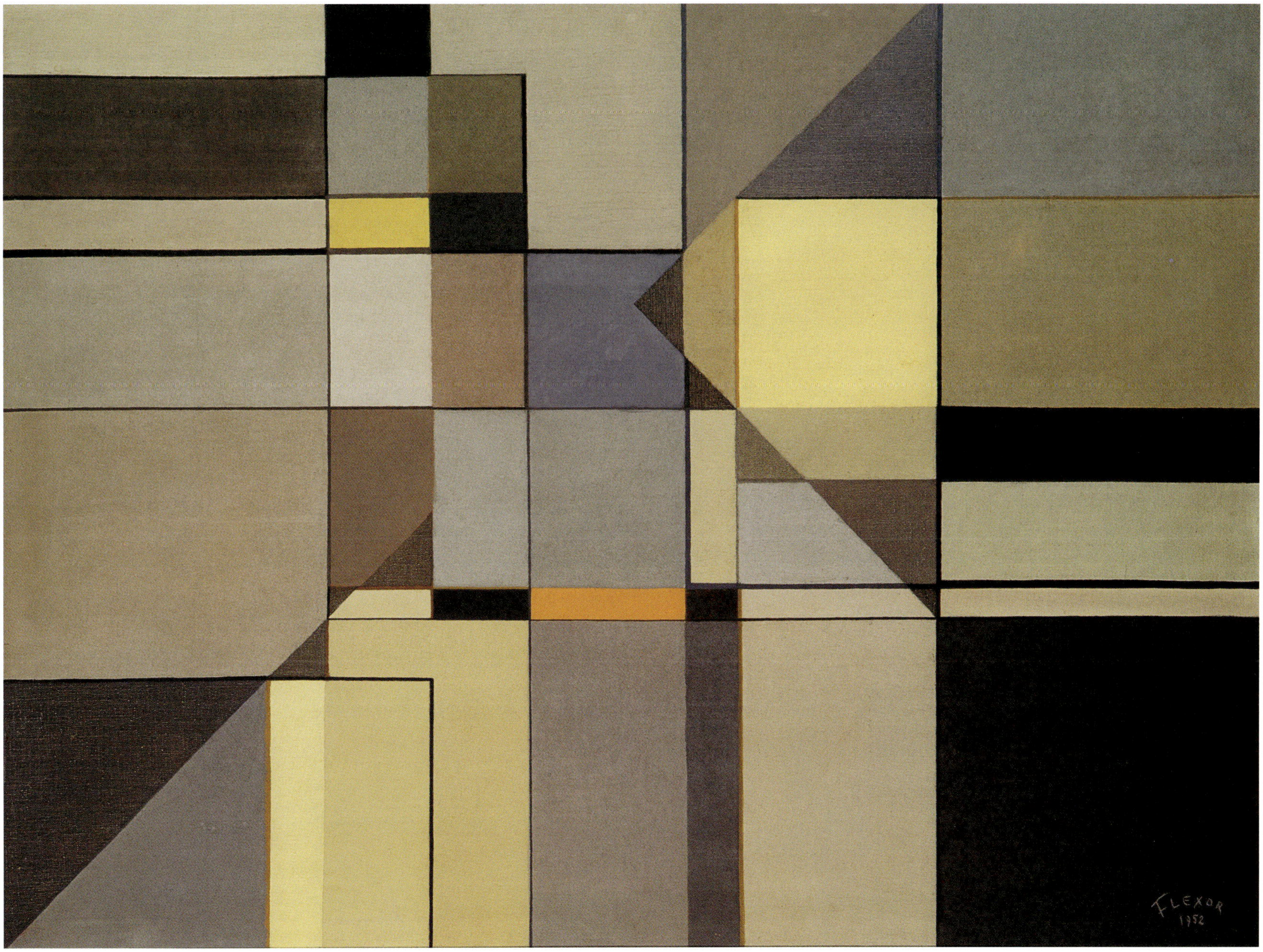
FLEXOR
1952

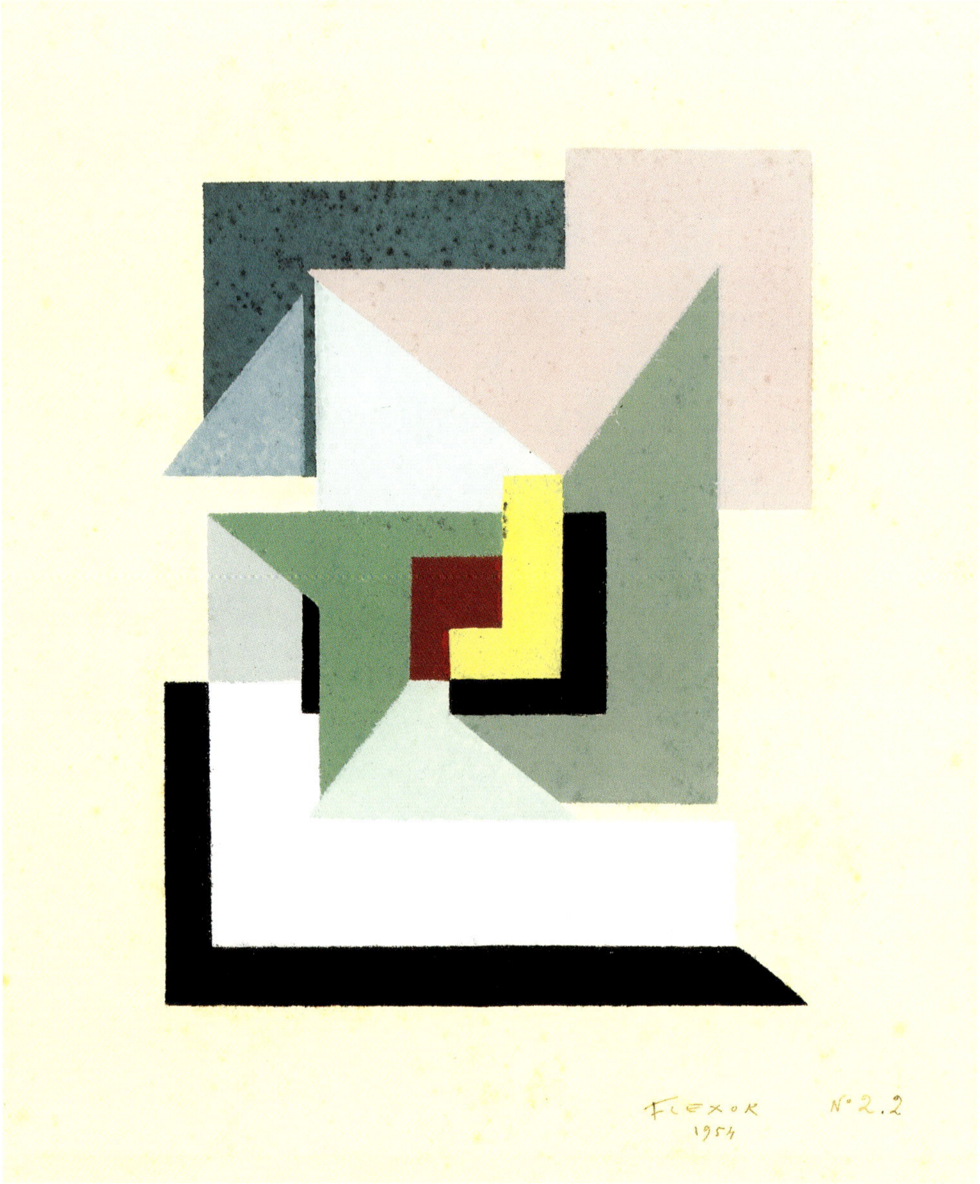

LEFT
Samson Flexor
Abstrato geométrico no. 22
[*Abstract and Geometric no. 22*],
1954
Screenprint
Image: 10 x 7 7/8 inches
(25.4 x 20 cm)
Sheet: 25 x 18 1/8 inches
(63.5 x 46 cm)
The Adolpho Leirner Collection
of Brazilian Constructive Art,
gift of the Caroline Wiess Law
Foundation
2005.1004
PHOTO: Tom Jenkins

RIGHT
Alberto Teixeira
Intensidade [*Intensity*], 1954
Oil on canvas
28 5/8 x 28 5/8 inches
(72.6 x 72.6 cm)
The Adolpho Leirner Collection
of Brazilian Constructive Art,
museum purchase with funds
provided by the Caroline Wiess
Law Accessions Endowment
Fund
2005.1031
PHOTO: Rômulo Fialdini

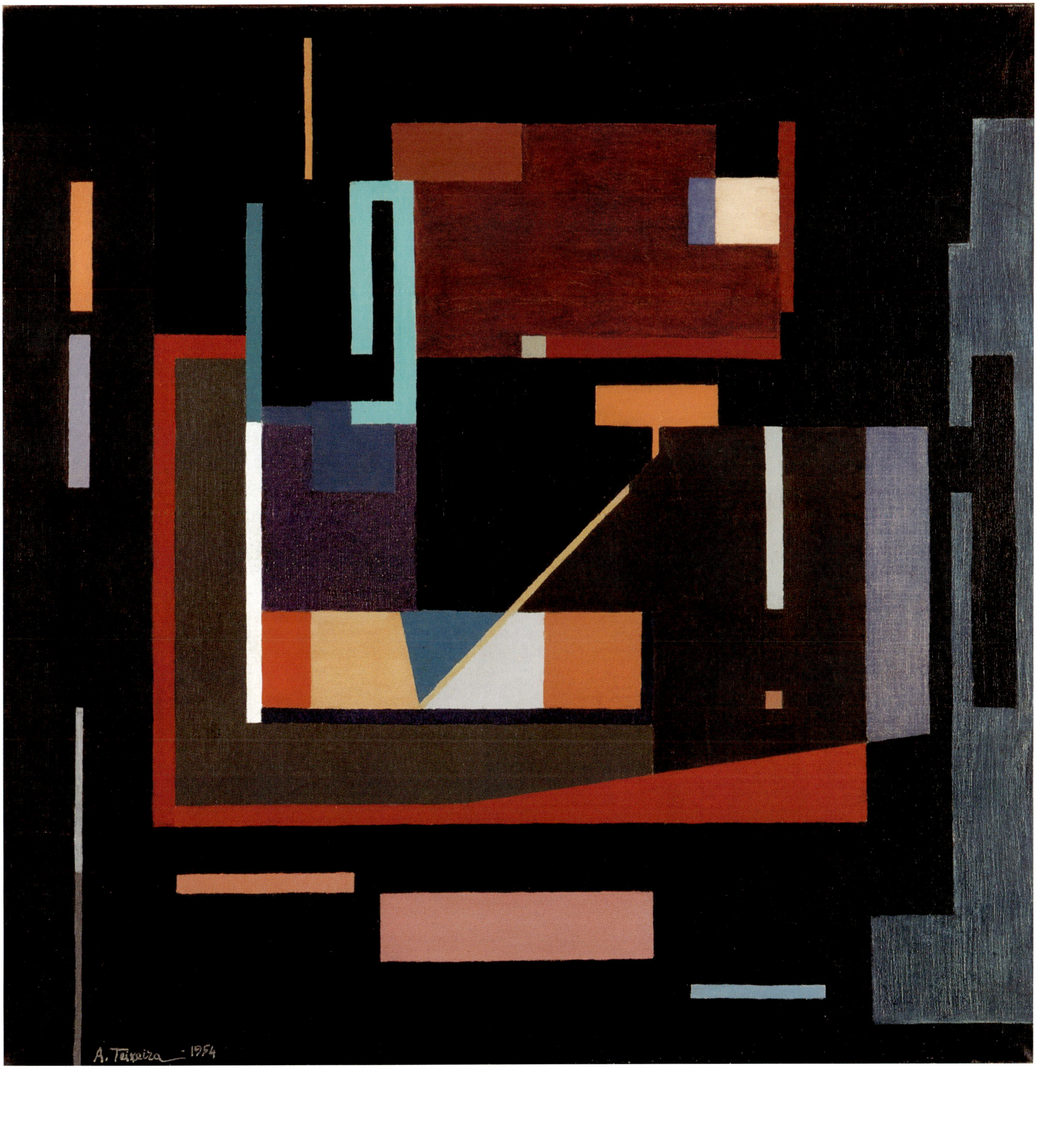
A. Teixeira - 1954

Wega Nery
Composição no. 4
[*Composition no. 4*], 1953
Oil on canvas
23 1/2 x 28 5/8 inches
(59.7 x 72.7 cm)
The Adolpho Leirner Collection
of Brazilian Constructive Art,
gift of the Caroline Wiess Law
Foundation
2005.1020
PHOTO: Tom Jenkins

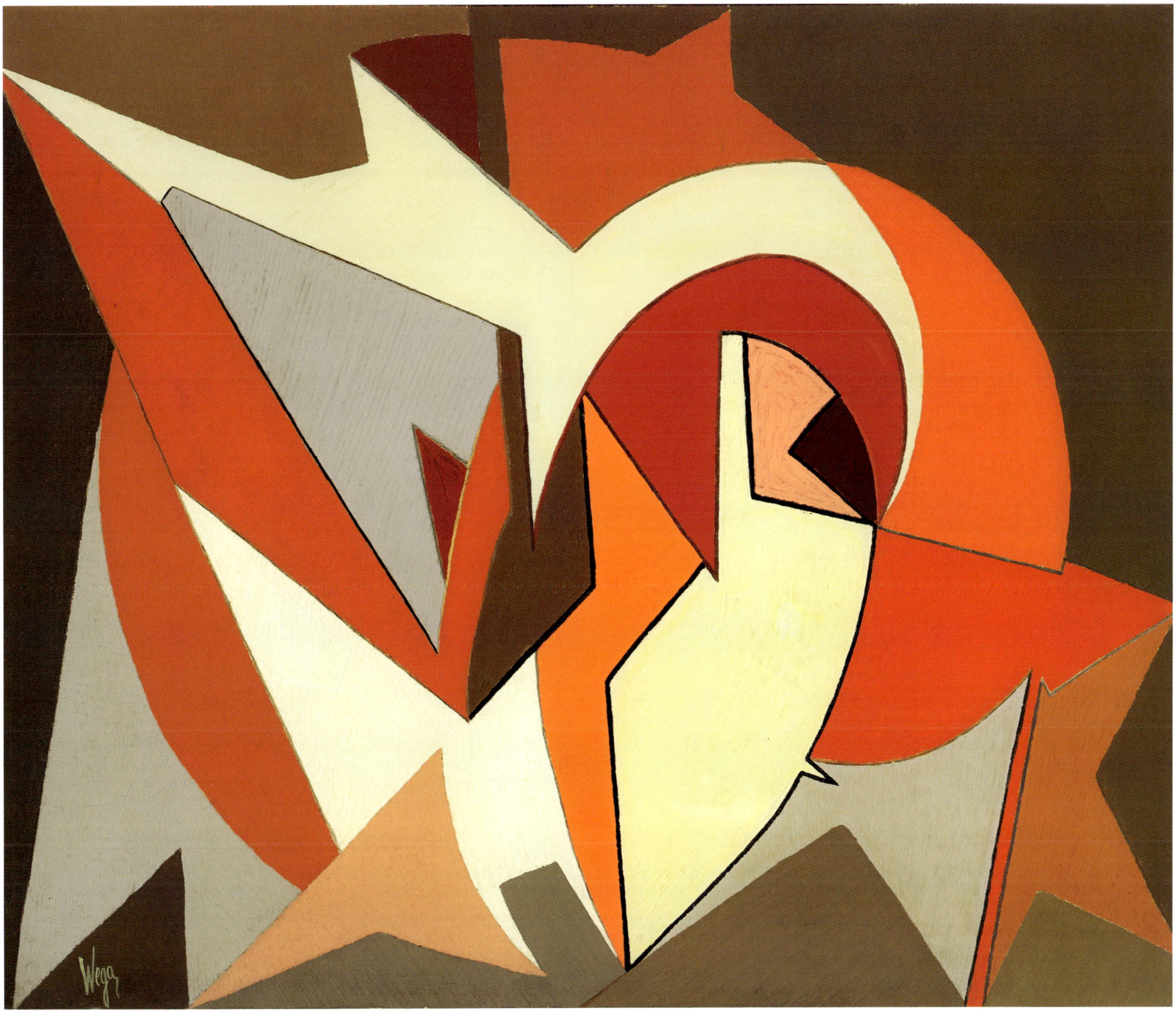

Leopoldo Raimo
Triangulação [*Triangulation*],
1956
Oil on canvas
19 5/8 x 33 inches
(49.8 x 83.8 cm)
The Adolpho Leirner Collection
of Brazilian Constructive Art,
gift of the Caroline Wiess Law
Foundation
2005.1025
PHOTO: Rômulo Fialdini

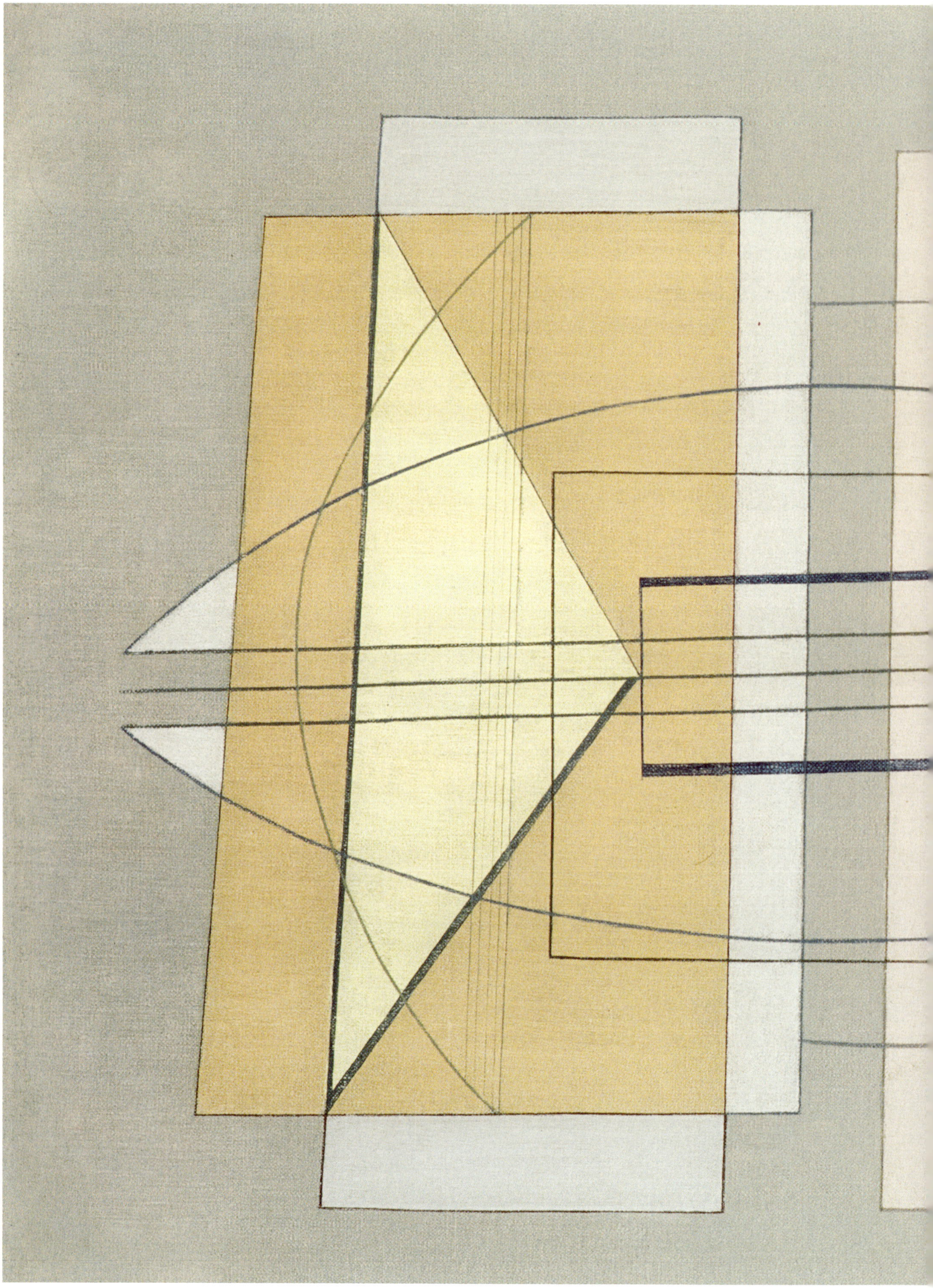

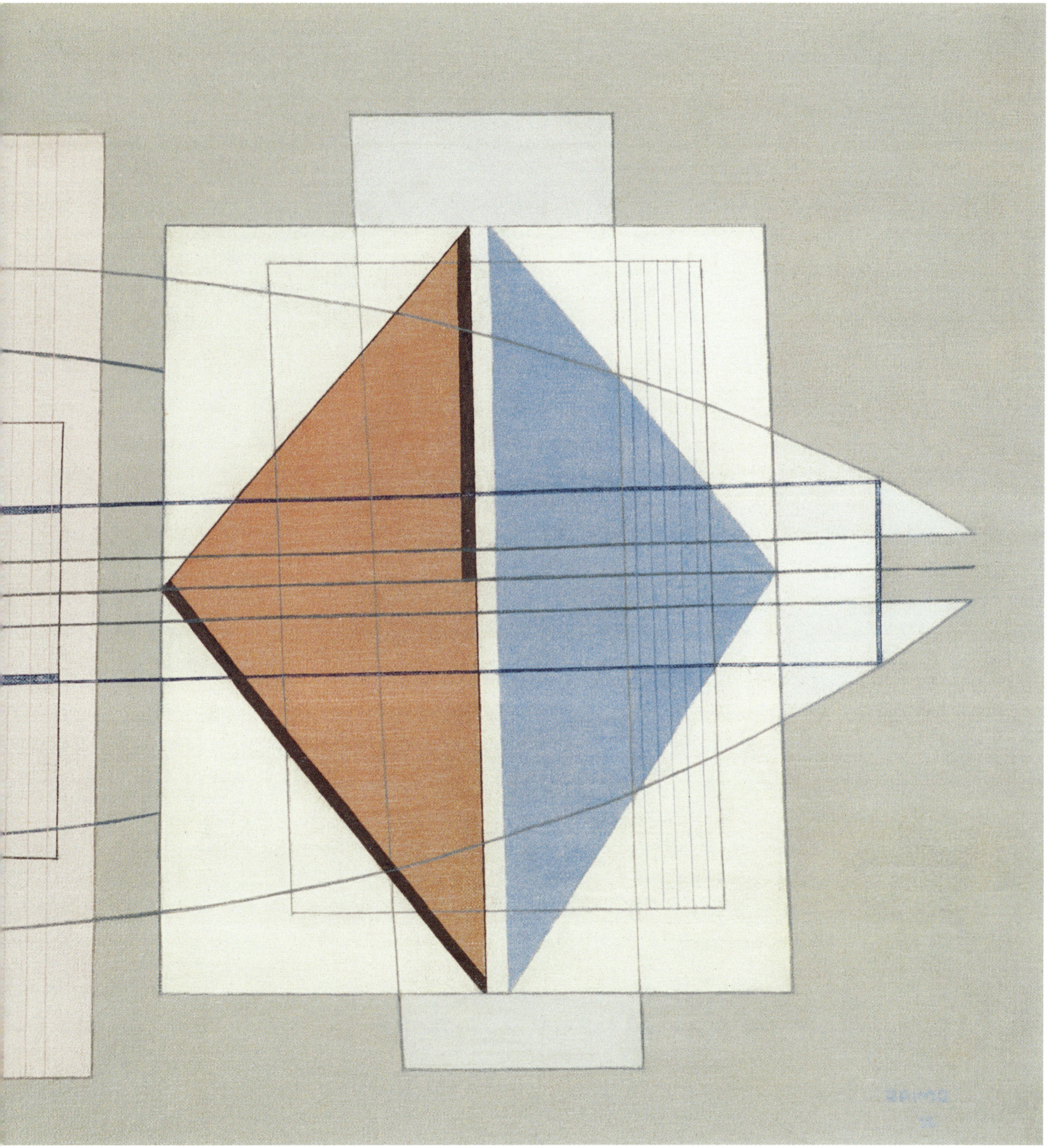

Samson Flexor
Puro e diagonal
[*Pure and Diagonal*], 1957
Oil on canvas
24 x 24 inches (61 x 61 cm)
The Adolpho Leirner Collection
of Brazilian Constructive Art,
gift of the Caroline Wiess Law
Foundation
2005.1006

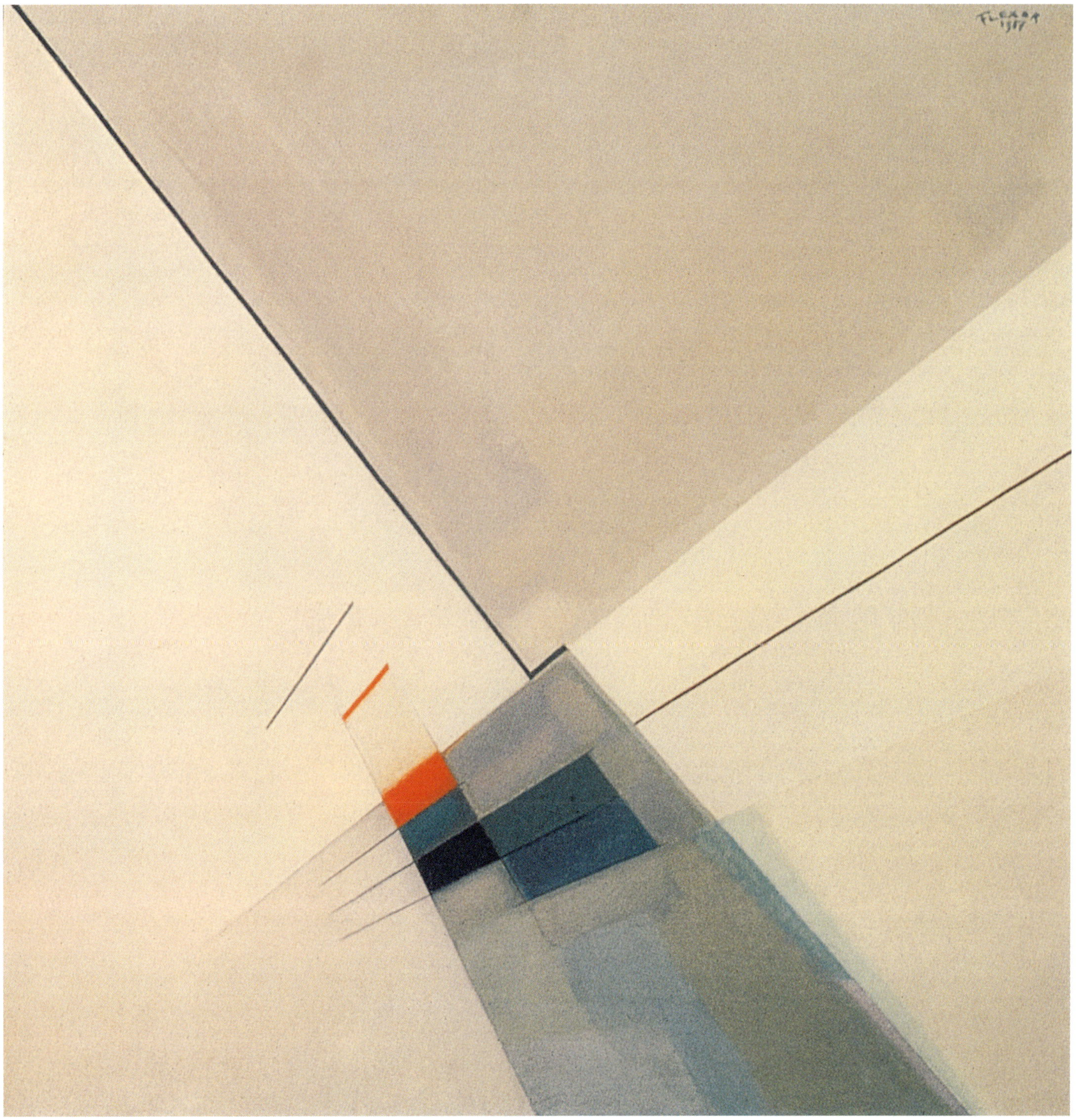

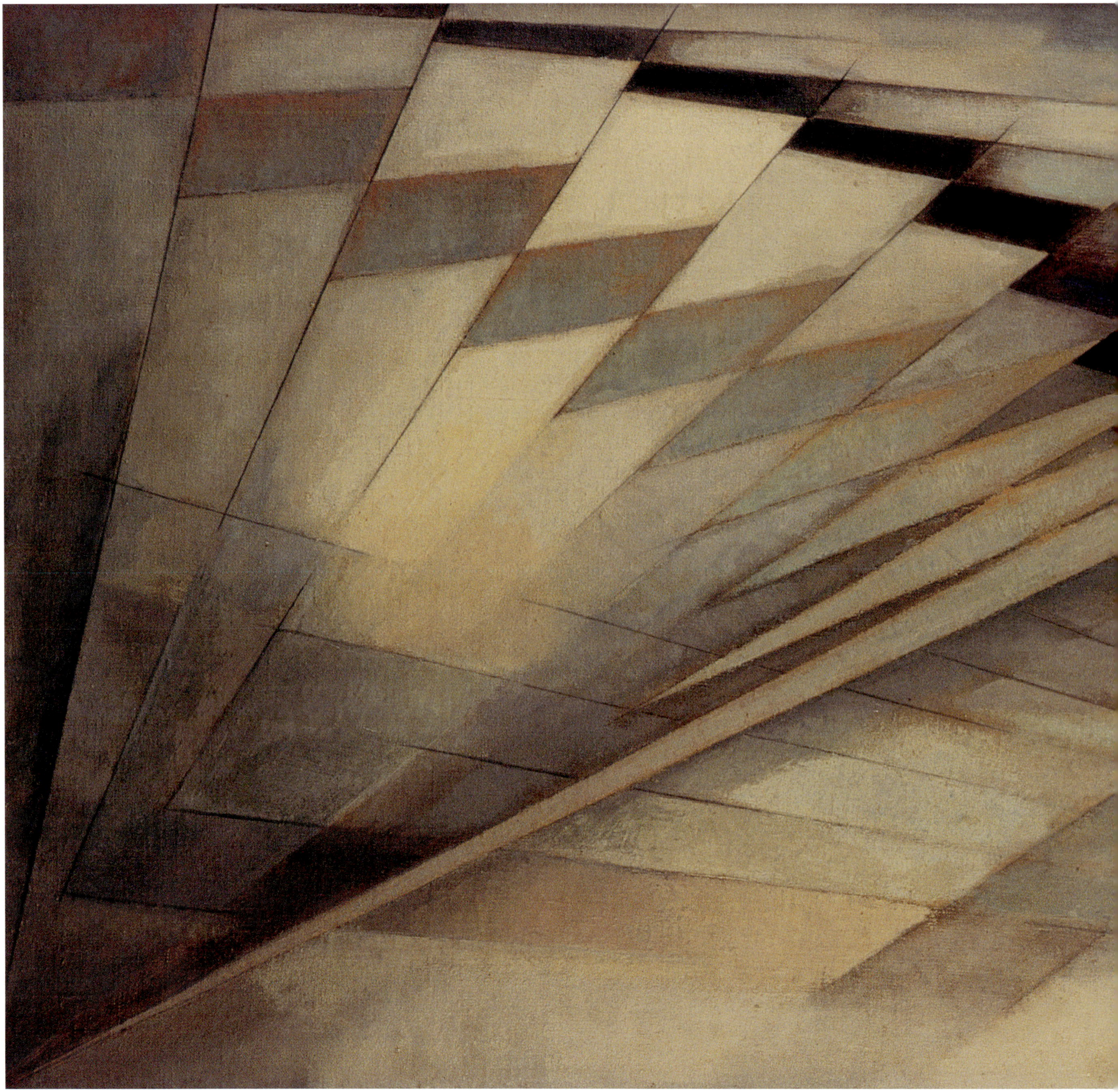

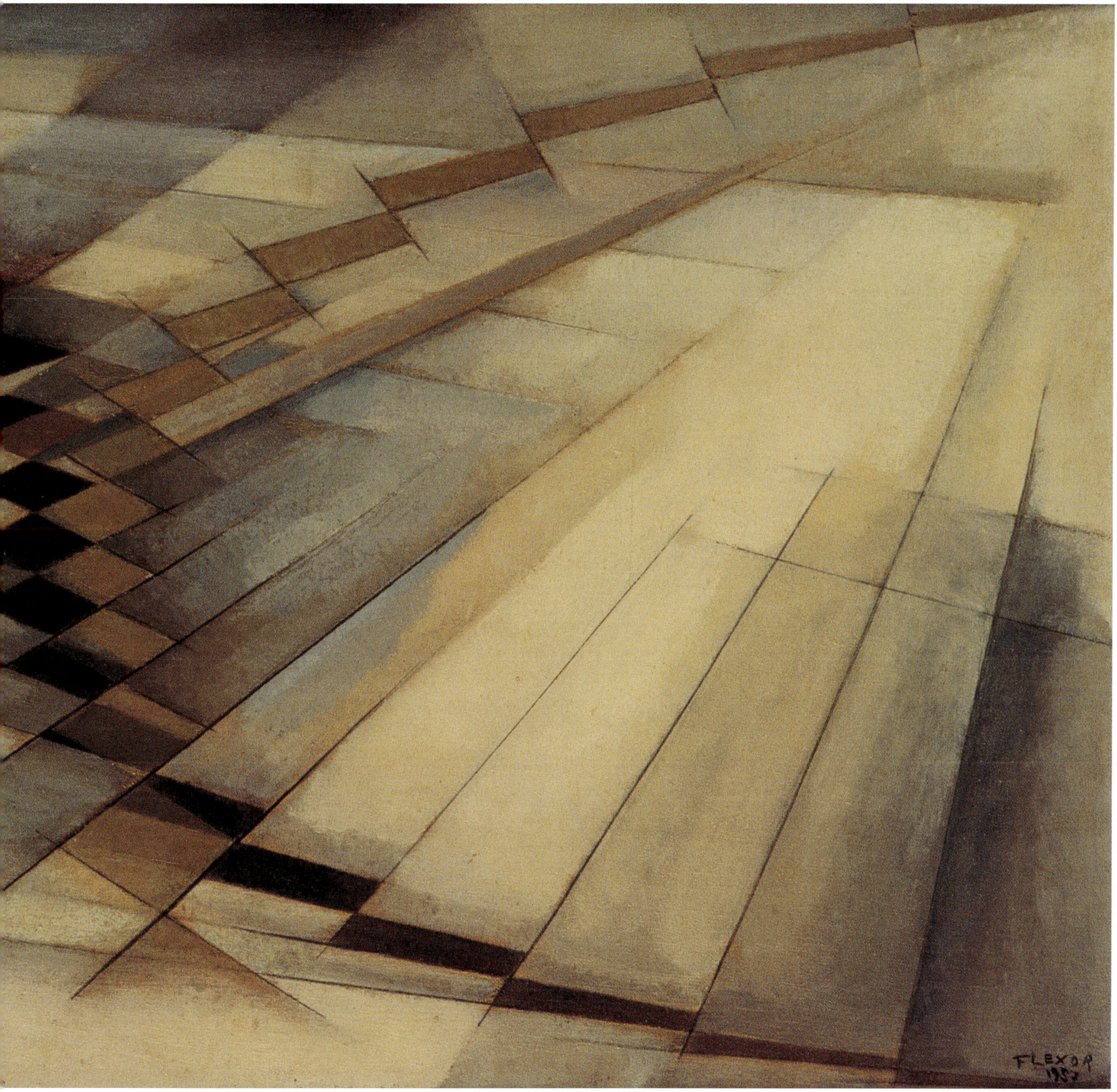
FLEXOR

PREVIOUS PAGES
Samson Flexor
Abstrato [*Abstract*], 1957
Oil on canvas
16 1/2 x 35 1/2 inches
(41.9 x 90.2 cm)
The Adolpho Leirner Collection of Brazilian Constructive Art, gift of the Caroline Wiess Law Foundation
2005.1007
PHOTO: Rômulo Fialdini

Norberto Nicola
Trama ativa [*Active Web*], 1955
Mixed media on wood
29 1/4 x 12 inches
(74.3 x 30.5 cm)
The Adolpho Leirner Collection of Brazilian Constructive Art, gift of the Caroline Wiess Law Foundation
2005.1021
PHOTO: Rômulo Fialdini

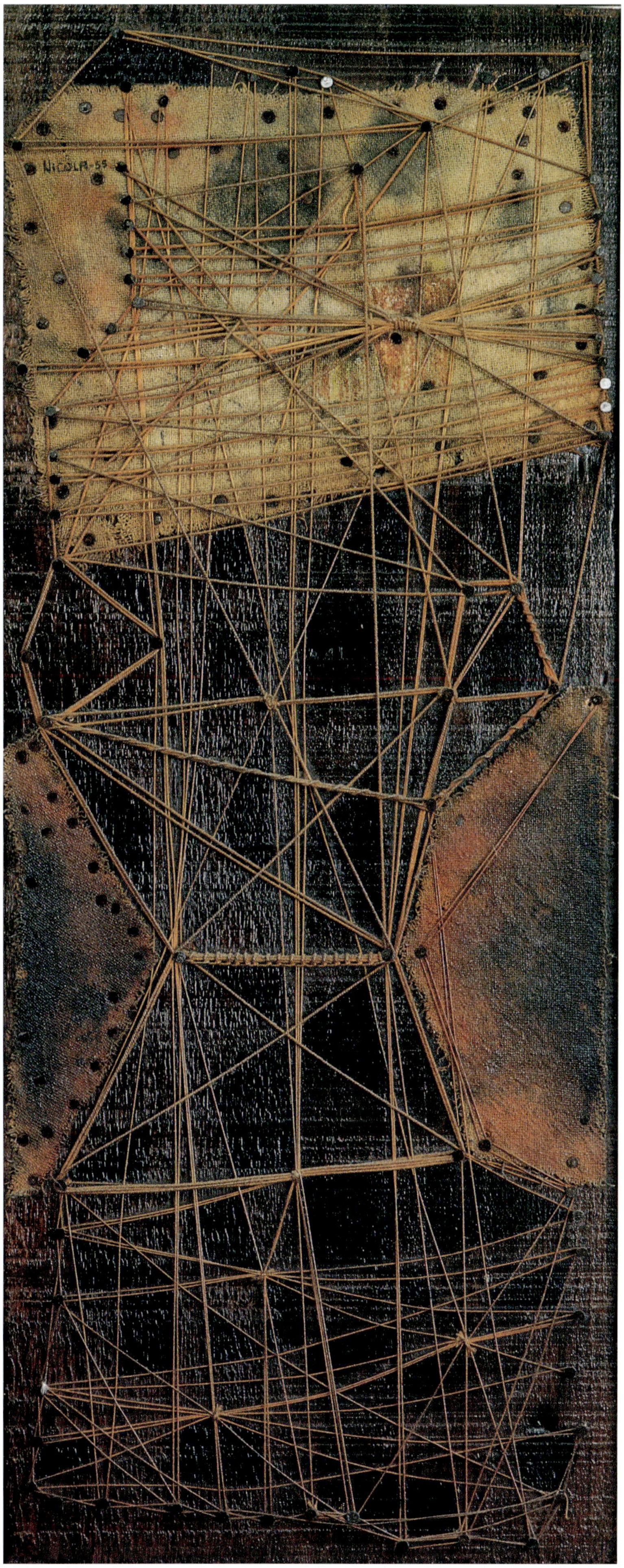
NICOLA-55

Grupo ruptura
and
Arte Concreto

Anatol Wladyslaw
Composição ortogonal no. 2
[*Orthogonal Composition no. 2*],
1952
Oil on canvas
28 3/4 x 23 3/8 inches
(73 x 59.4 cm)
The Adolpho Leirner Collection
of Brazilian Constructive Art,
museum purchase with funds
provided by the Caroline Wiess
Law Accessions Endowment
Fund
2005.1042
PHOTO: Rômulo Fialdini

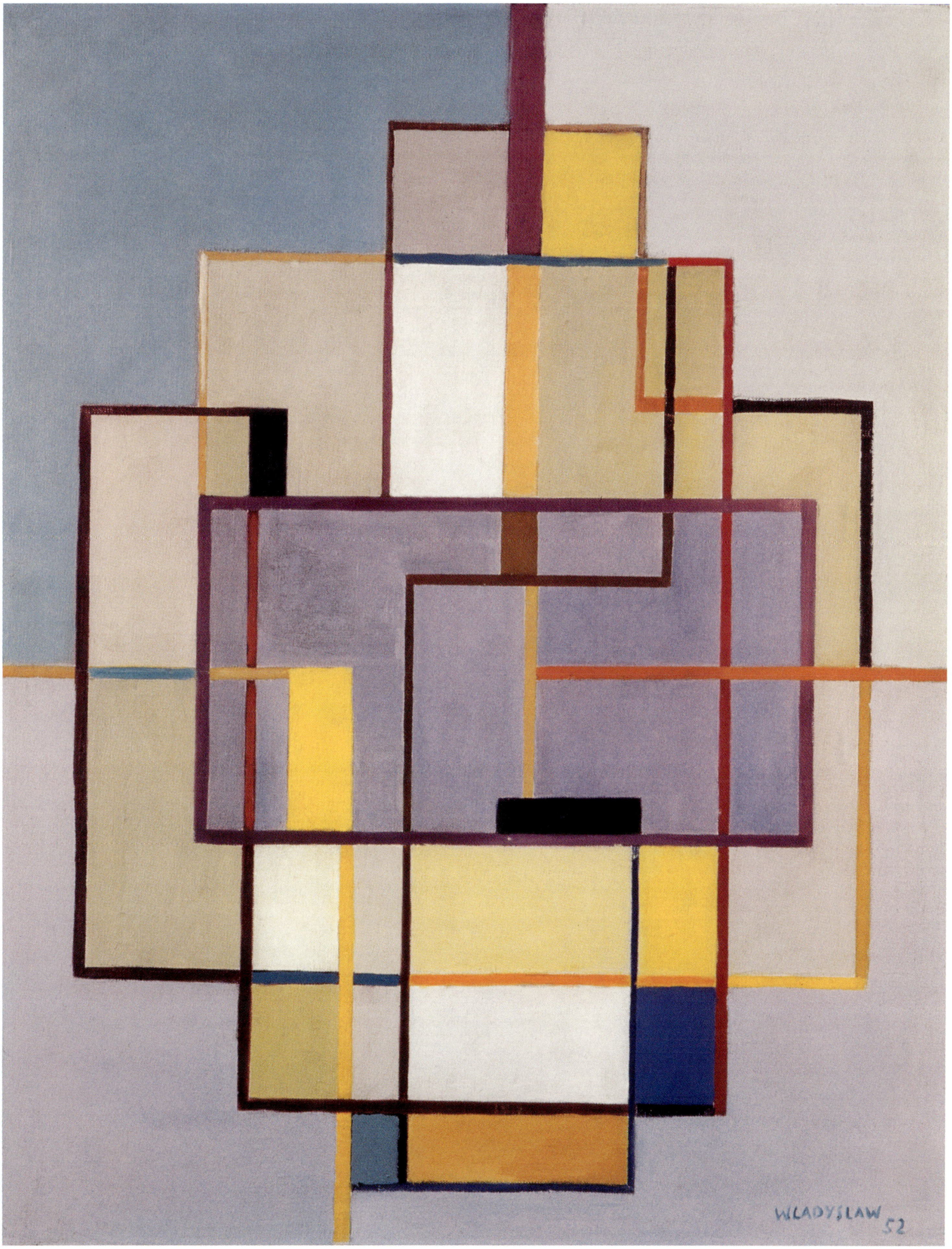
WLADYSLAW
52

Lothar Charoux
Abstrato geométrico
[*Abstract and Geometric*],
1952
Oil on canvas
24 x 19 5/8 inches
(61 x 49.8 cm)
The Adolpho Leirner Collection
of Brazilian Constructive Art,
gift of the Caroline Wiess Law
Foundation
2005.989
PHOTO: Tom Jenkins

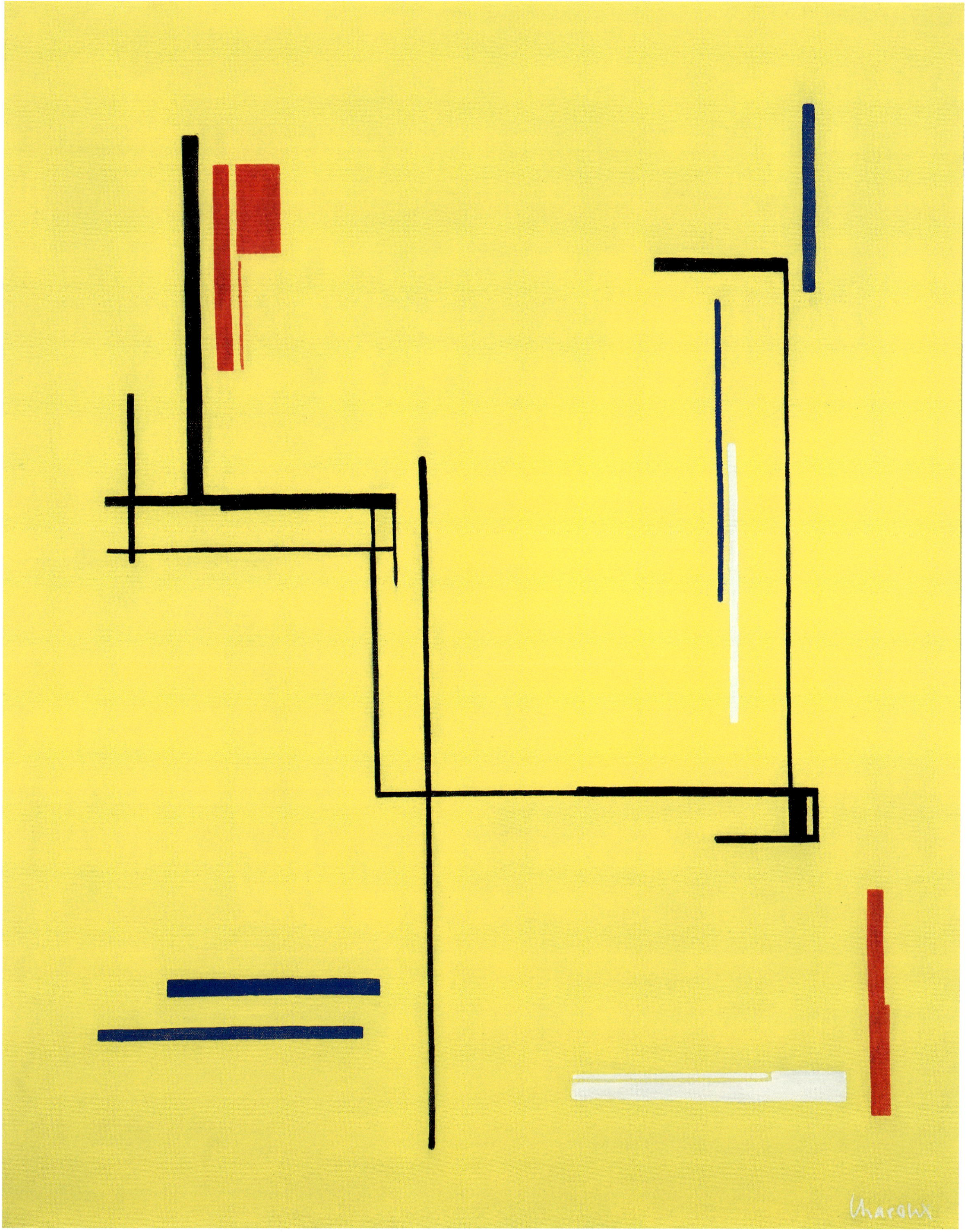
Charchoune

Anatol Wladyslaw
Composição [*Composition*],
1952
Oil on canvas
21 5/8 x 21 5/8 inches
(55 x 55 cm)
The Adolpho Leirner Collection
of Brazilian Constructive Art,
museum purchase with funds
provided by the Caroline Wiess
Law Accessions Endowment
Fund
2005.1043

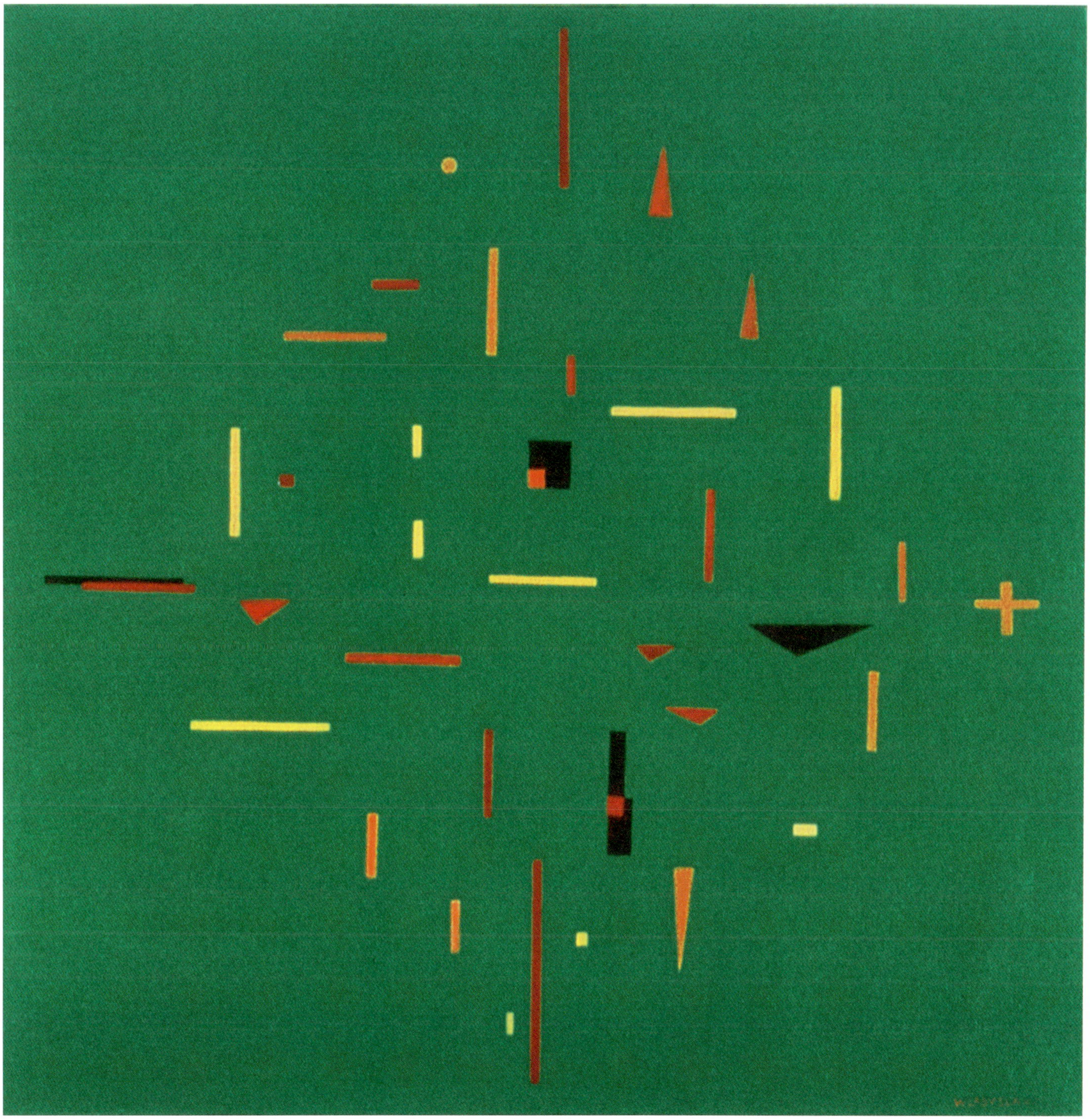

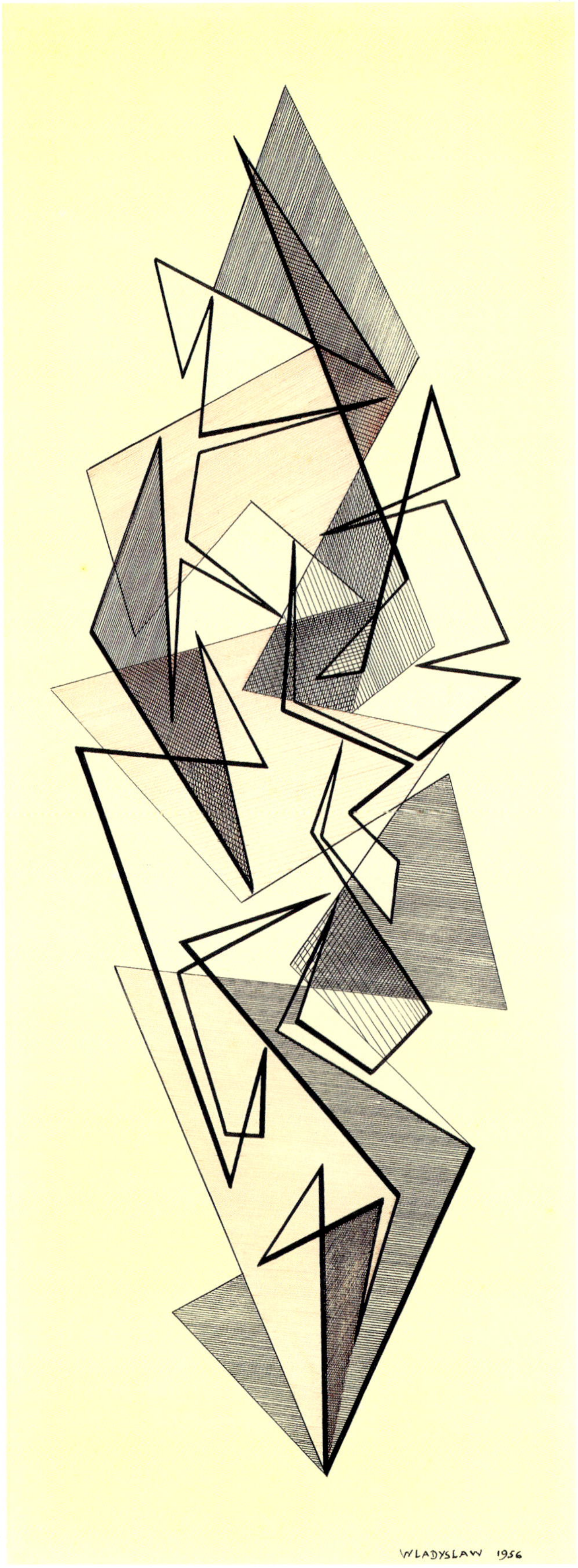

LEFT
Anatol Wladyslaw
Sem título [*Untitled*], 1956
India ink on paper
18 15/16 x 8 1/2 inches
(48.1 x 21.6 cm)
The Adolpho Leirner Collection of Brazilian Constructive Art, museum purchase with funds provided by the Caroline Wiess Law Accessions Endowment Fund
2005.1045
PHOTO: Tom Jenkins

RIGHT
Anatol Wladyslaw
Composição linear [*Linear Composition*], 1953
Oil on canvas
27 1/2 x 27 5/8 inches
(69.9 x 70.1 cm)
The Adolpho Leirner Collection of Brazilian Constructive Art, museum purchase with funds provided by the Caroline Wiess Law Accessions Endowment Fund
2005.1044
PHOTO: Tom Jenkins

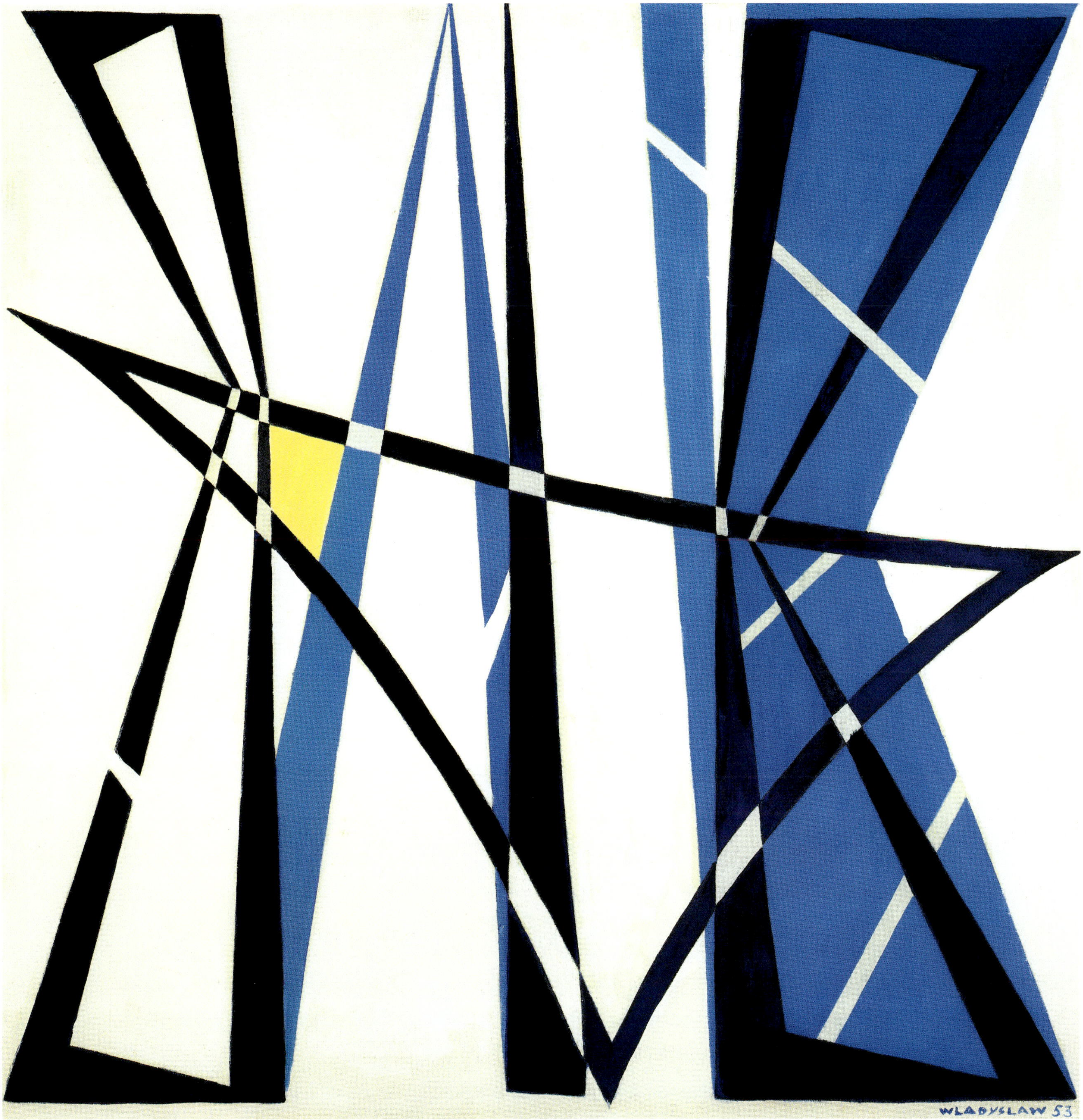
WLADYSLAW 53

Maurício Nogueira Lima
Composição 1 [*Composition no. 1*],
1952
Oil on canvas
28 3/4 x 19 5/8 inches
(73 x 49.8 cm)
The Adolpho Leirner Collection
of Brazilian Constructive Art,
gift of the Caroline Wiess Law
Foundation
2005.1012
PHOTO: Rômulo Fialdini

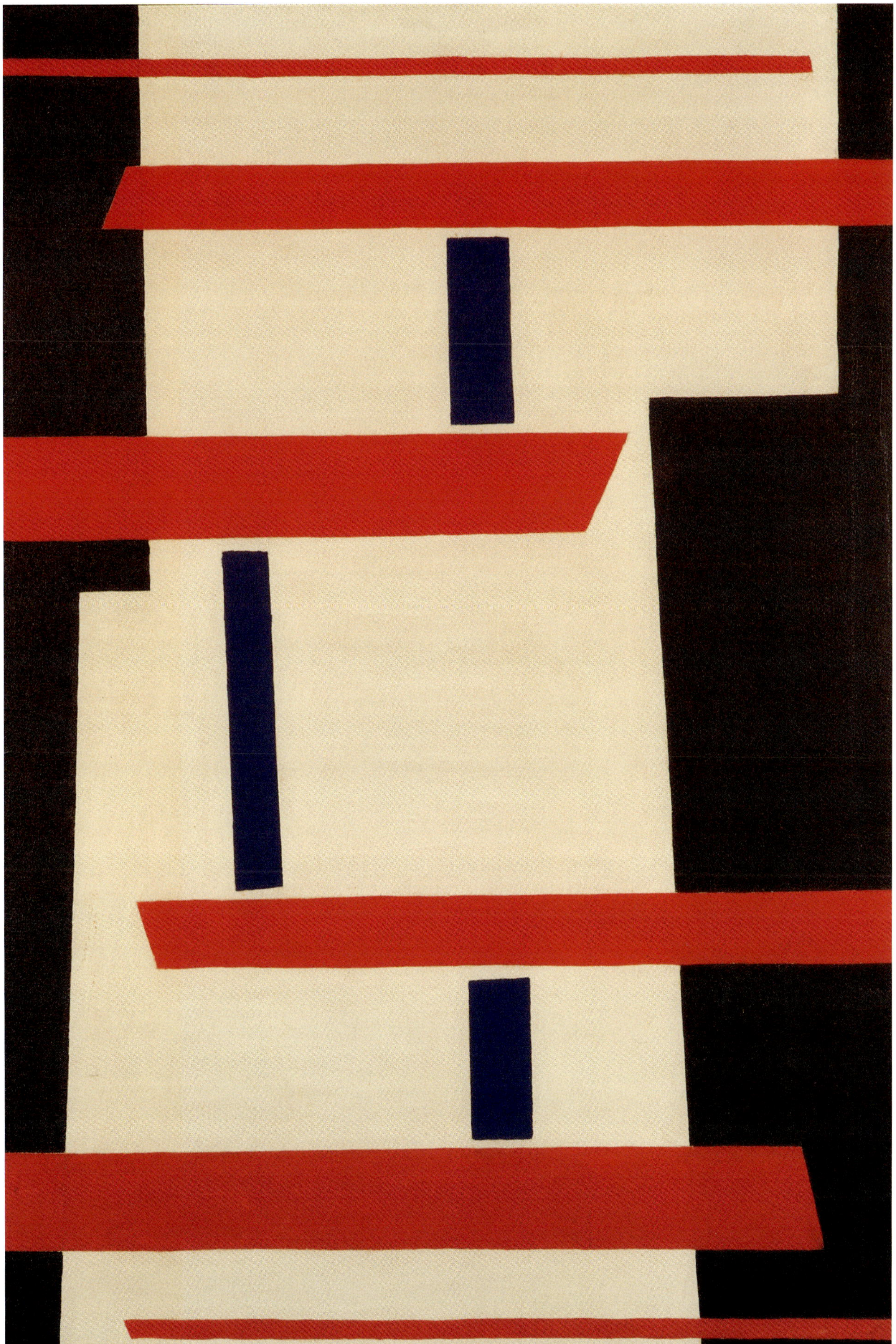
Mauricio N. Lima 52

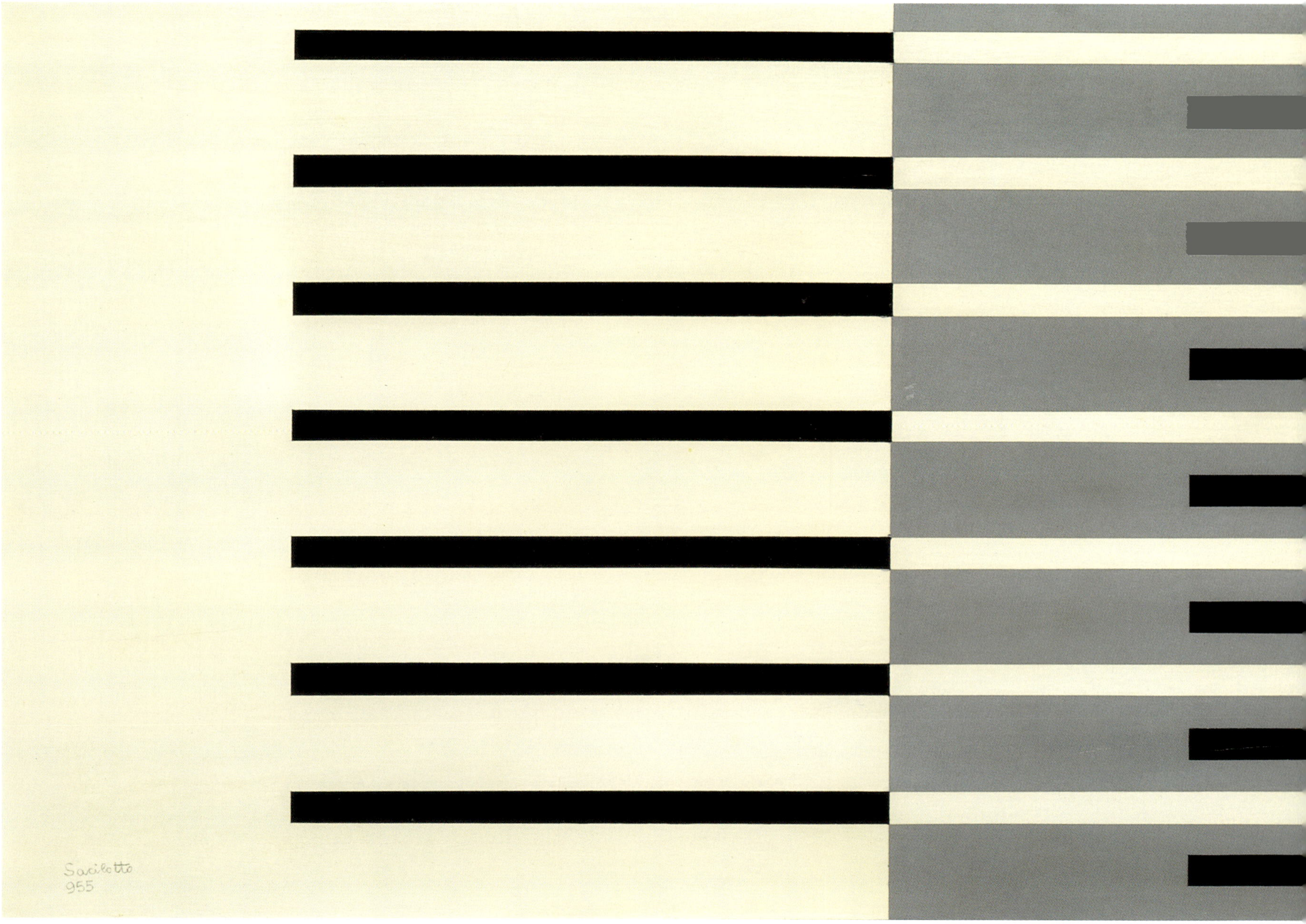
Sacilotto
955

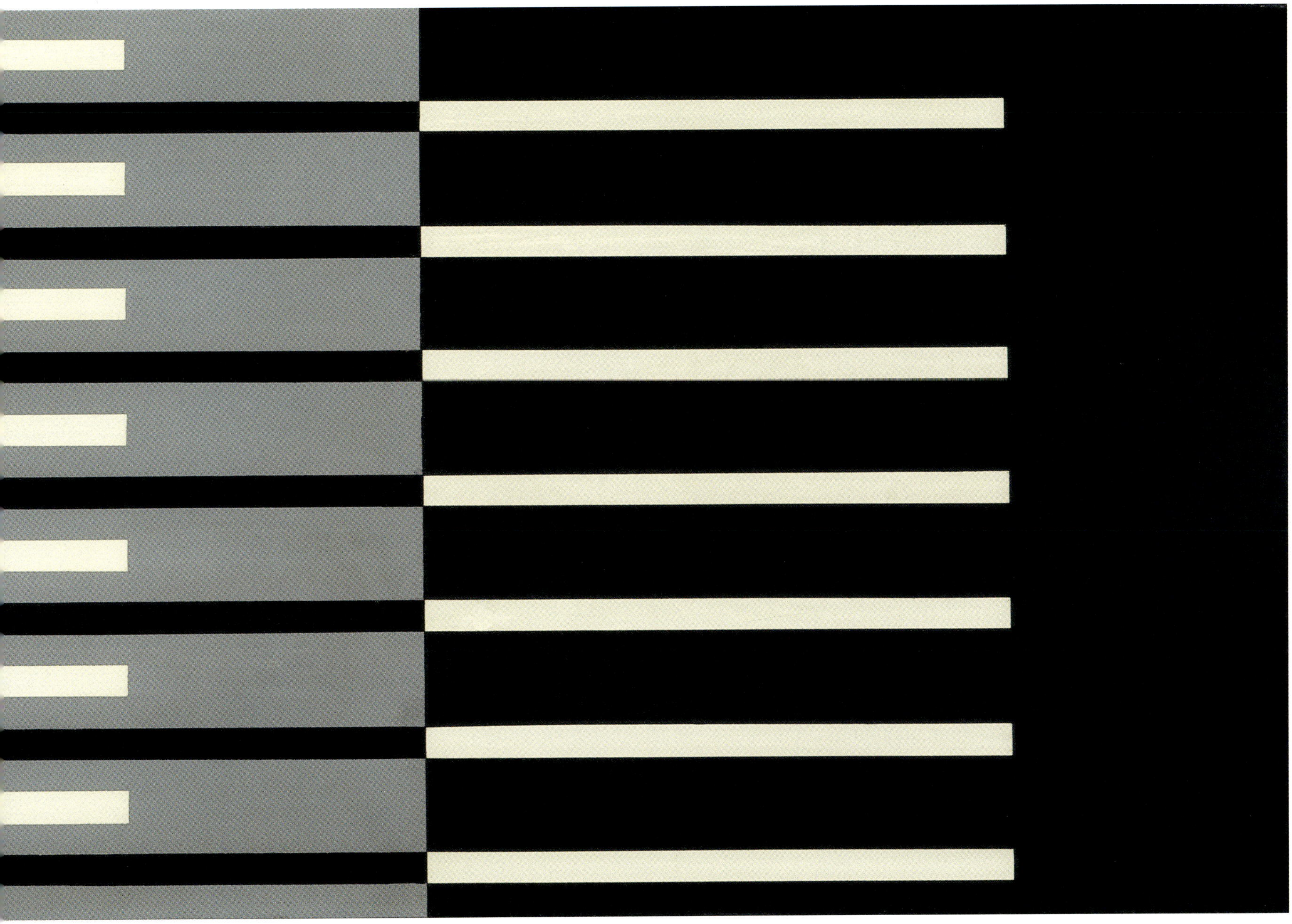

PREVIOUS PAGES
Luís Sacilotto
Concreção 5521
[*Concretion 5521*], 1955
Enamel on wood
11 3/4 x 35 1/2 inches
(30 x 90 cm)
The Adolpho Leirner Collection of Brazilian Constructive Art, museum purchase with funds provided by the Caroline Wiess Law Accessions Endowment Fund
2005.1027
PHOTO: Tom Jenkins

Alexandre Wollner
Sem título [*Untitled*], 1957
Enamel on hardboard
23 5/8 x 23 5/8 inches
(60 x 60 cm)
The Adolpho Leirner Collection of Brazilian Constructive Art, museum purchase with funds provided by the Caroline Wiess Law Accessions Endowment Fund
2005.1046
PHOTO: Tom Jenkins

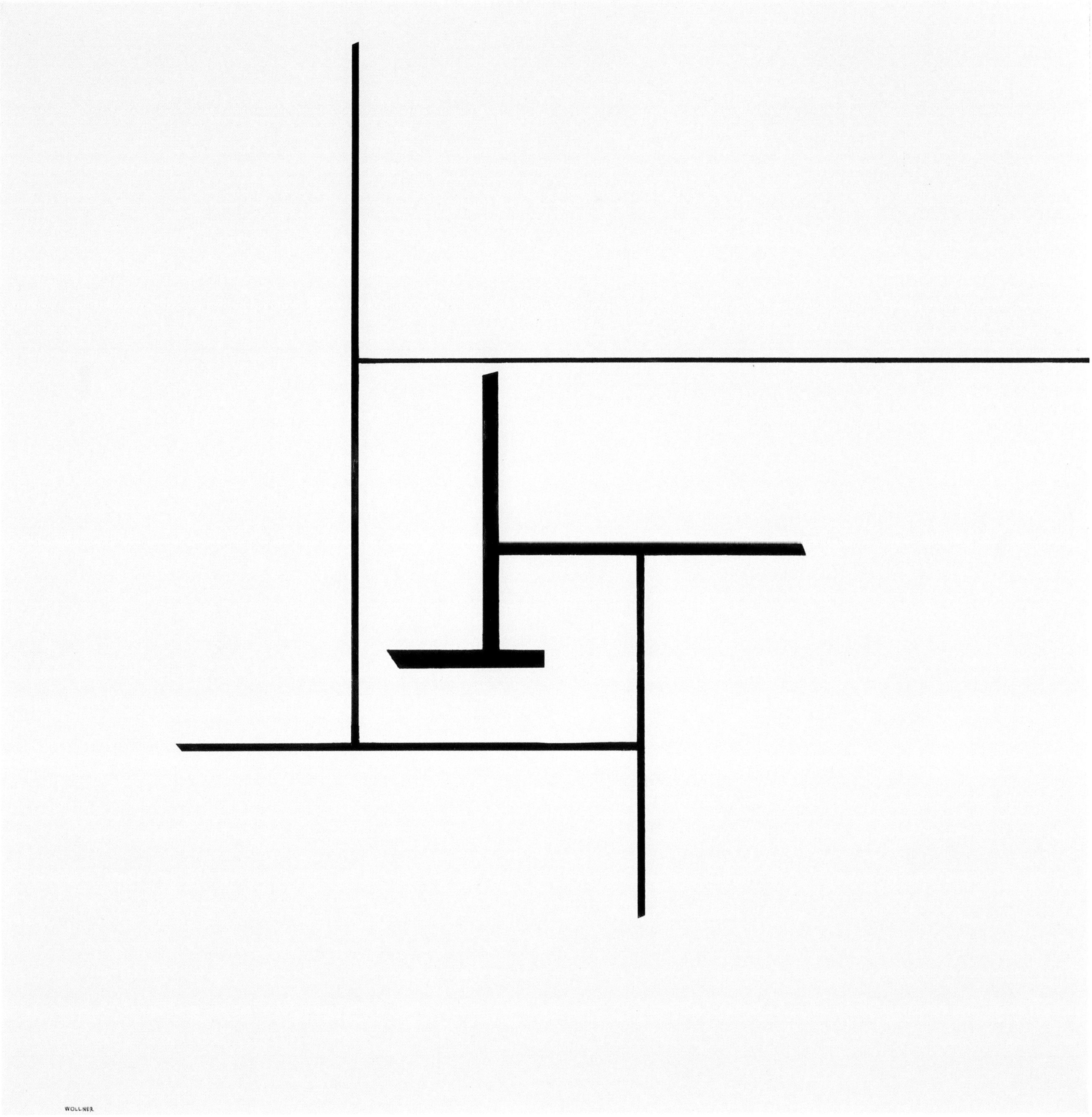
WOLLNER

Waldemar Cordeiro
Idéia visível [*Visible Idea*], 1956
Wood plastered with paint
39 1/2 x 39 9/16 inches
(100.3 x 100.5 cm)
The Adolpho Leirner Collection of Brazilian Constructive Art, museum purchase with funds provided by the Caroline Wiess Law Accessions Endowment Fund
2007.15
PHOTO: Tom Jenkins

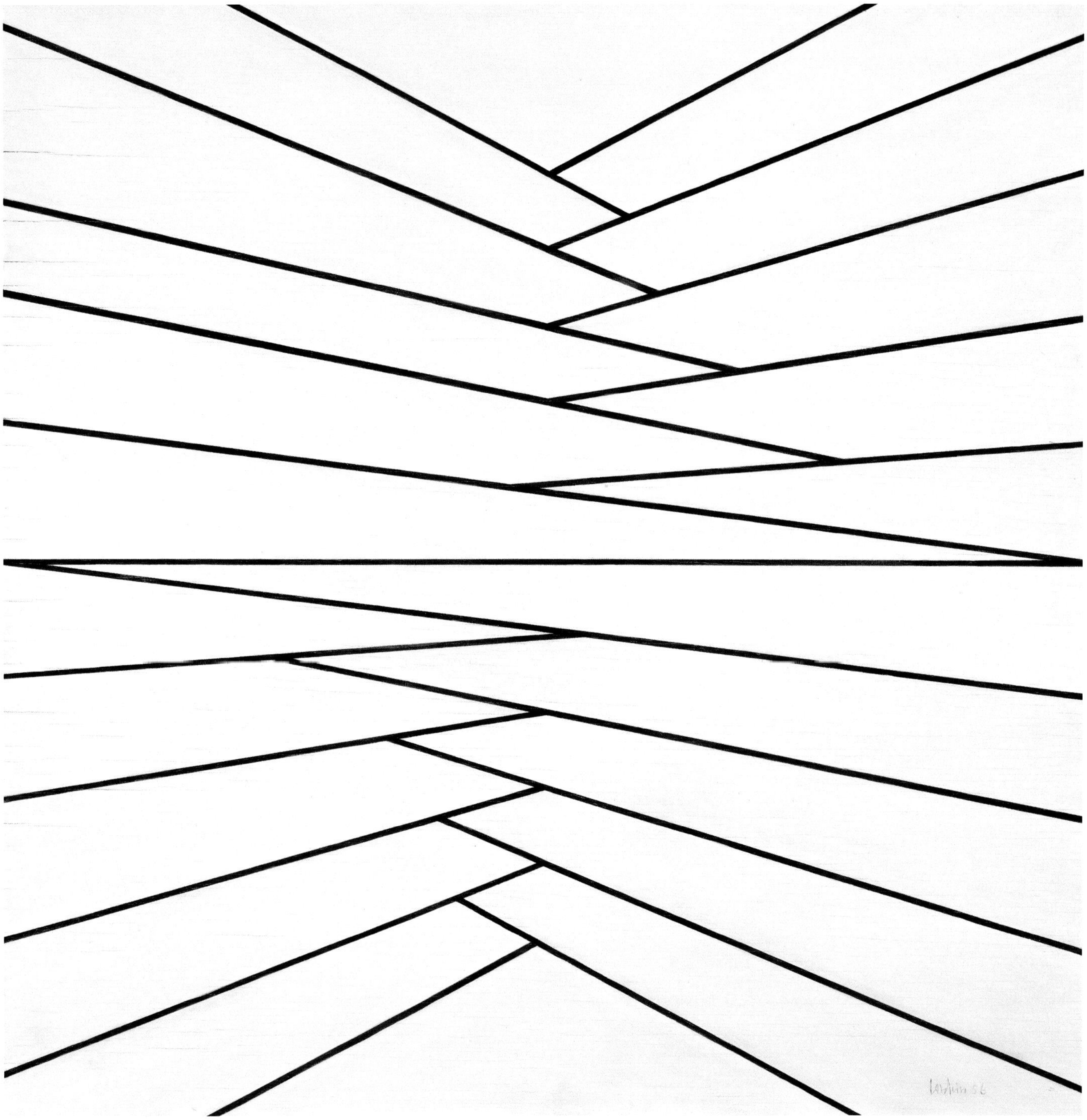

Luís Sacilotto
Concreção 6045
[*Concretion 6045*], 1960
Painted iron
12 1/4 x 35 1/2 x 15 1/2 inches
(31.1 x 90.2 x 39.4 cm)
The Adolpho Leirner Collection of Brazilian Constructive Art, museum purchase with funds provided by the Caroline Wiess Law Accessions Endowment Fund
2007.24
PHOTO: Rômulo Fialdini

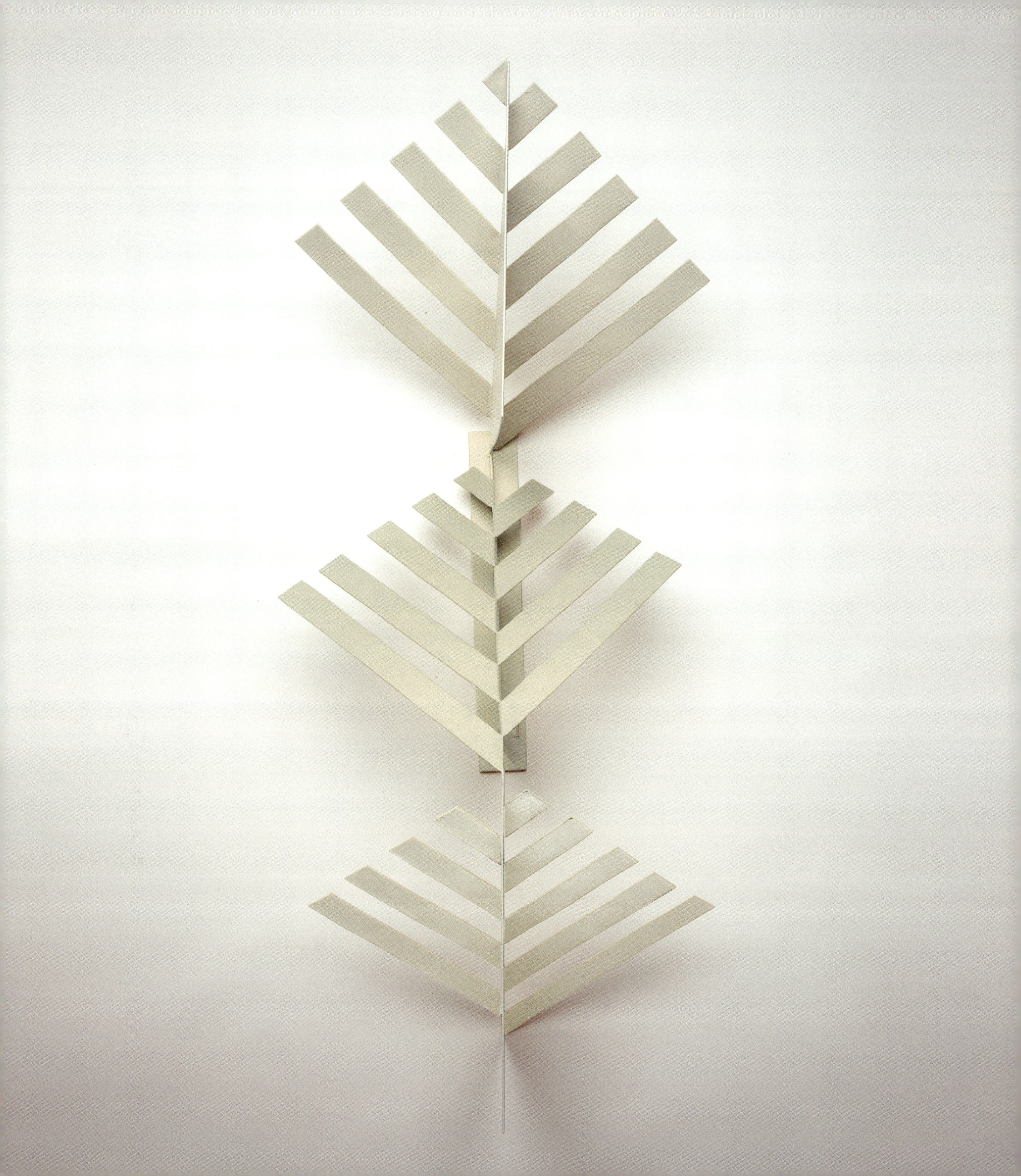

Lothar Charoux
Sem título [*Untitled*], 1950s
India ink on paper
12 7/8 x 13 inches (32.7 x 33 cm)
The Adolpho Leirner Collection
of Brazilian Constructive Art,
gift of the Caroline Wiess Law
Foundation
2005.990
PHOTO: Tom Jenkins

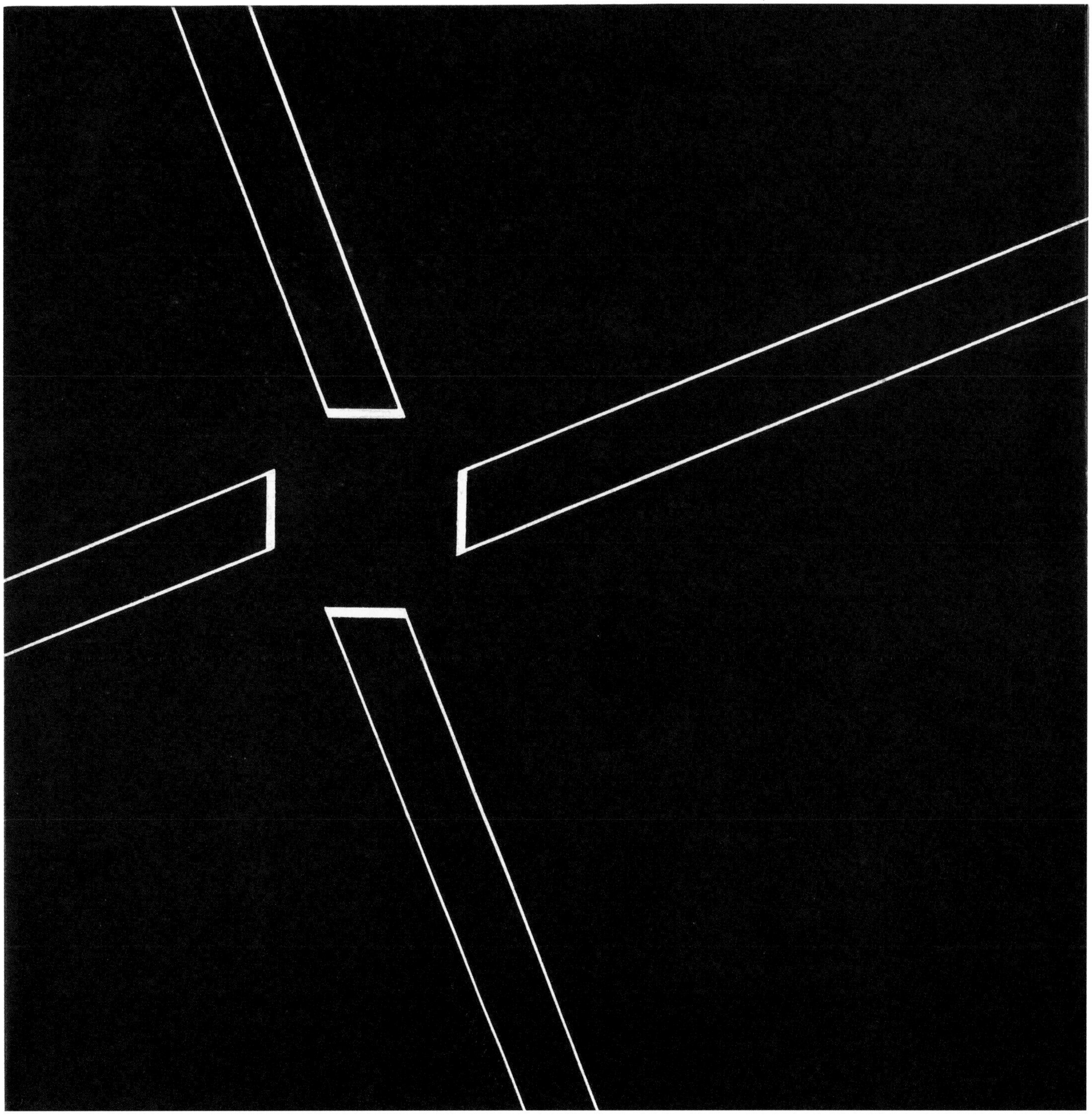

Luís Sacilotto
Concreção 5730
[*Concretion 5730*], 1957
Aluminum
14 1/4 x 19 3/4 x 19 5/8 inches
(36.2 x 50.2 x 49.8 cm)
The Adolpho Leirner Collection of Brazilian Constructive Art, museum purchase with funds provided by the Caroline Wiess Law Accessions Endowment Fund
2007.22
PHOTO: Rômulo Fialdini

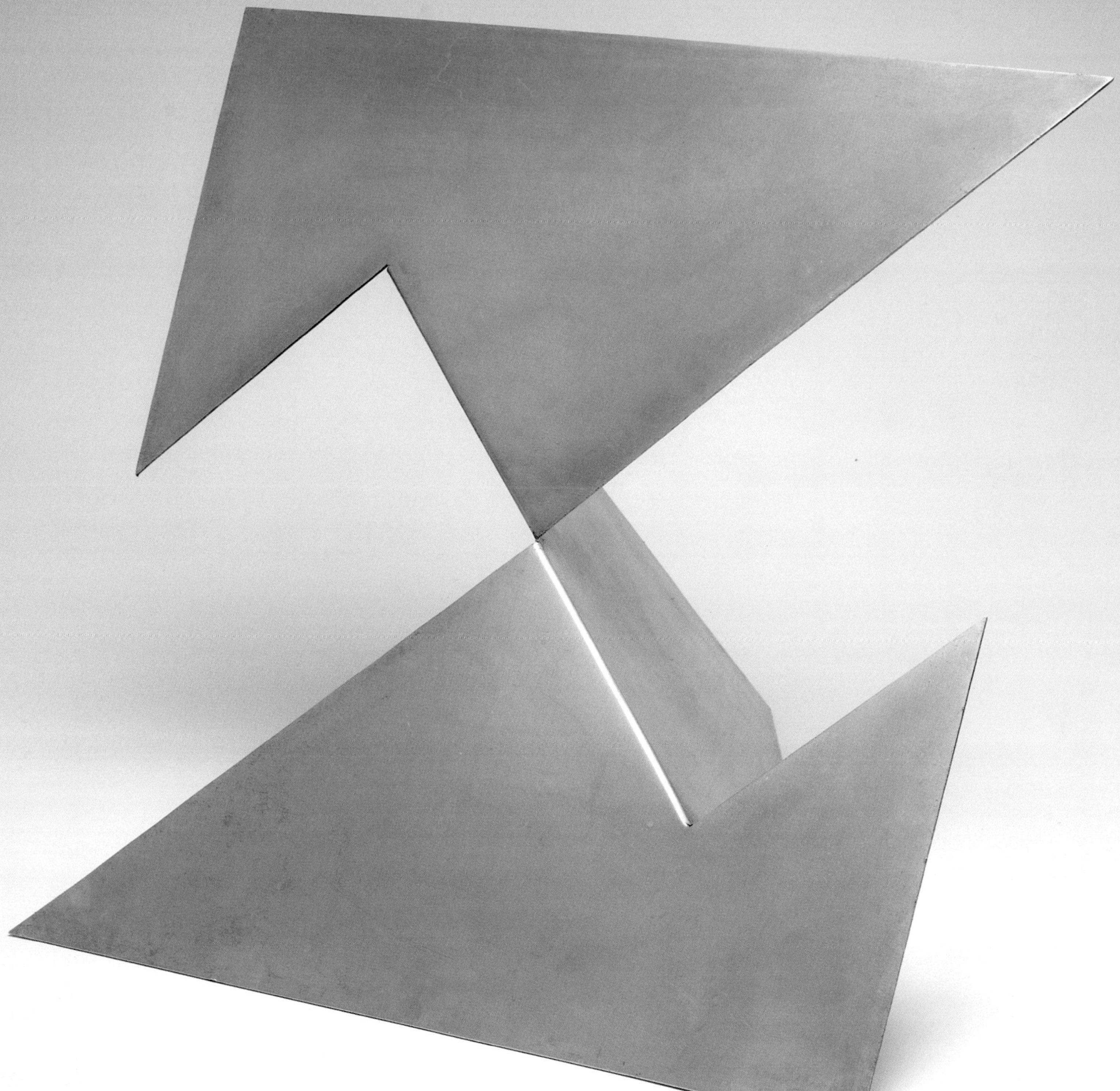

Maurício Nogueira Lima
Objeto rítmico no. 2 (segunda versão) [*Rhythmic Object no. 2 (second version)*], 1970s;
first version, 1952
Plastered paint on hardboard
15 3/4 x 15 3/4 inches
(40 x 40 cm)
The Adolpho Leirner Collection of Brazilian Constructive Art, museum purchase with funds provided by the Caroline Wiess Law Accessions Endowment Fund
2005.471
PHOTO: Tom Jenkins

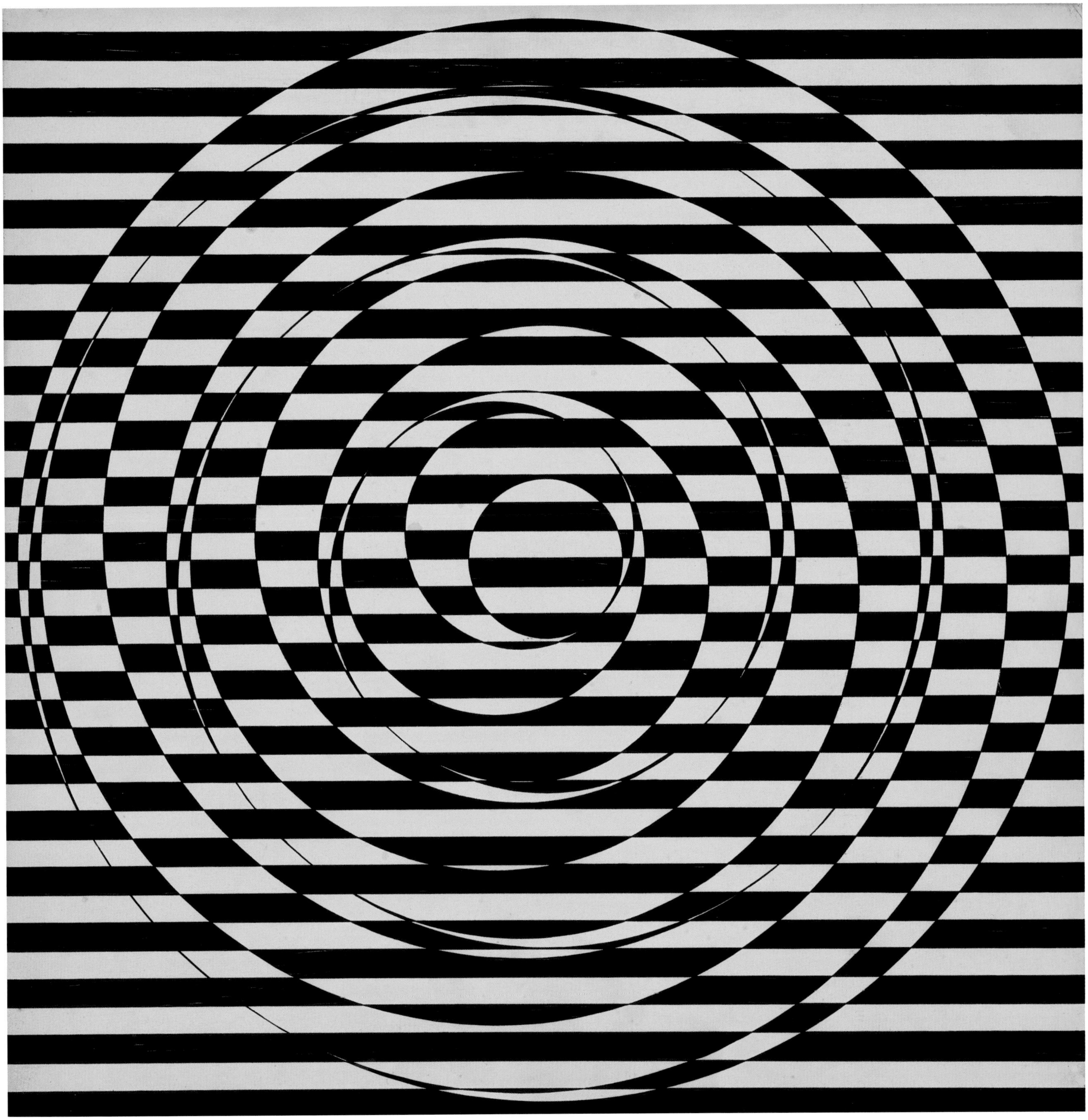

Luís Sacilotto
Concreção 5942
[*Concretion 5942*], 1959
Painted aluminum
11 3/4 x 11 3/4 x 6 5/8 inches
(30 x 30 x 17 cm)
The Adolpho Leirner Collection
of Brazilian Constructive Art,
museum purchase with funds
provided by the Caroline Wiess
Law Accessions Endowment
Fund
2007.23
PHOTO: Tom Jenkins

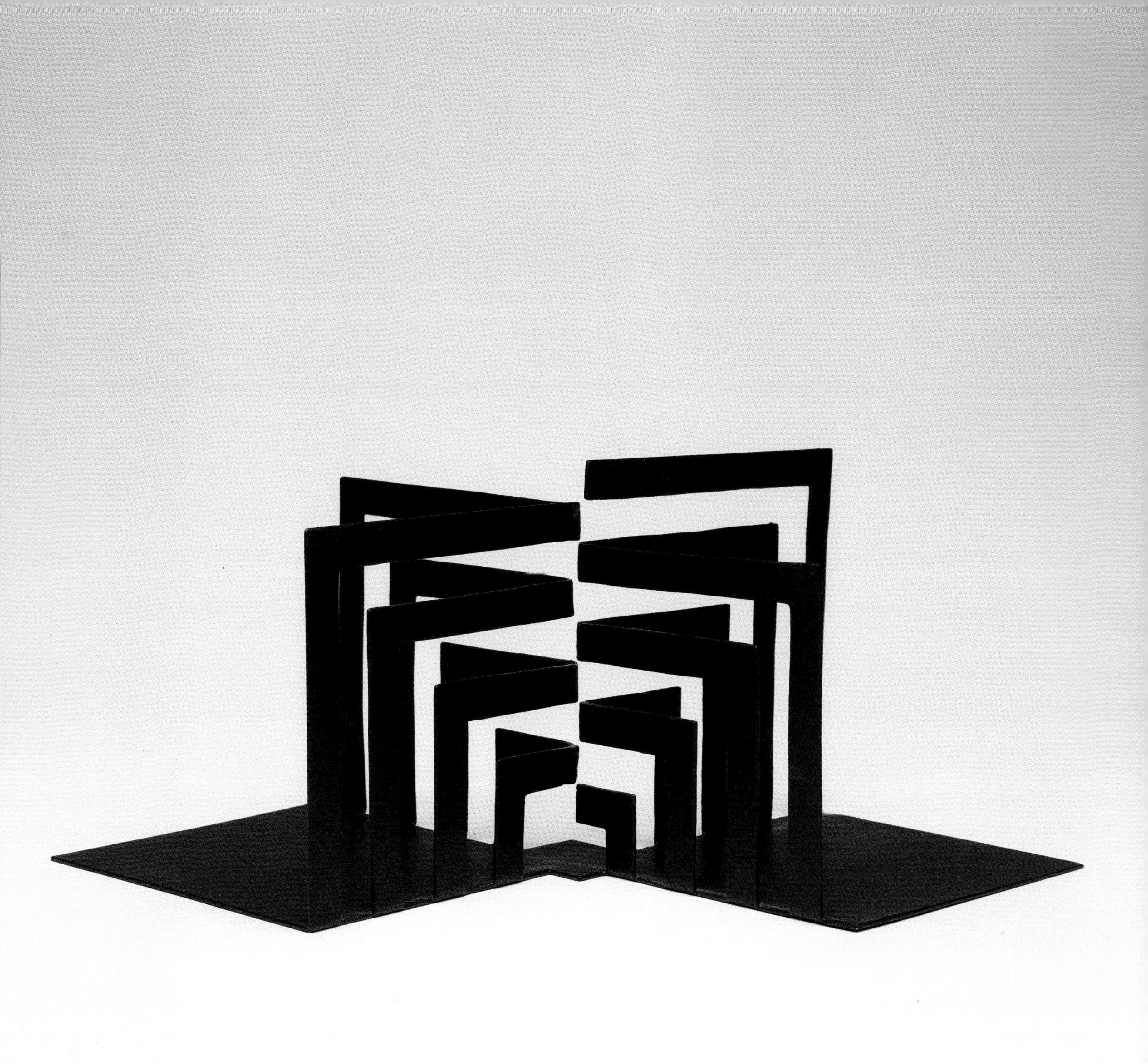

Antônio Maluf
Progressões [*Progressions*], 1953
Tempera on cardboard
16 1/8 x 27 5/8 inches
(41 x 70.2 cm)
The Adolpho Leirner Collection of Brazilian Constructive Art, gift of the Caroline Wiess Law Foundation
2005.1017
PHOTO: Tom Jenkins

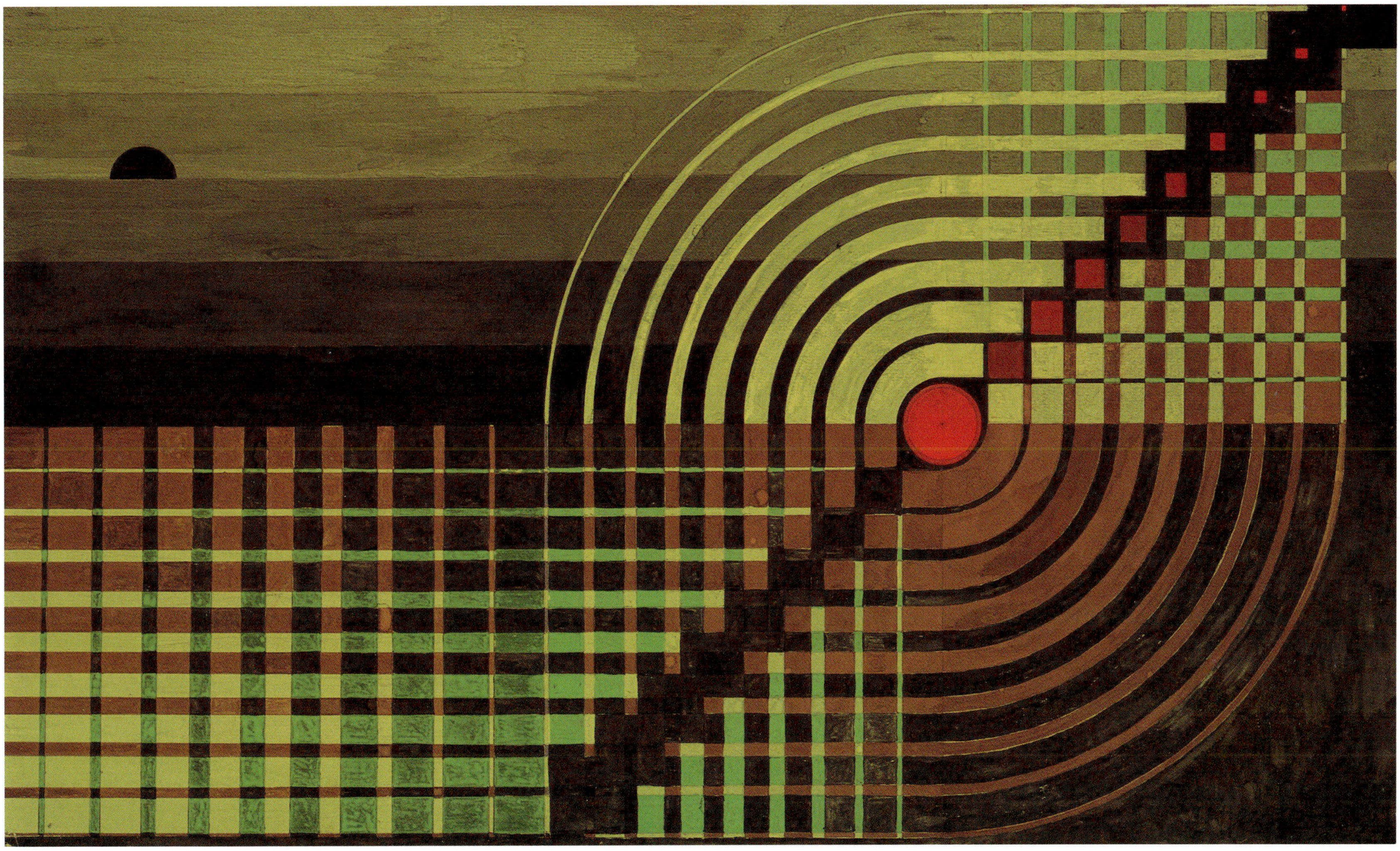

Maurício Nogueira Lima
Sem título [*Untitled*], 1962
Oil on canvas
27 9/16 x 19 1/2 inches
(70 x 49.5 cm)
The Adolpho Leirner Collection
of Brazilian Constructive Art,
gift of the Caroline Wiess Law
Foundation
2005.1013
PHOTO: Rômulo Fialdini

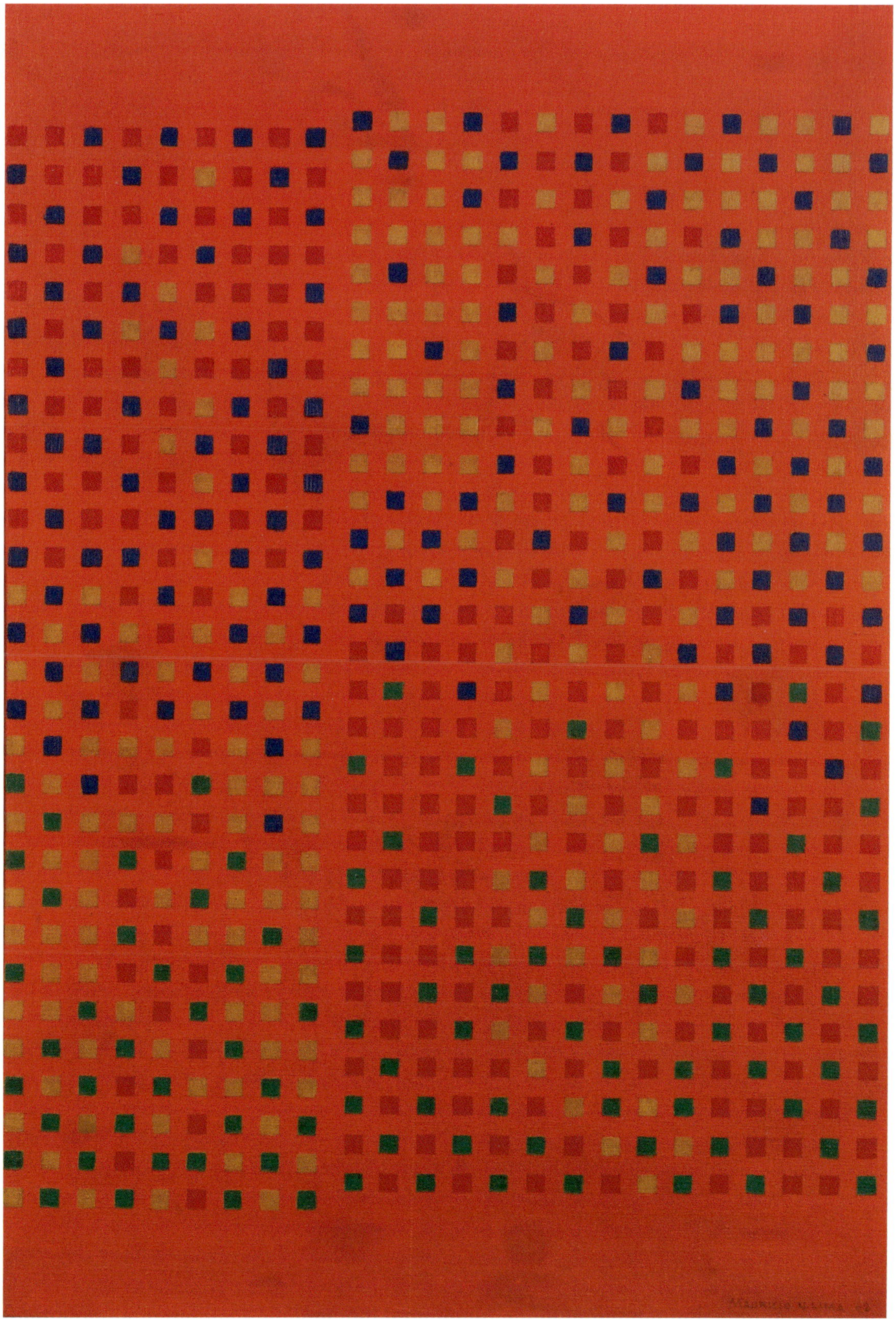

LEFT
Maurício Nogueira Lima
Pintura 2 [*Painting no. 2*], 1961
Oil on canvas
21 5/8 x 15 inches
(55 x 38 cm)
The Adolpho Leirner Collection of Brazilian Constructive Art, gift of the Caroline Wiess Law Foundation
2005.1014
PHOTO: Rômulo Fialdini

RIGHT
Maurício Nogueira Lima
Retícula [*Grid*], 1960
Oil on canvas
19 5/8 x 15 3/4 inches
(49.8 x 40 cm)
The Adolpho Leirner Collection of Brazilian Constructive Art, museum purchase with funds provided by the Caroline Wiess Law Accessions Endowment Fund
2006.49
PHOTO: Rômulo Fialdini

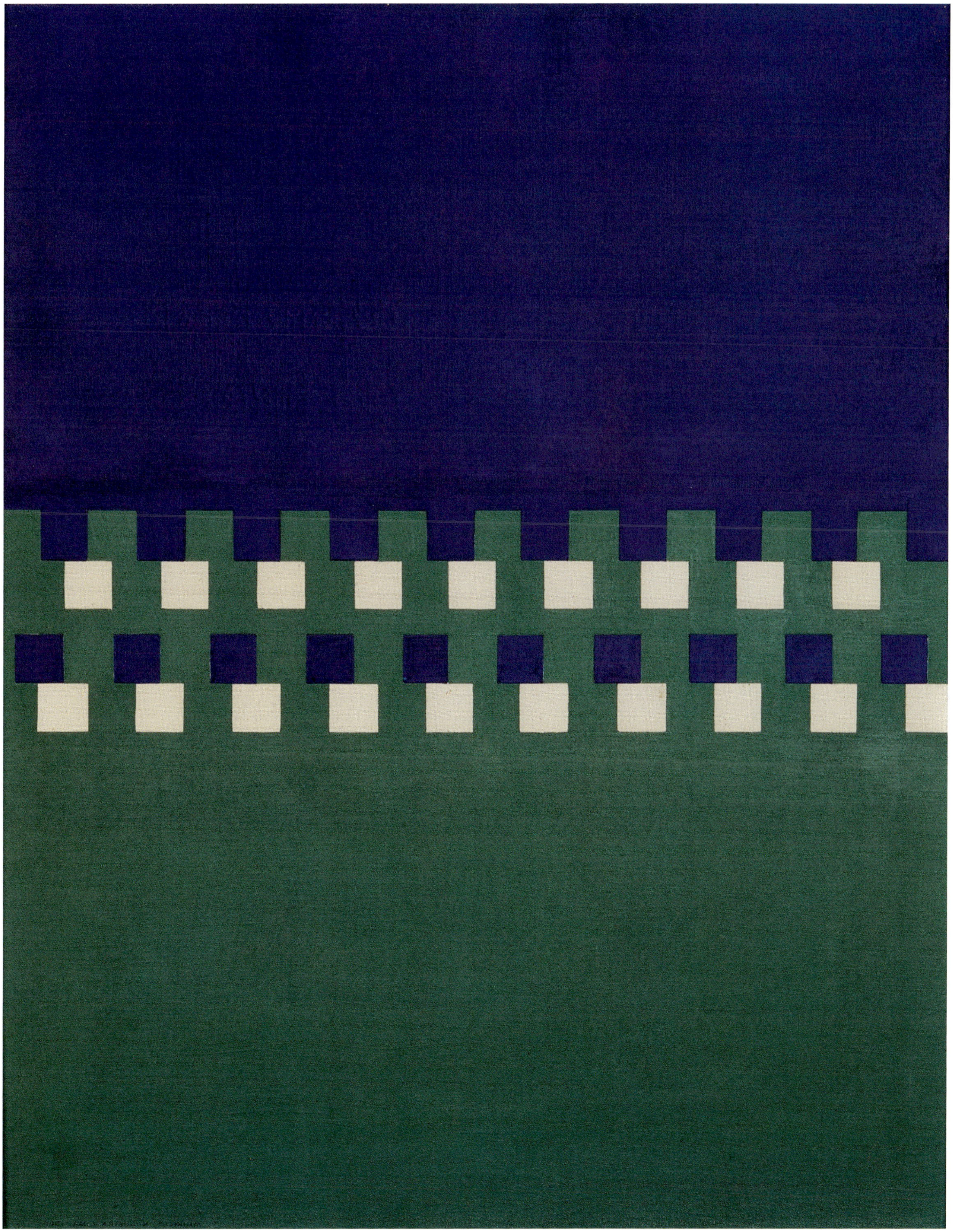

Judith Lauand
Variação de quadrados
[*Variations of Squares*], 1957
Enamel on hardboard
23 3/4 x 23 3/4 inches
(60.3 x 60.3 cm)
The Adolpho Leirner Collection
of Brazilian Constructive Art,
gift of the Caroline Wiess Law
Foundation
2005.1010

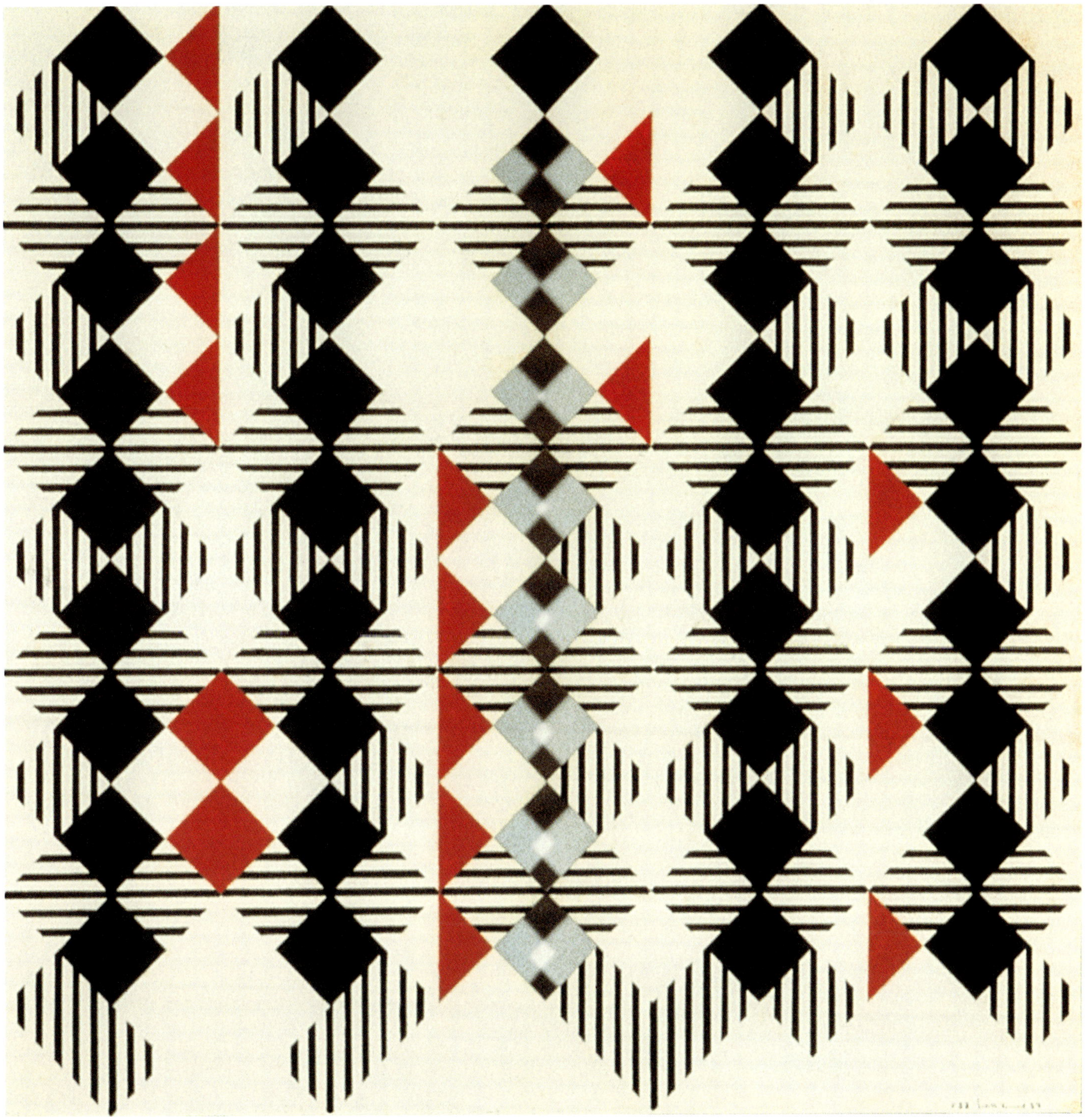

Hermelindo Fiaminghi
Virtual XIV [*Virtual no. 14*], 1958
Enamel on hardboard
23 5/8 x 23 5/8 inches
[60 x 60 cm]
The Adolpho Leirner Collection of Brazilian Constructive Art, gift of the Caroline Wiess Law Foundation
2005.1000
PHOTO: Rômulo Fialdini

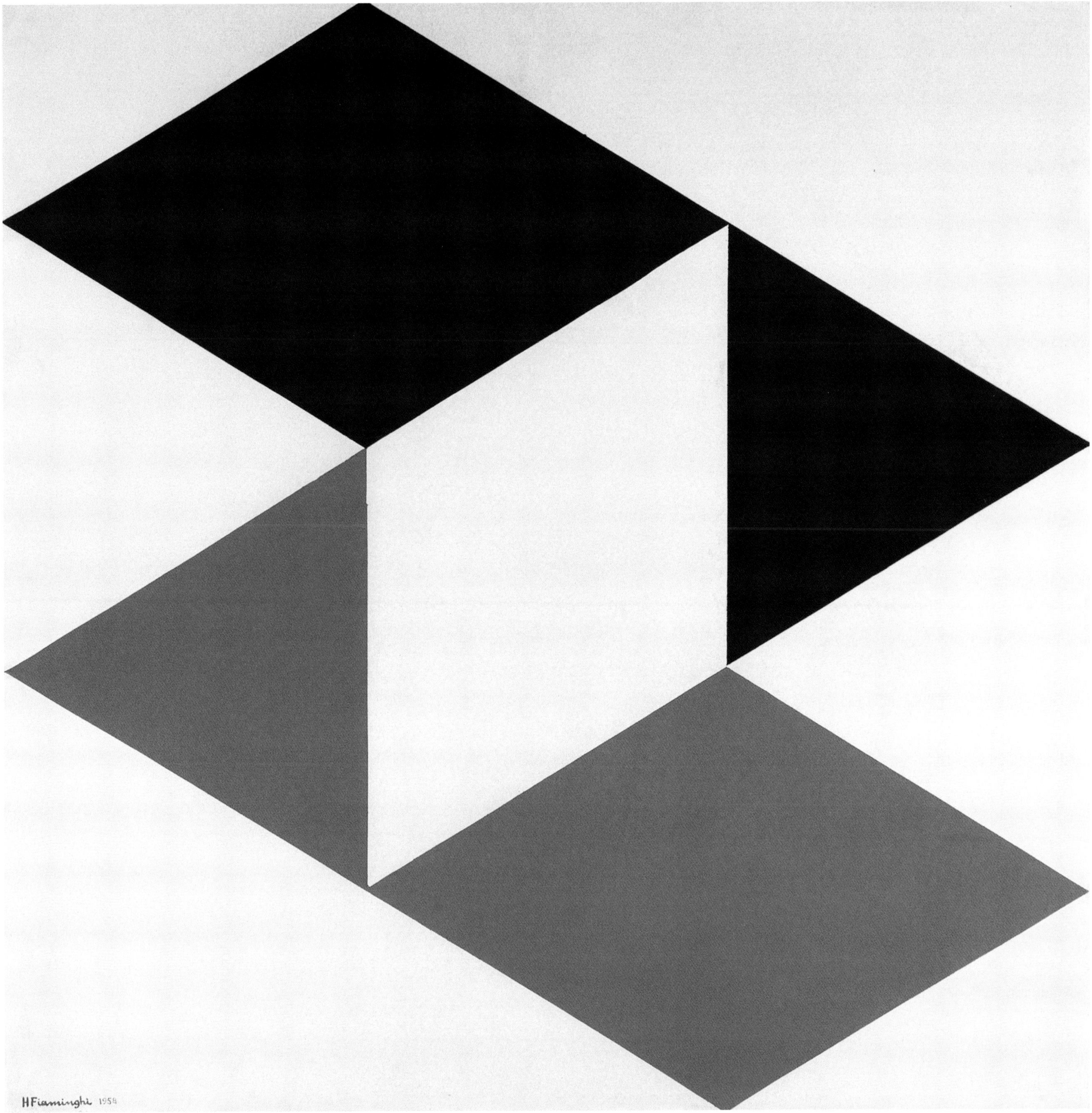
HFiaminghi 1958

Geraldo de Barros
Concreto [*Concrete*], 1958
Enamel on hardboard
19 3/8 x 27 15/16 inches
(49.2 x 71 cm)
The Adolpho Leirner Collection of Brazilian Constructive Art, gift of the Caroline Wiess Law Foundation
2005.979
PHOTO: Rômulo Fialdini

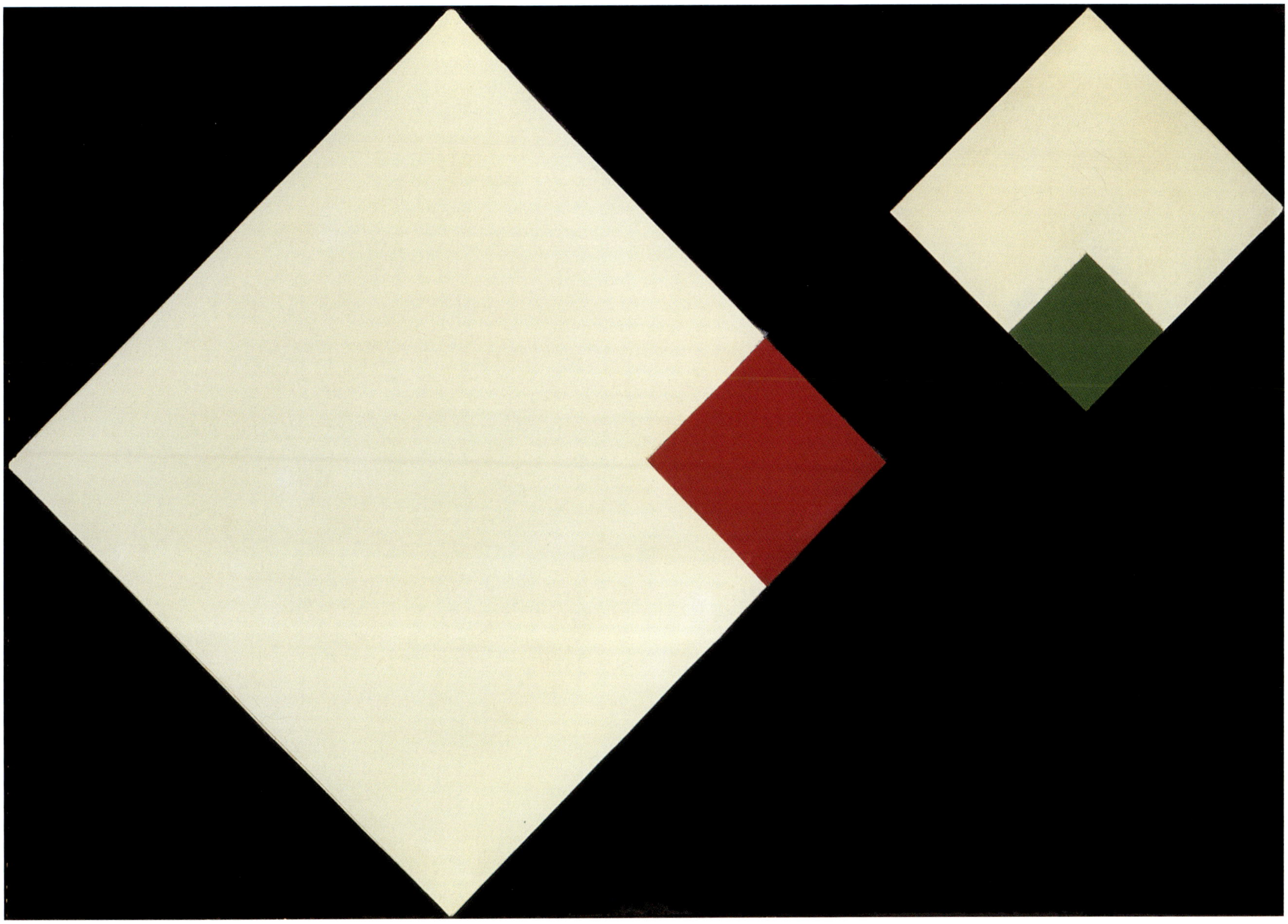

Hermelindo Fiaminghi
Virtual XII [*Virtual no. 12*], 1958
Enamel on hardboard
19 11/16 x 19 11/16 inches
(50 x 50 cm)
The Adolpho Leirner Collection of Brazilian Constructive Art, gift of the Caroline Wiess Law Foundation
2005.999
PHOTO: Rômulo Fialdini

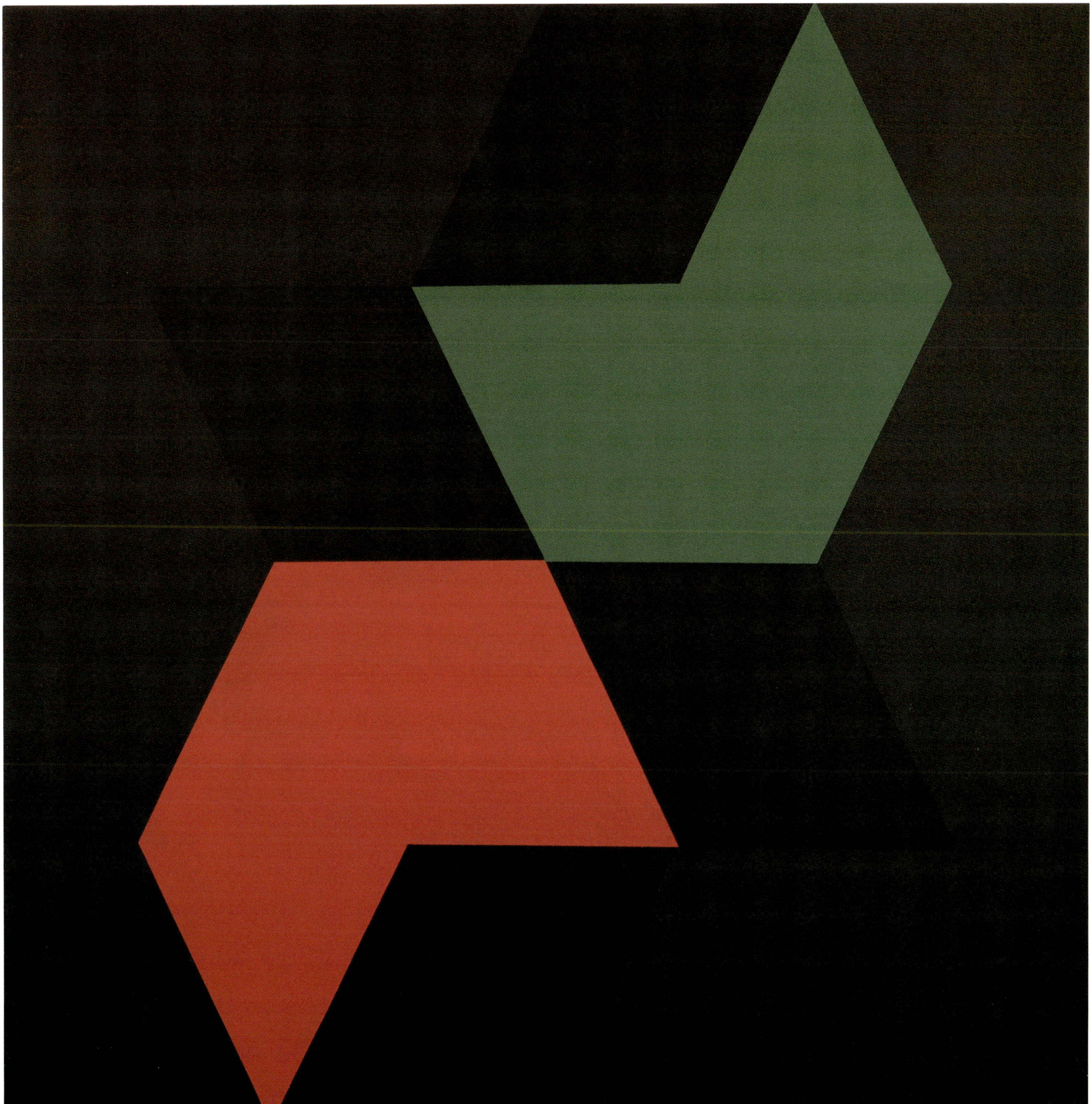

Raul Porto
Sem título [*Untitled*], 1960
India ink on paper
19 3/4 x 19 11/16 inches
(50.2 x 50 cm)
The Adolpho Leirner Collection
of Brazilian Constructive Art,
gift of the Caroline Wiess Law
Foundation
2005.1019
PHOTO: Tom Jenkins

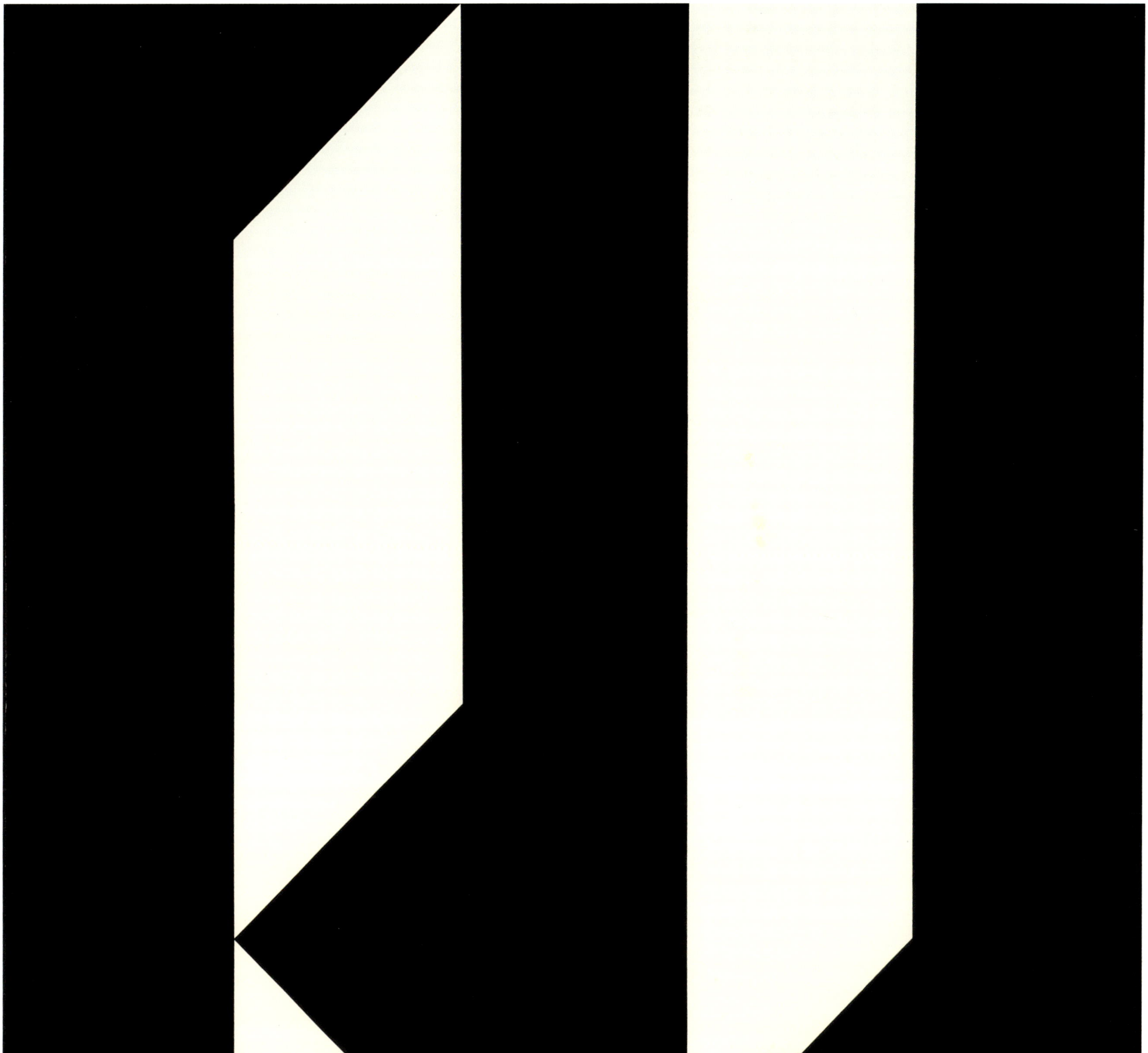

Grupo Frente

Ivan Serpa
Faixas ritmadas
[*Rhythmic Strips*], 1953
Industrial paint on hardboard
48 1/4 x 35 3/8 inches
(122.6 x 89.9 cm)
The Adolpho Leirner Collection of Brazilian Constructive Art, museum purchase with funds provided by the Caroline Wiess Law Accessions Endowment Fund
2005.473
PHOTO: Tom Jenkins

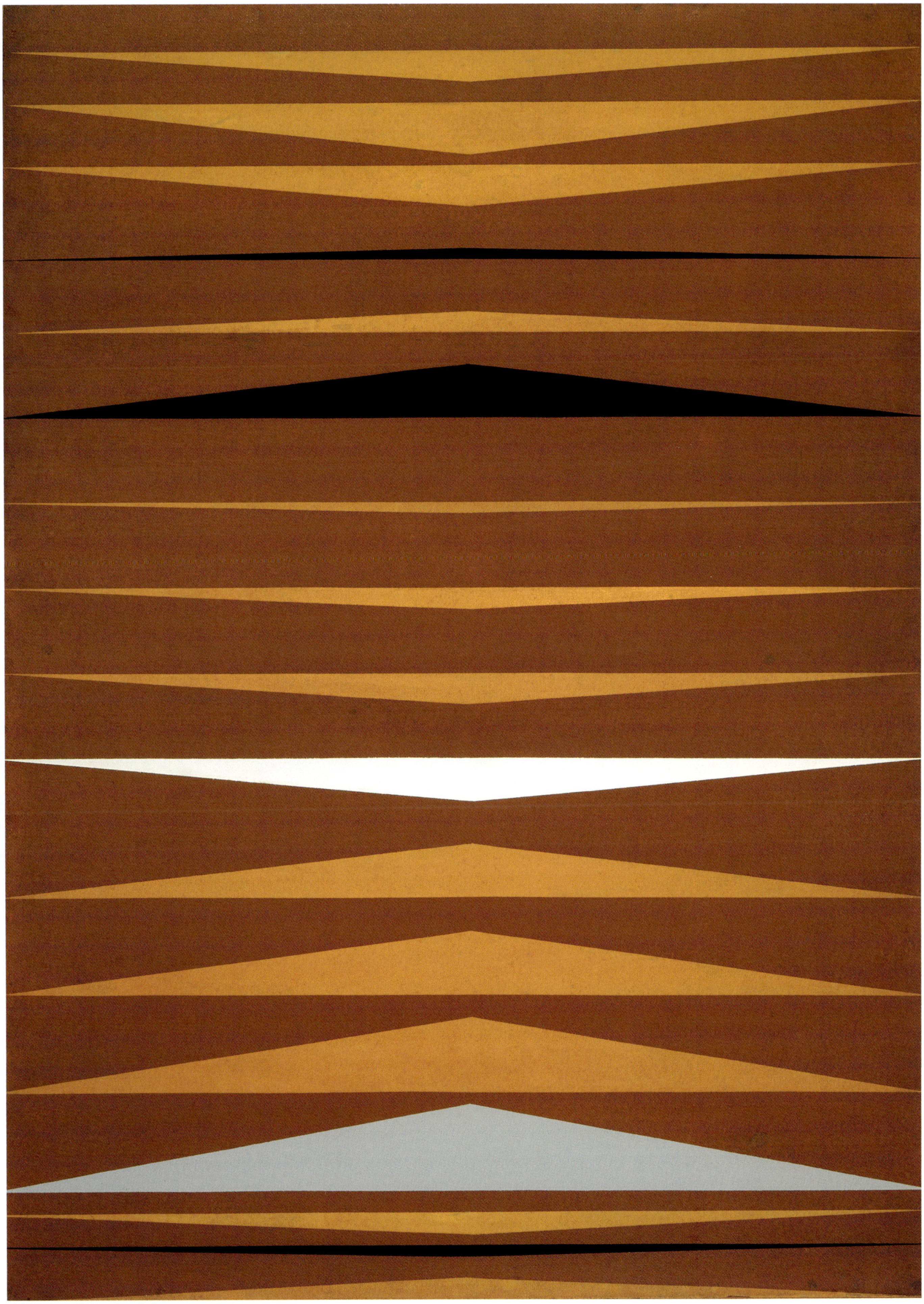

João José da Silva Costa
Idéia múltipla [*Multiple Idea*],
1956
Oil on canvas
25 1/4 x 25 1/4 inches
(64.1 x 64.1 cm)
The Adolpho Leirner Collection
of Brazilian Constructive Art,
gift of the Caroline Wiess Law
Foundation
2005.991
PHOTO: Rômulo Fialdini

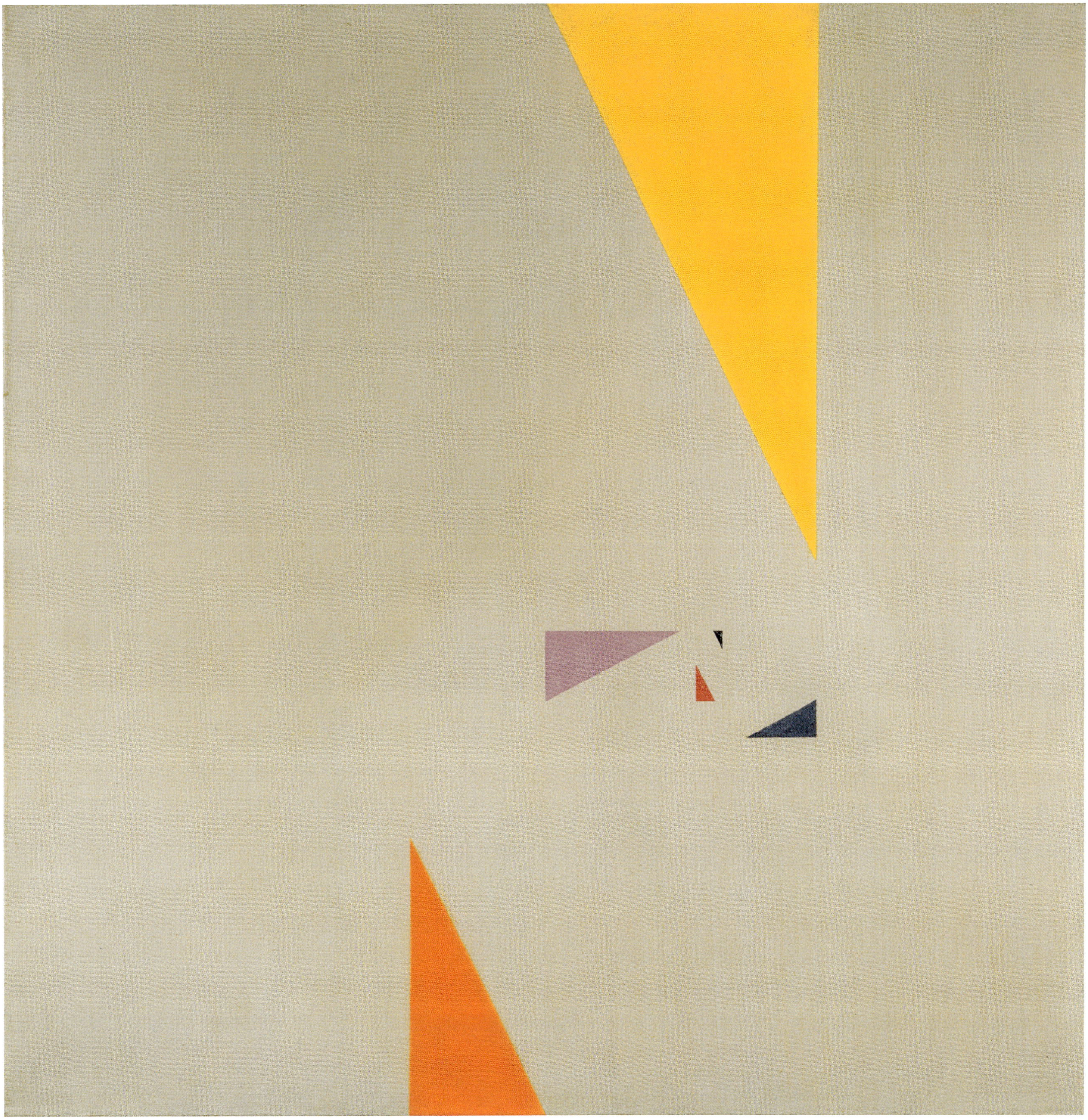

Aluísio Carvão
Tema circular 1
[*Circular Theme no. 1*], 1957
Oil on hardboard
32 x 25 3/8 inches
(81.3 x 64.5 cm)
The Adolpho Leirner Collection
of Brazilian Constructive Art,
gift of the Caroline Wiess Law
Foundation
2005.985

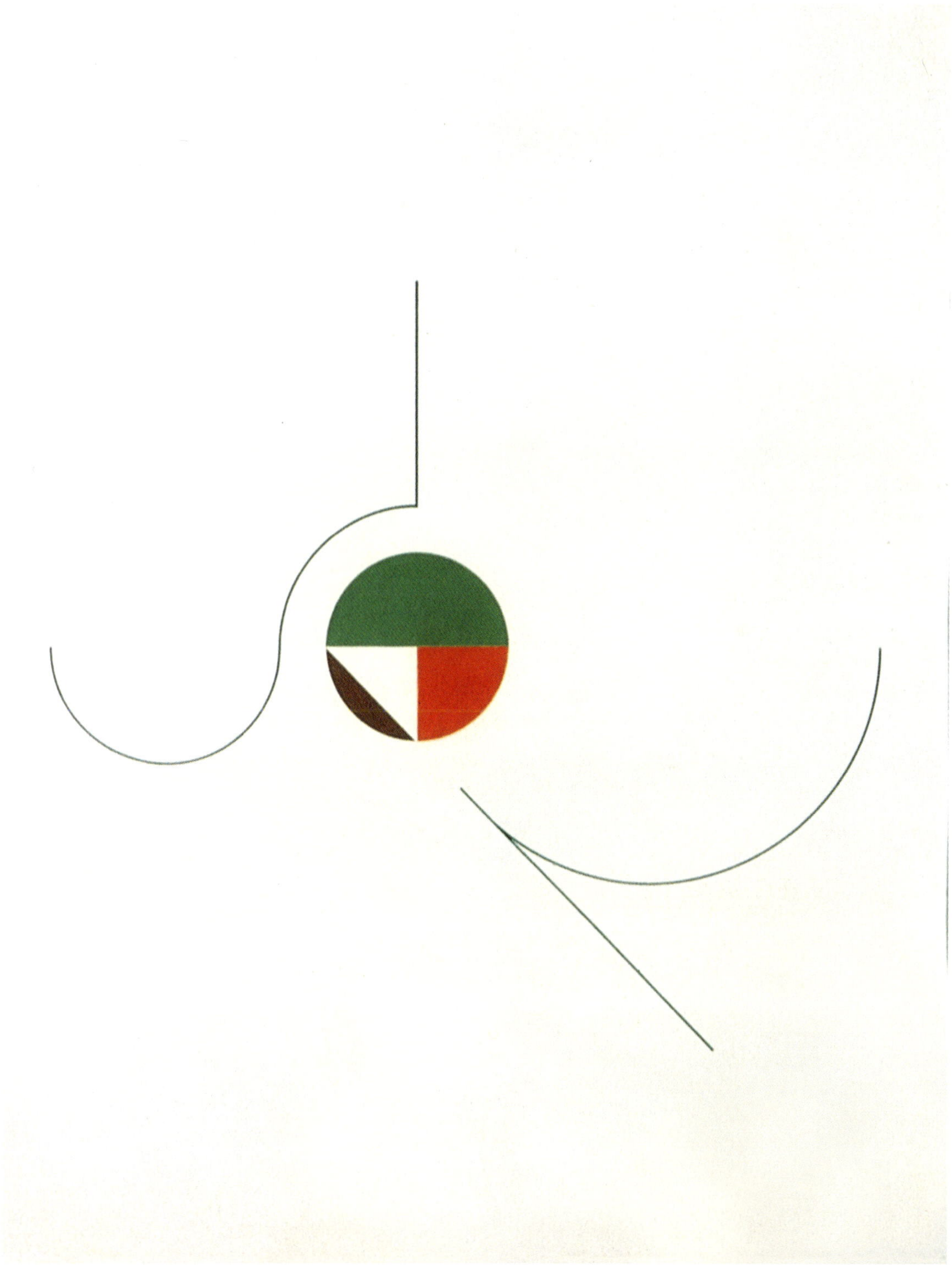

Rubem Ludolf
Sem título [*Untitled*], 1958
Gouache on paper
21 1/8 x 21 7/8 inches
(53.7 x 55.6 cm)
The Adolpho Leirner Collection
of Brazilian Constructive Art,
gift of the Caroline Wiess Law
Foundation
2005.1015
PHOTO: Tom Jenkins

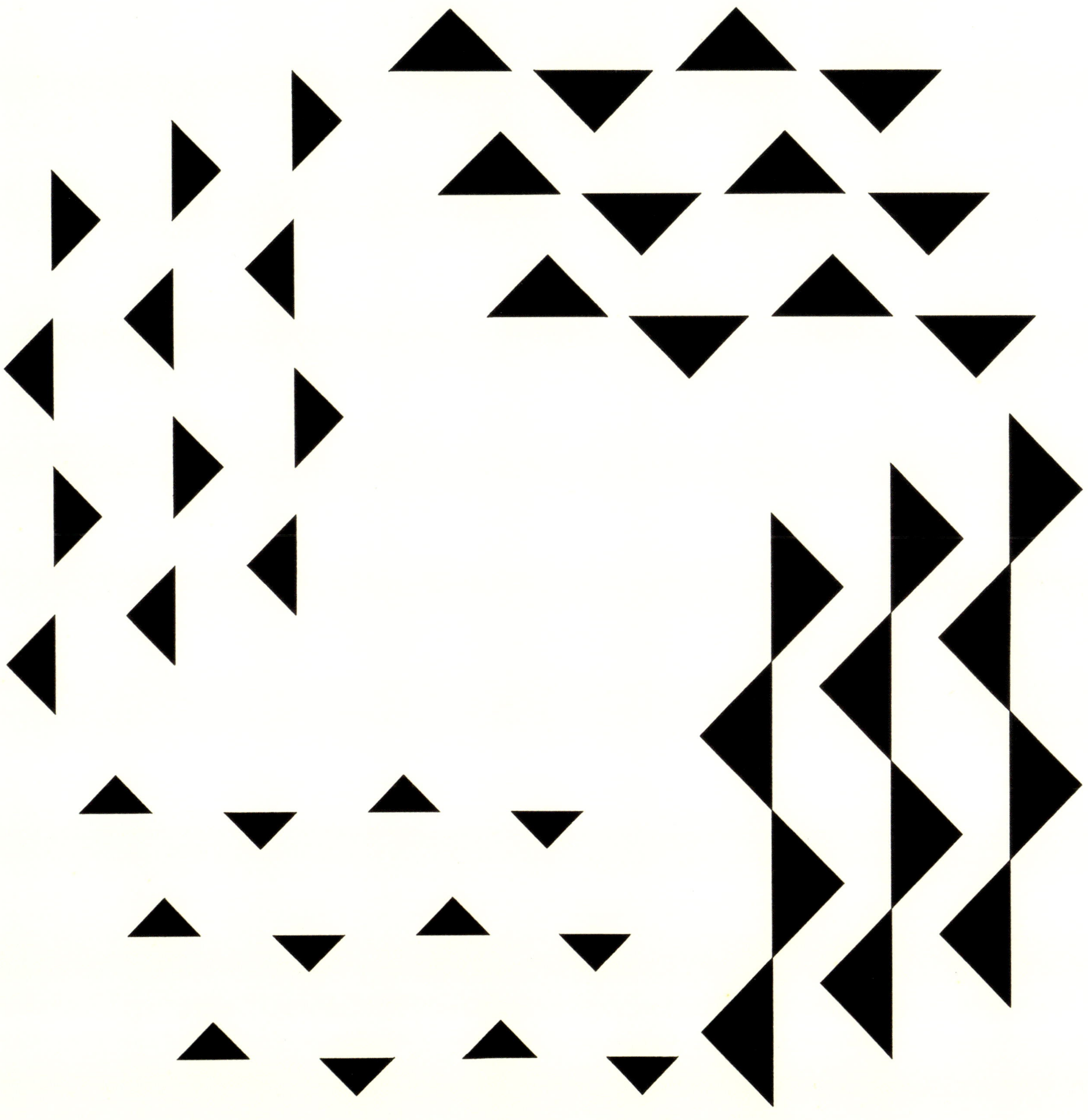

Lygia Pape
Sem título [*Untitled*], 1958
Woodcut on paper
11 13/16 x 16 9/16 inches
(30 x 42 cm)
The Adolpho Leirner Collection
of Brazilian Constructive Art,
gift of the Caroline Wiess Law
Foundation
2005.1024
PHOTO: Rômulo Fialdini

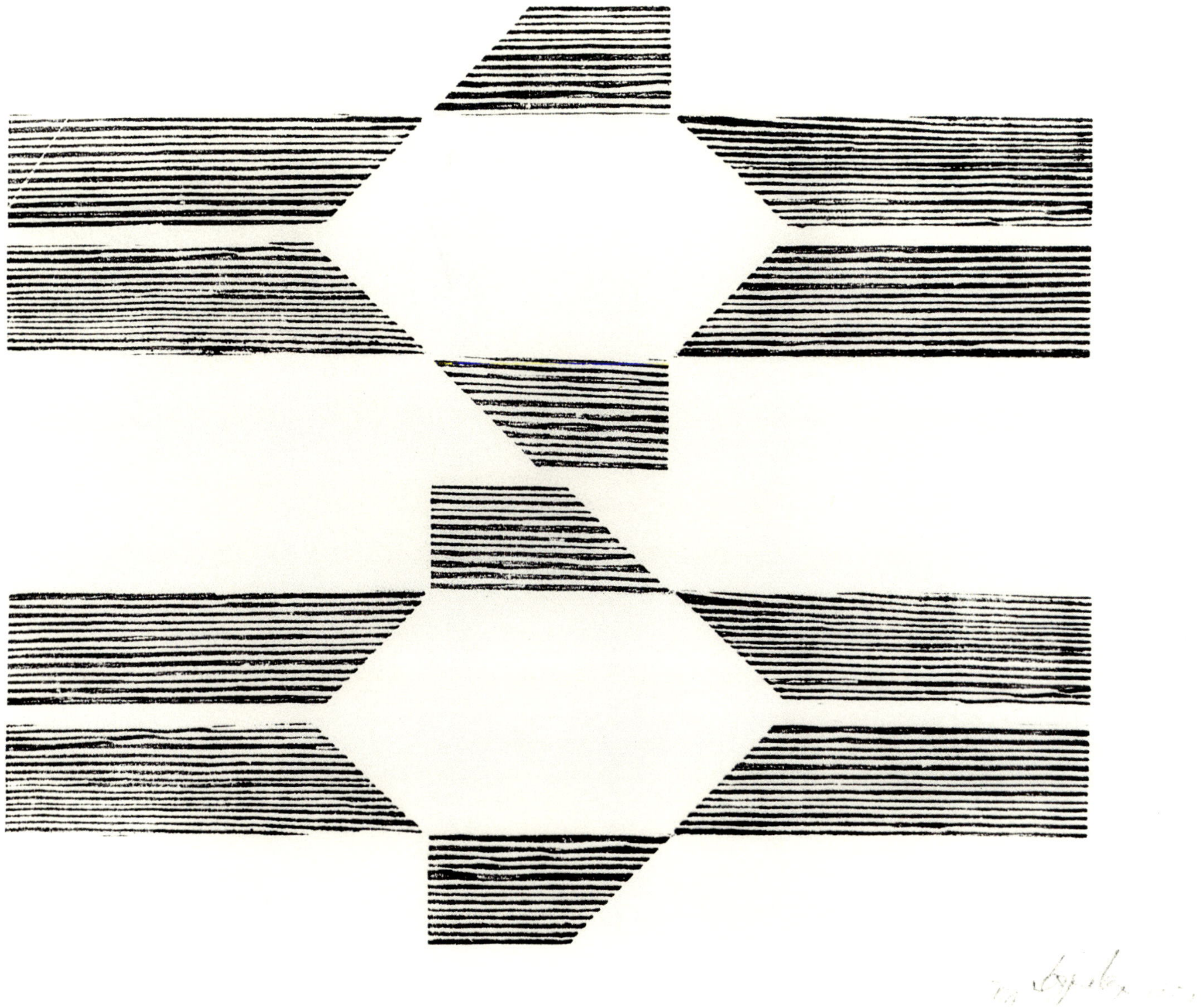

Décio Vieira
Sem título [*Untitled*], 1958
Pastel on paper
39 1/4 x 27 3/4 inches
(99.7 x 70.5 cm)
The Adolpho Leirner Collection of Brazilian Constructive Art, museum purchase with funds provided by the Caroline Wiess Law Accessions Endowment Fund
2005.1034
PHOTO: Rômulo Fialdini

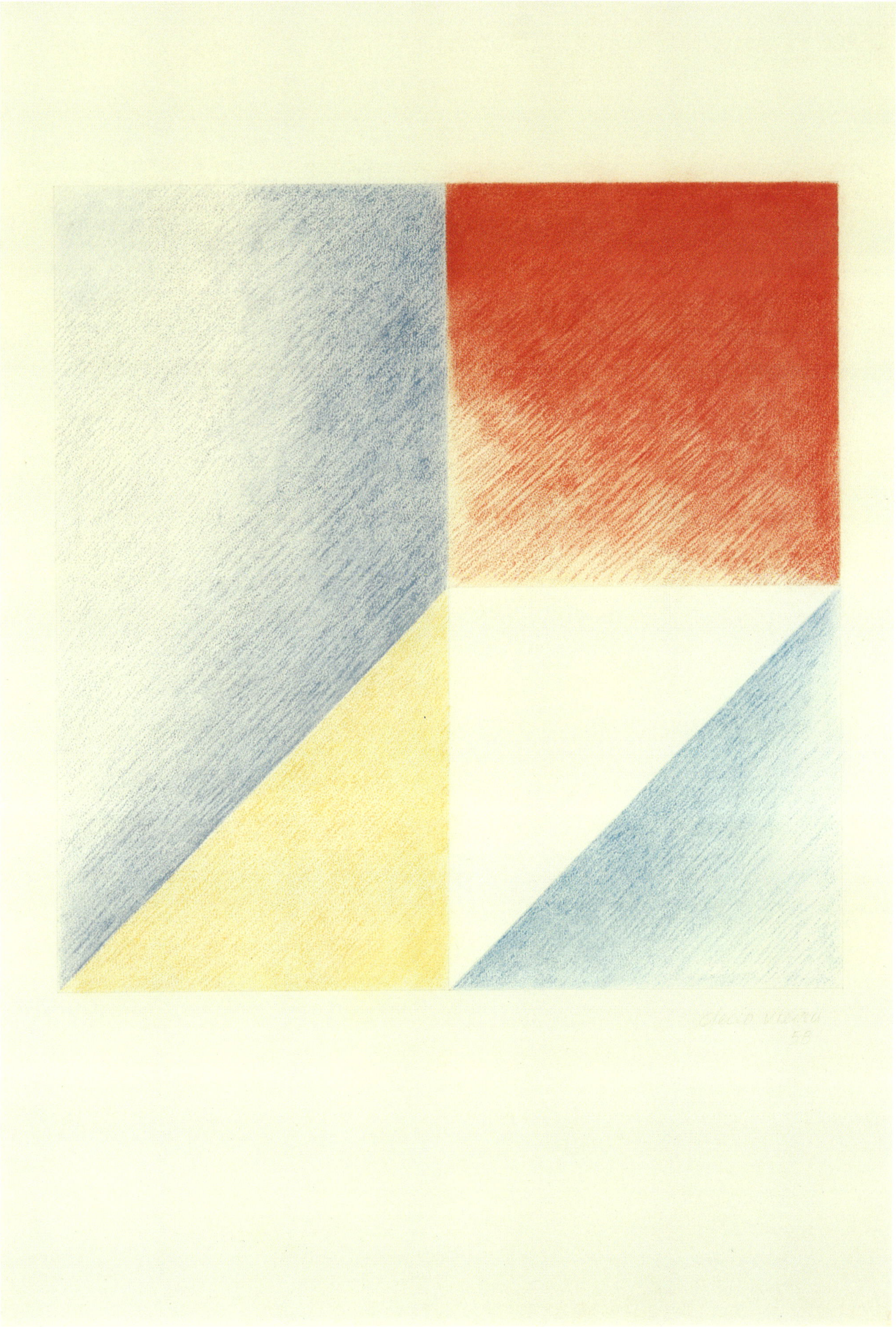

Abraham Palatnik
Aparelho cinecromático
[*Chromo-Kinetic Set*], 1964
Canvas and wood boxes with two motors, colored lightbulbs linked to a programmed electric circuit, and iron-articulated wood blades
38 1/8 x 28 3/4 x 7 1/2 inches
(96.8 x 73 x 19.1 cm)
The Adolpho Leirner Collection of Brazilian Constructive Art, museum purchase with funds provided by the Caroline Wiess Law Accessions Endowment Fund
2007.21
PHOTO: Fernando Chaves

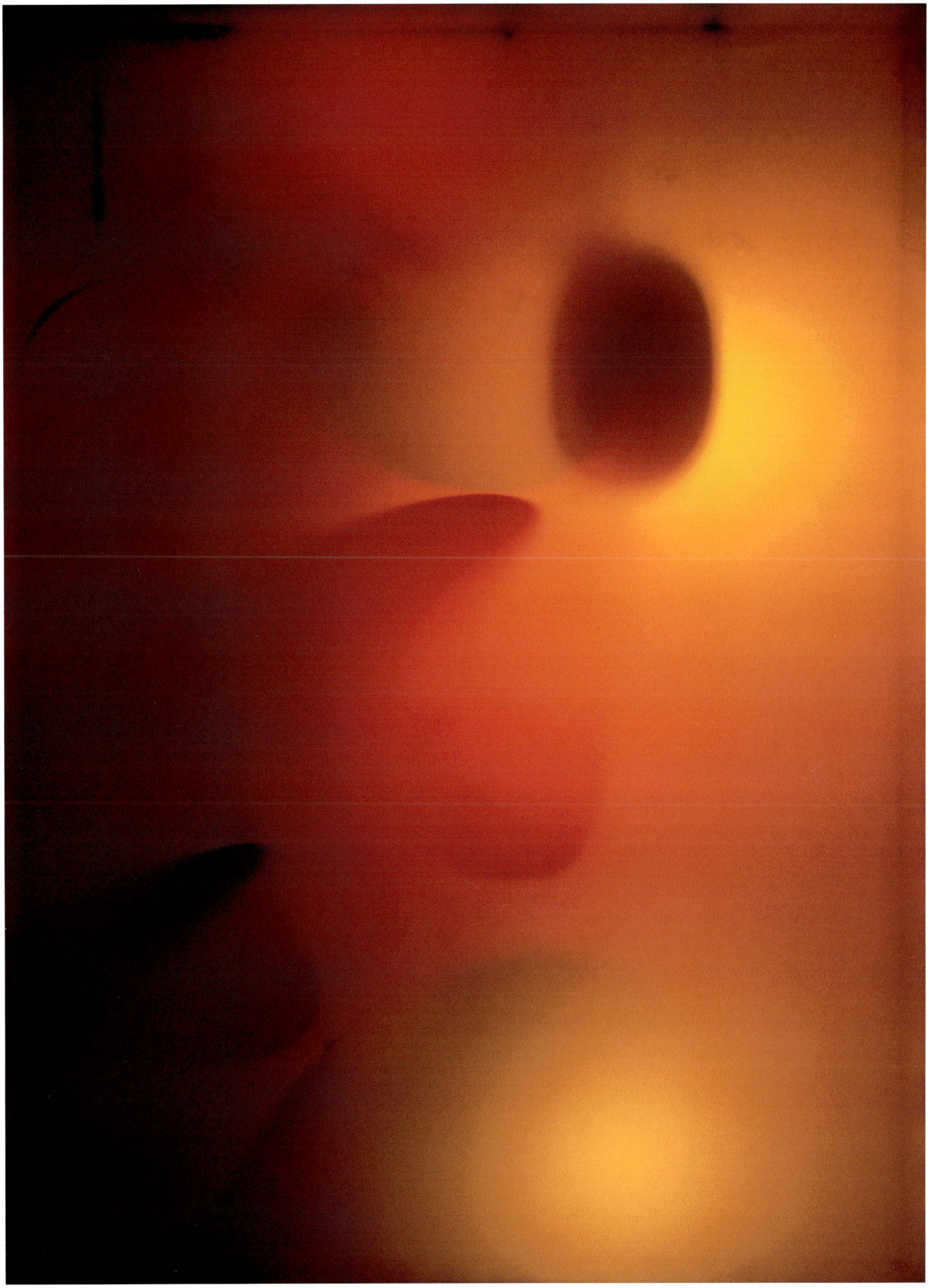

Neo-Concrete

Hércules Barsotti
Branco/Preto [*White/Black*],
1960
Oil on canvas
39 1/4 x 19 5/8 inches
(99.7 x 49.8 cm)
The Adolpho Leirner Collection
of Brazilian Constructive Art,
museum purchase with funds
provided by the Caroline Wiess
Law Accessions Endowment
Fund
2007.10
PHOTO: Rômulo Fialdini

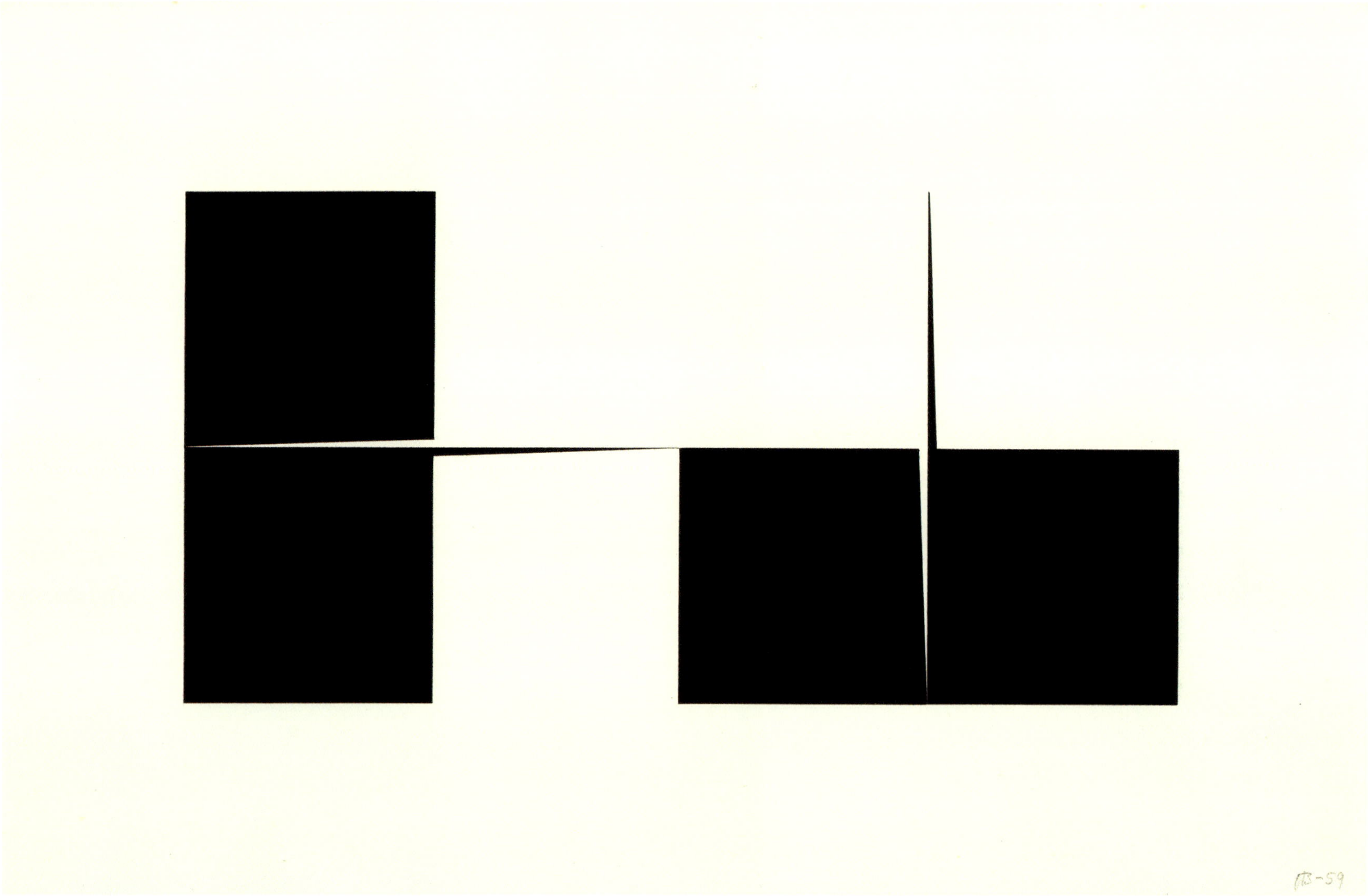

Hércules Barsotti
Sem título [*Untitled*], 1959
India ink on paper
8 1/4 x 13 inches (21 x 33 cm)
The Adolpho Leirner Collection of Brazilian Constructive Art, gift of the Caroline Wiess Law Foundation
2005.982
PHOTO: Tom Jenkins

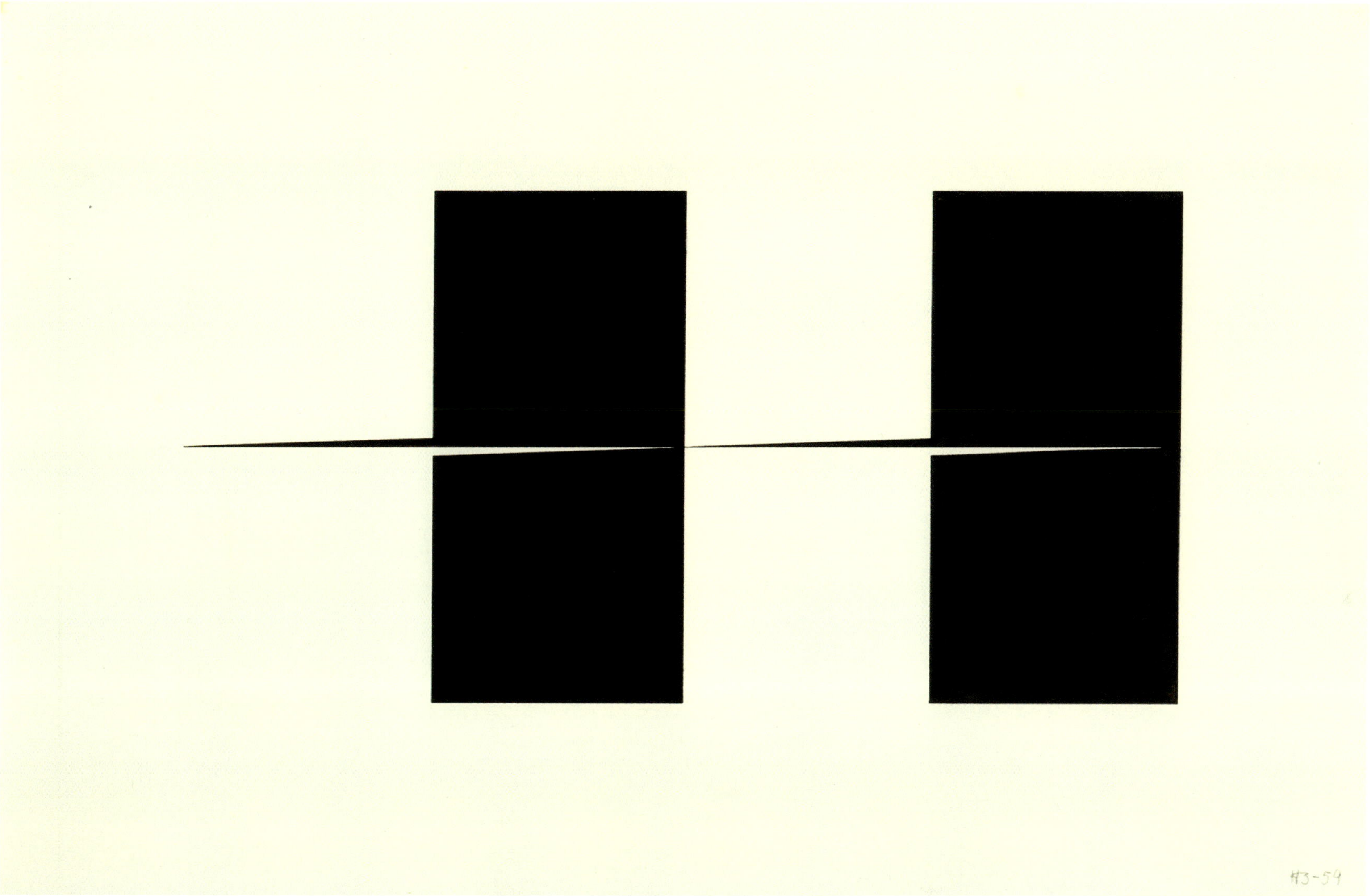

Hércules Barsotti
Sem título [*Untitled*], 1959
India ink on paper
8 1/4 x 13 inches (21 x 33 cm)
The Adolpho Leirner Collection of Brazilian Constructive Art, gift of the Caroline Wiess Law Foundation
2005.981
PHOTO: Tom Jenkins

Willys de Castro
Objeto ativo [*Active Object*],
c. 1960
Oil on wood
27 1/8 x 7/8 x 2 11/16 inches
(68.9 x 2.3 x 6.9 cm)
The Adolpho Leirner Collection
of Brazilian Constructive Art,
gift of the Caroline Wiess Law
Foundation
2005.988
PHOTO: Tom Jenkins

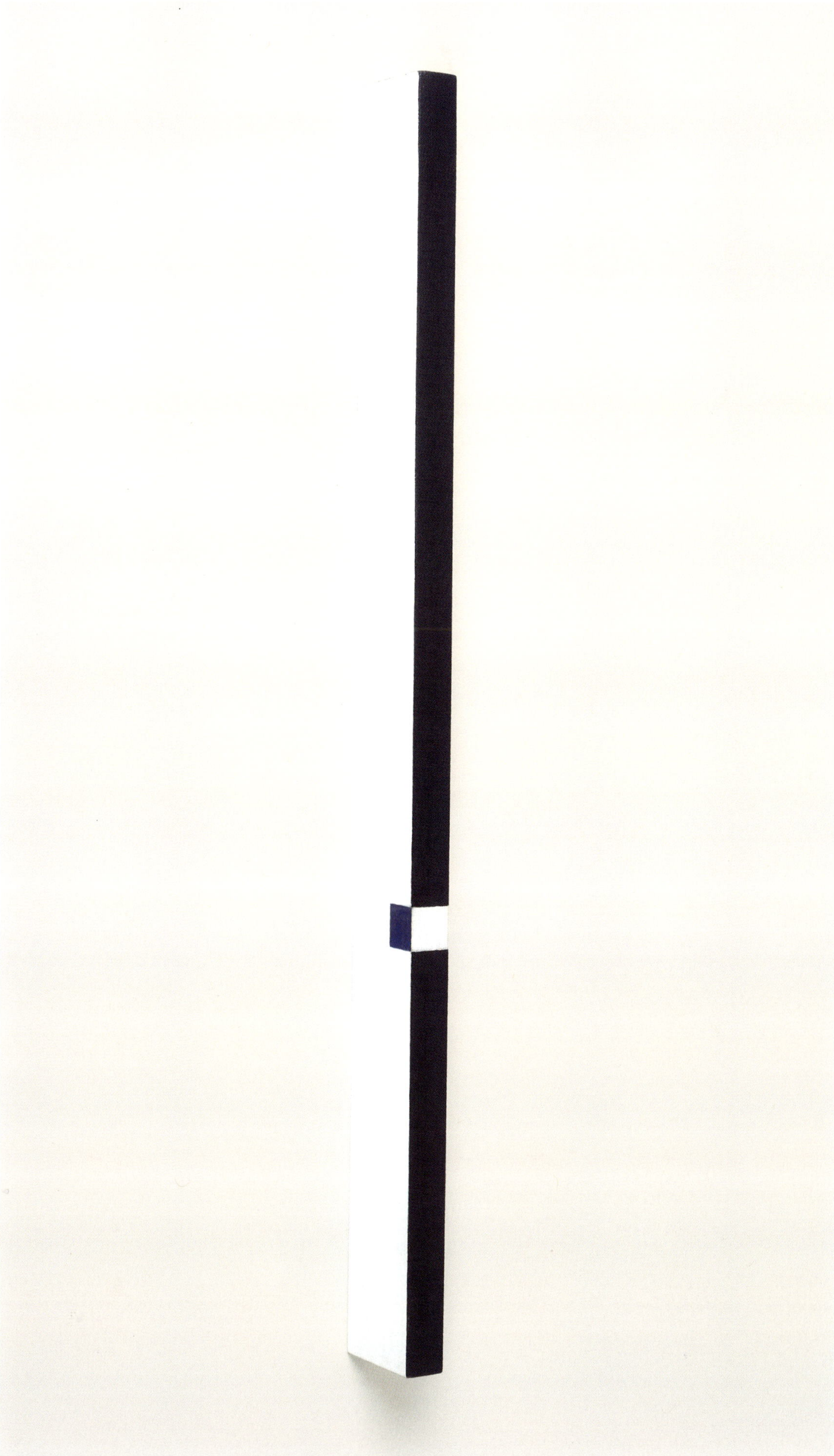

Willys de Castro
Pintura [*Painting*], 1957
Oil on canvas
22 7/8 x 30 3/4 inches
(58 x 78 cm)
The Adolpho Leirner Collection of Brazilian Constructive Art, museum purchase with funds provided by the Caroline Wiess Law Accessions Endowment Fund
2006.46
PHOTO: Tom Jenkins

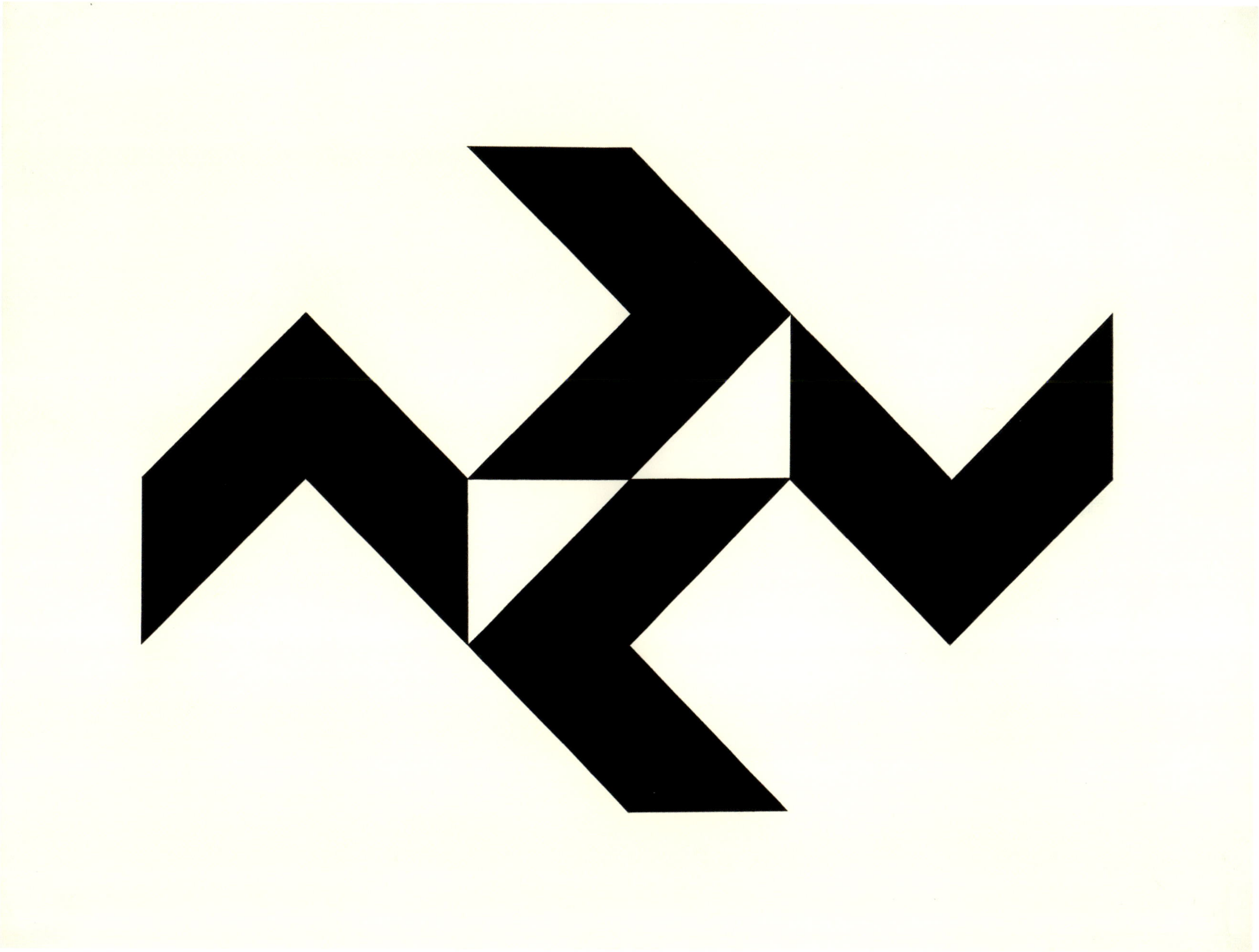

Willys de Castro
Pintura [*Painting*], 1958
Oil on canvas
27 1/2 x 27 1/2 inches
(69.9 x 69.9 cm)
The Adolpho Leirner Collection
of Brazilian Constructive Art,
gift of the Caroline Wiess Law
Foundation
2005.987
PHOTO: Tom Jenkins

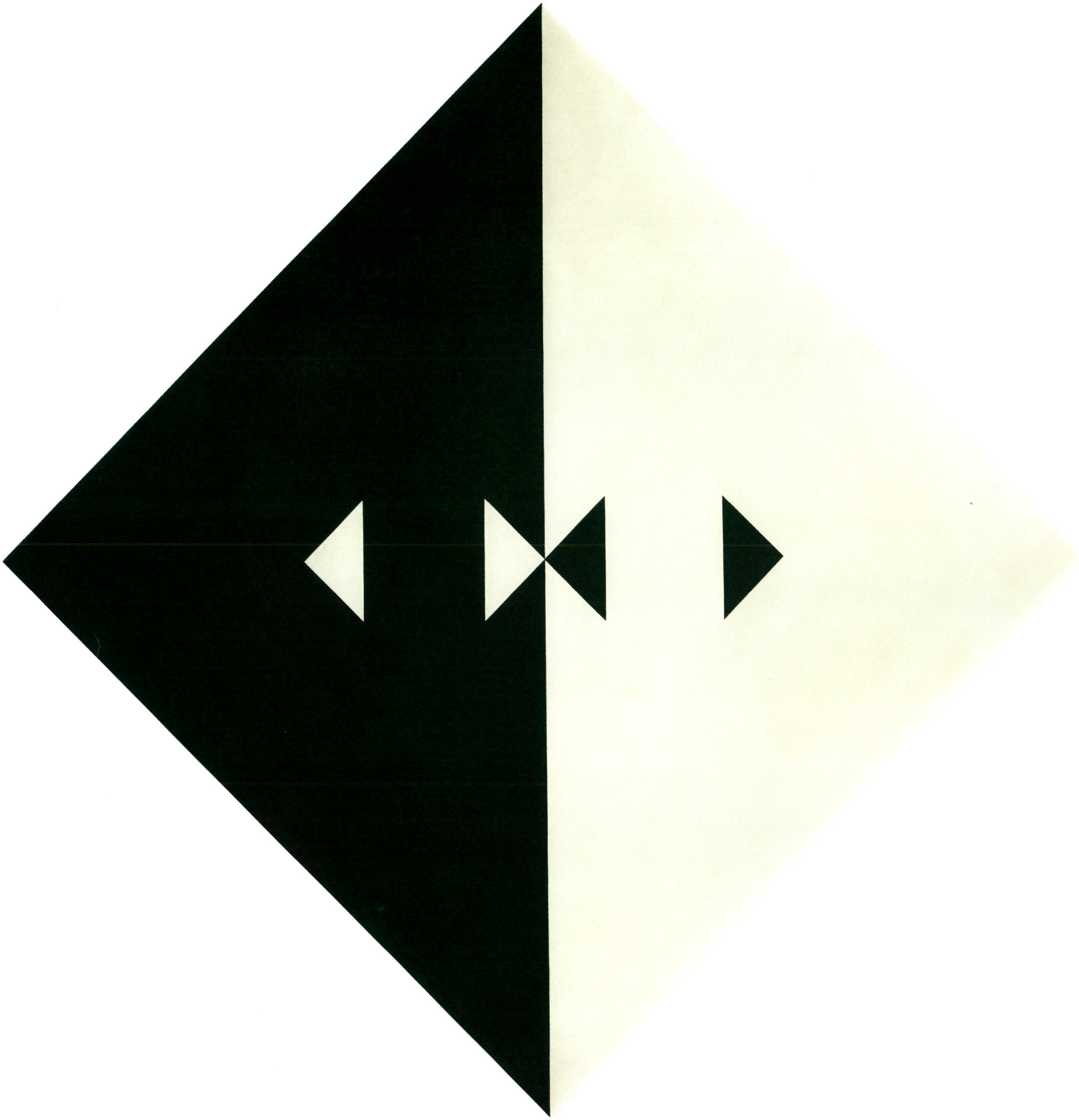

Amilcar de Castro
Sem título [*Untitled*], n.d.
Steel SAC50
19 3/4 x 28 x 31 inches
(50.2 x 71.1 x 78.7 cm)
The Adolpho Leirner Collection
of Brazilian Constructive Art,
gift of the Caroline Wiess Law
Foundation
2005.986

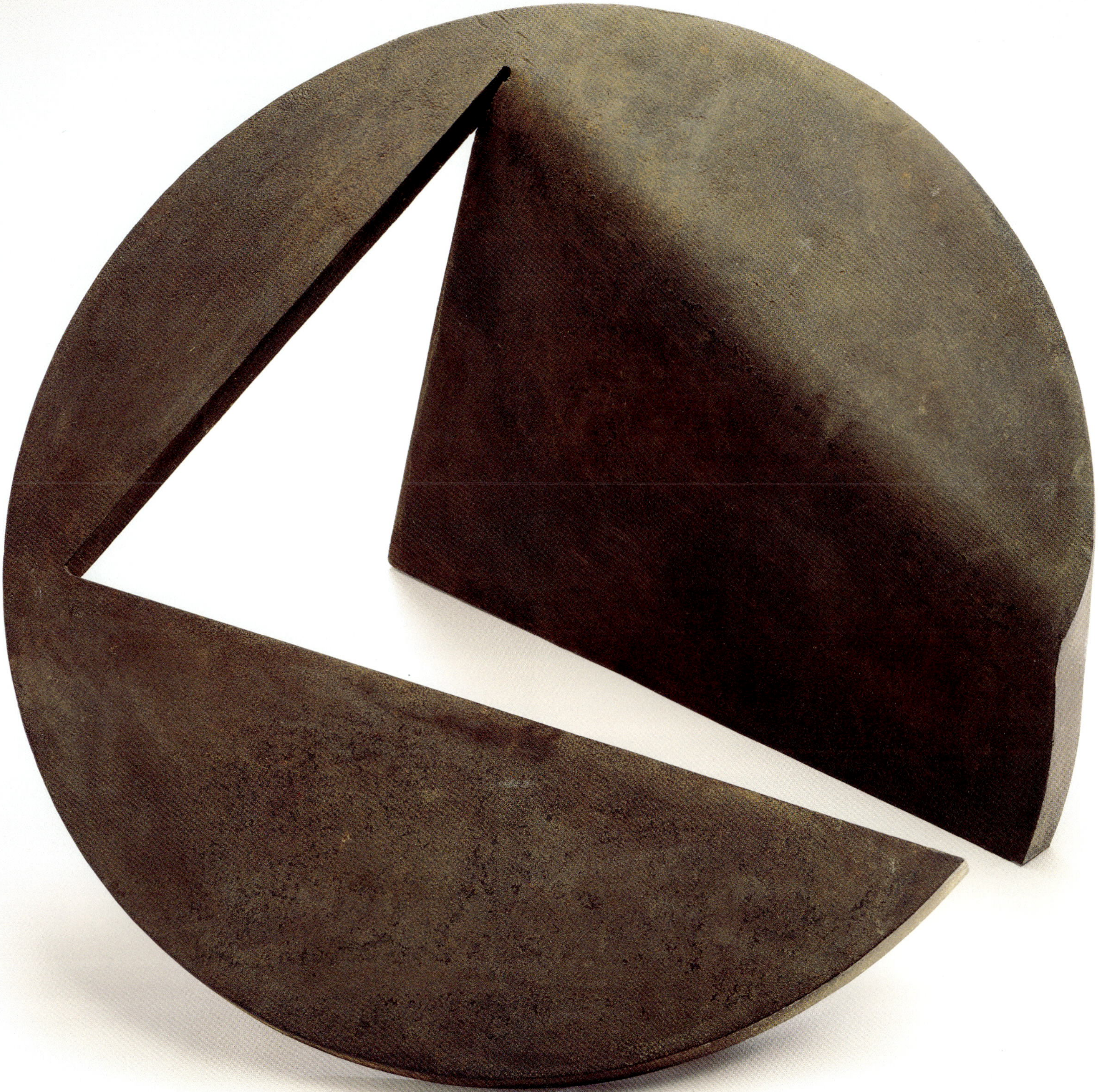

Franz Weissmann
Ponte [*Bridge*], 1958
Painted iron
18 5/8 x 18 5/8 x 26 5/8 inches
(47.3 x 47.3 x 67.6 cm)
The Adolpho Leirner Collection of Brazilian Constructive Art, museum purchase with funds provided by the Caroline Wiess Law Accessions Endowment Fund
2005.1040
PHOTO: Tom Jenkins

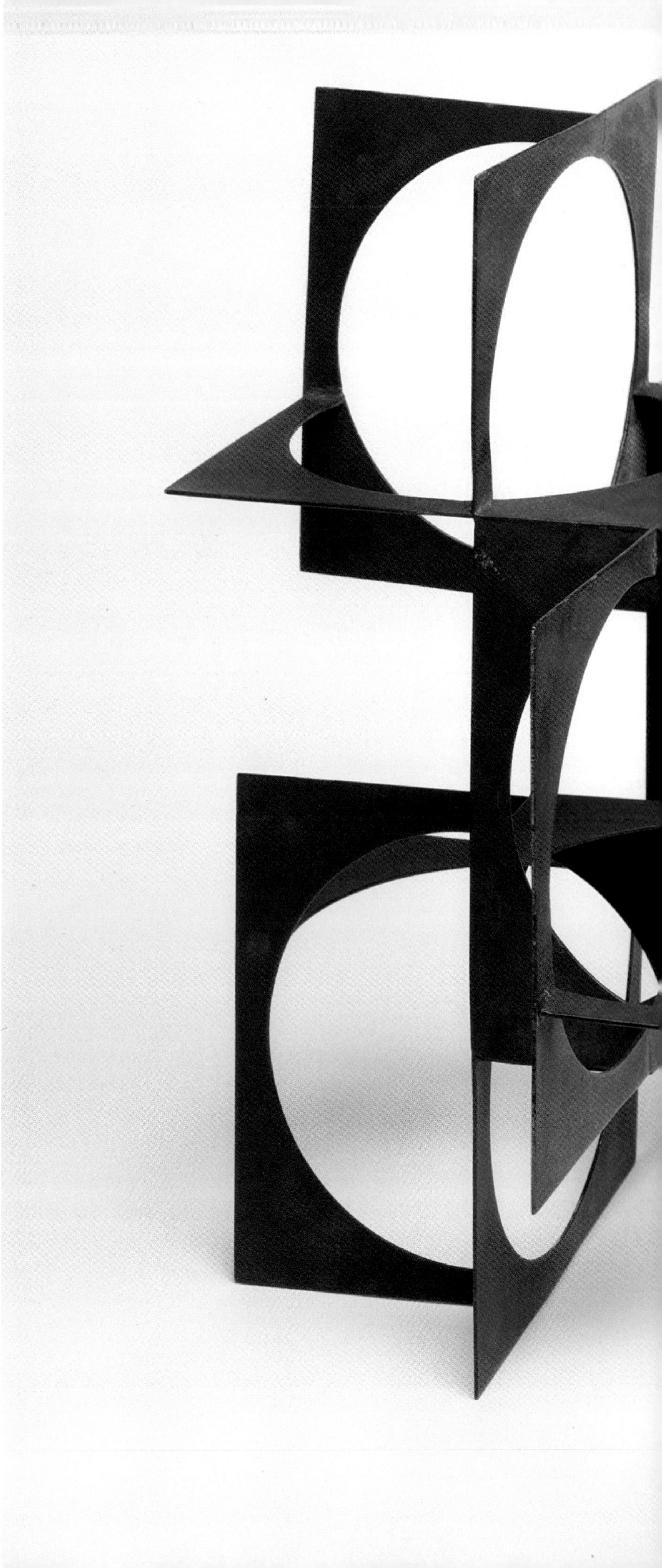

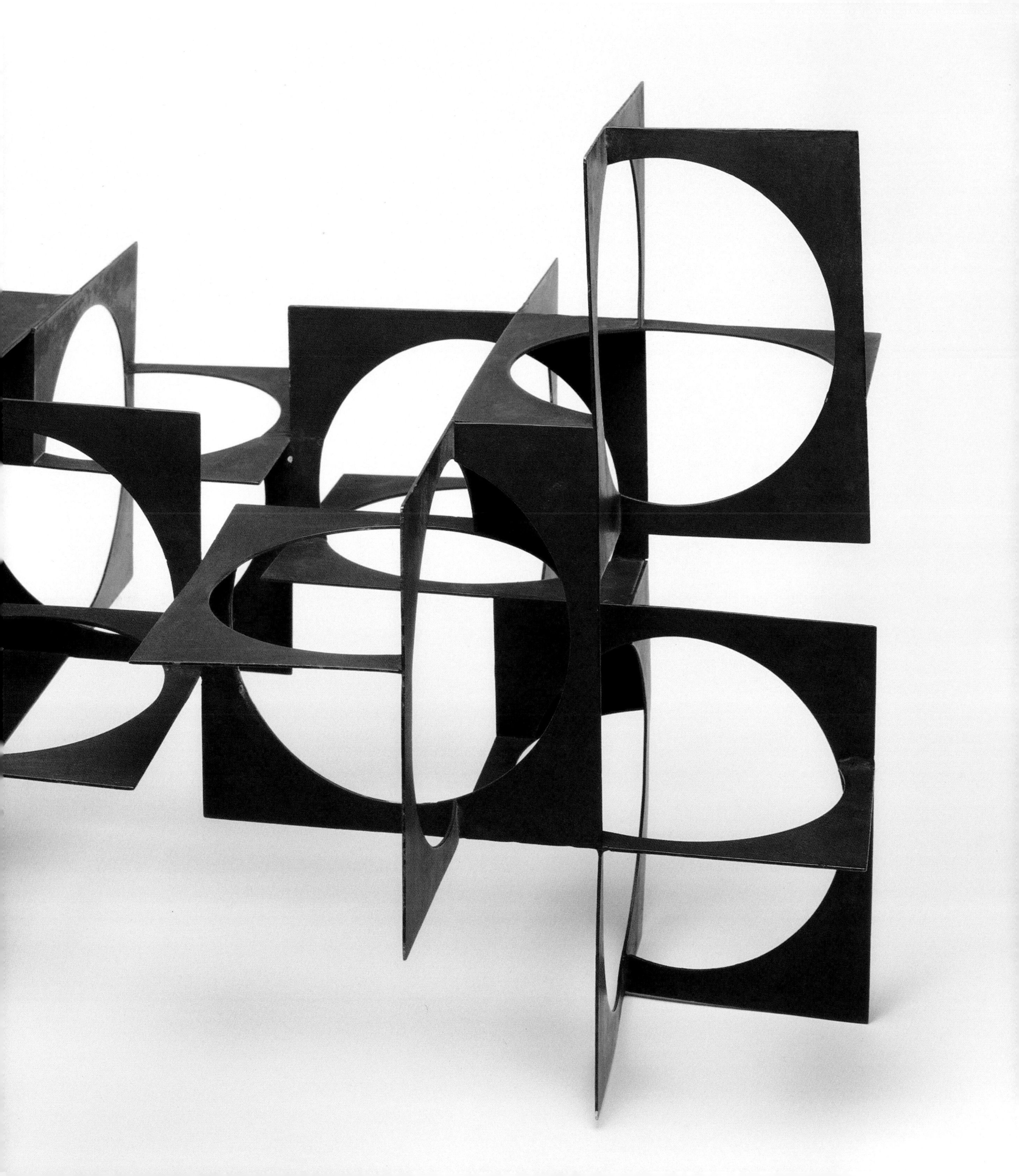

Independents

Cícero Dias
Meridianos [*Meridians*], 1953
Oil on canvas
31 7/8 x 21 5/16 inches
(81 x 54.1 cm)
The Adolpho Leirner Collection
of Brazilian Constructive Art,
gift of the Caroline Wiess Law
Foundation
2005.994
PHOTO: Rômulo Fialdini

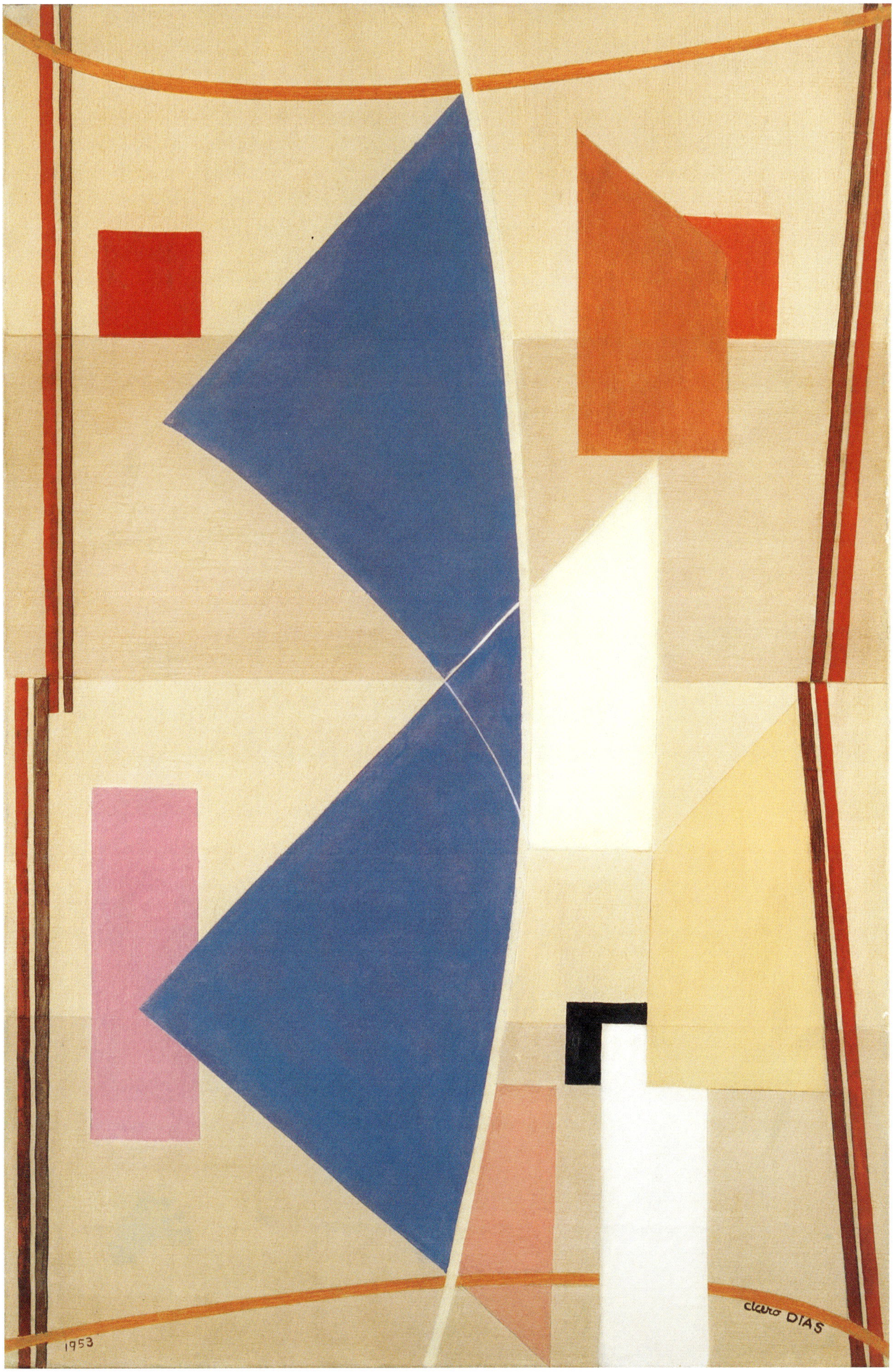
1953
cicero DIAS

Cícero Dias
Composição [*Composition*],
1954
Oil on canvas
32 x 21 3/8 inches
(81.3 x 54.4 cm)
The Adolpho Leirner Collection
of Brazilian Constructive Art,
gift of the Caroline Wiess Law
Foundation
2005.996
PHOTO: Rômulo Fialdini

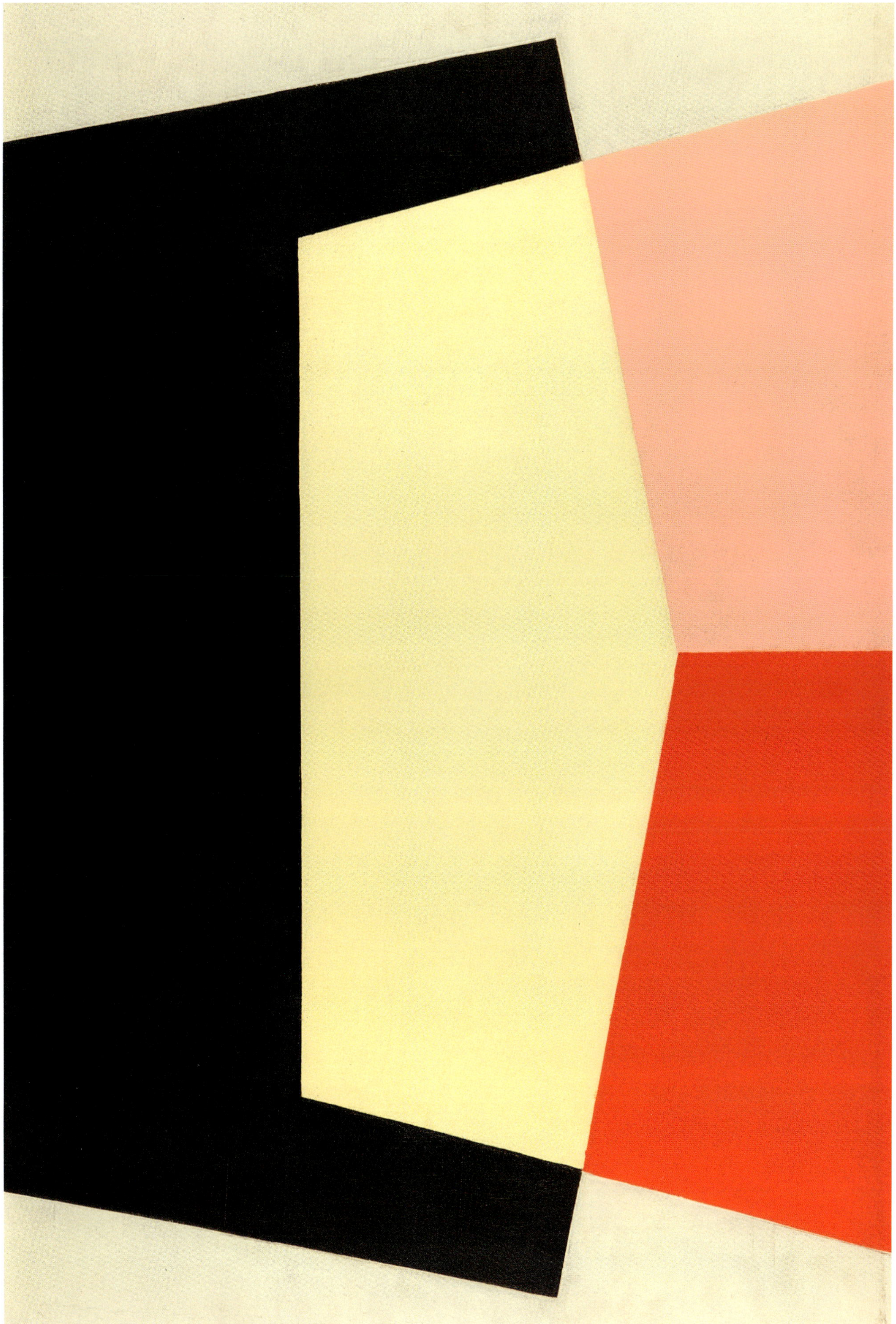

Cícero Dias
Sem título [*Untitled*], 1955
Oil on canvas
45 1/2 x 28 3/4 inches
(115.6 x 73 cm)
The Adolpho Leirner Collection of Brazilian Constructive Art, gift of the Caroline Wiess Law Foundation
2005.997

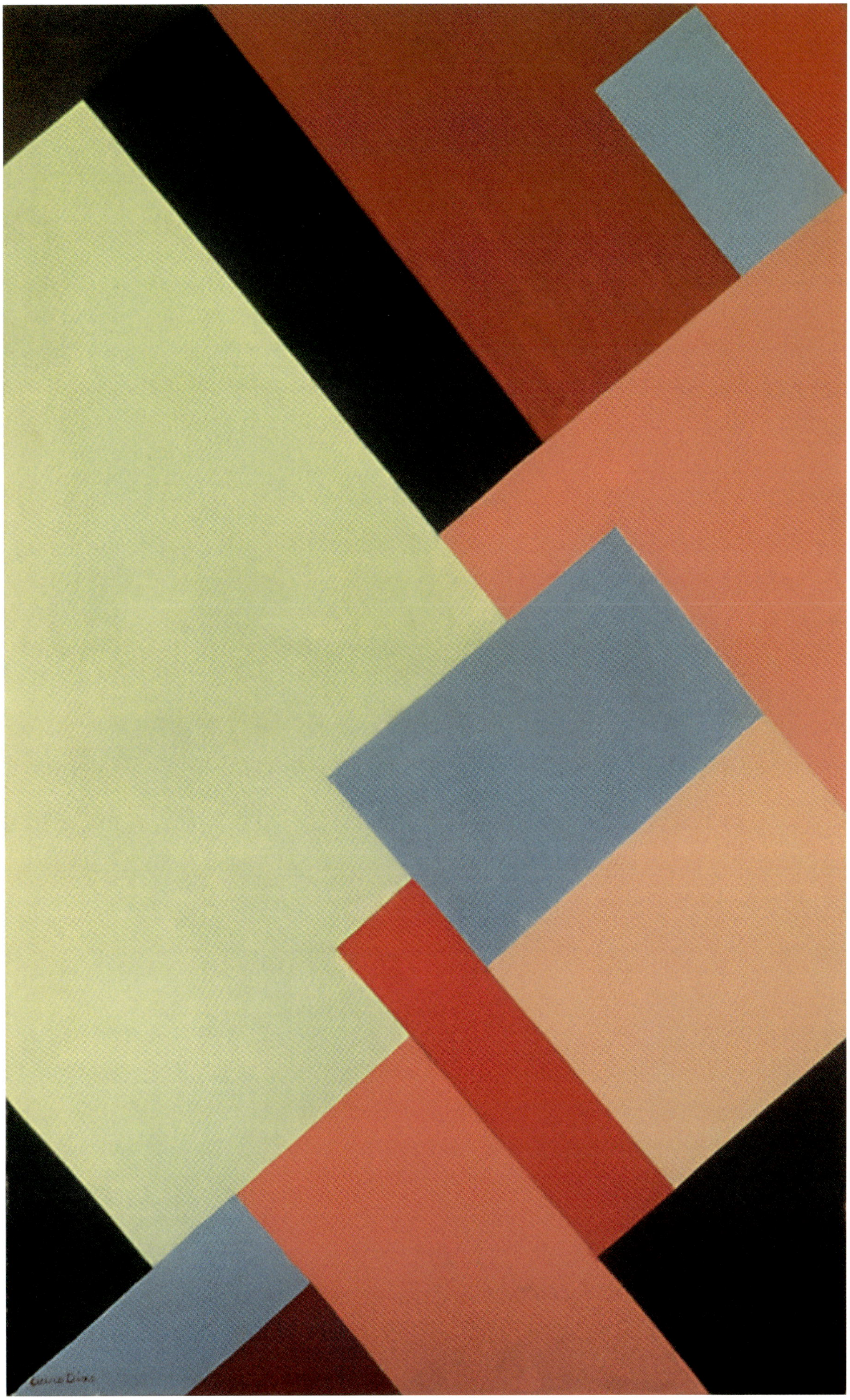

Cícero Dias
Sem título [*Untitled*], 1953
Oil on canvas
29 x 23 3/4 inches
(73.7 x 60.3 cm)
The Adolpho Leirner Collection
of Brazilian Constructive Art,
gift of the Caroline Wiess Law
Foundation
2005.995

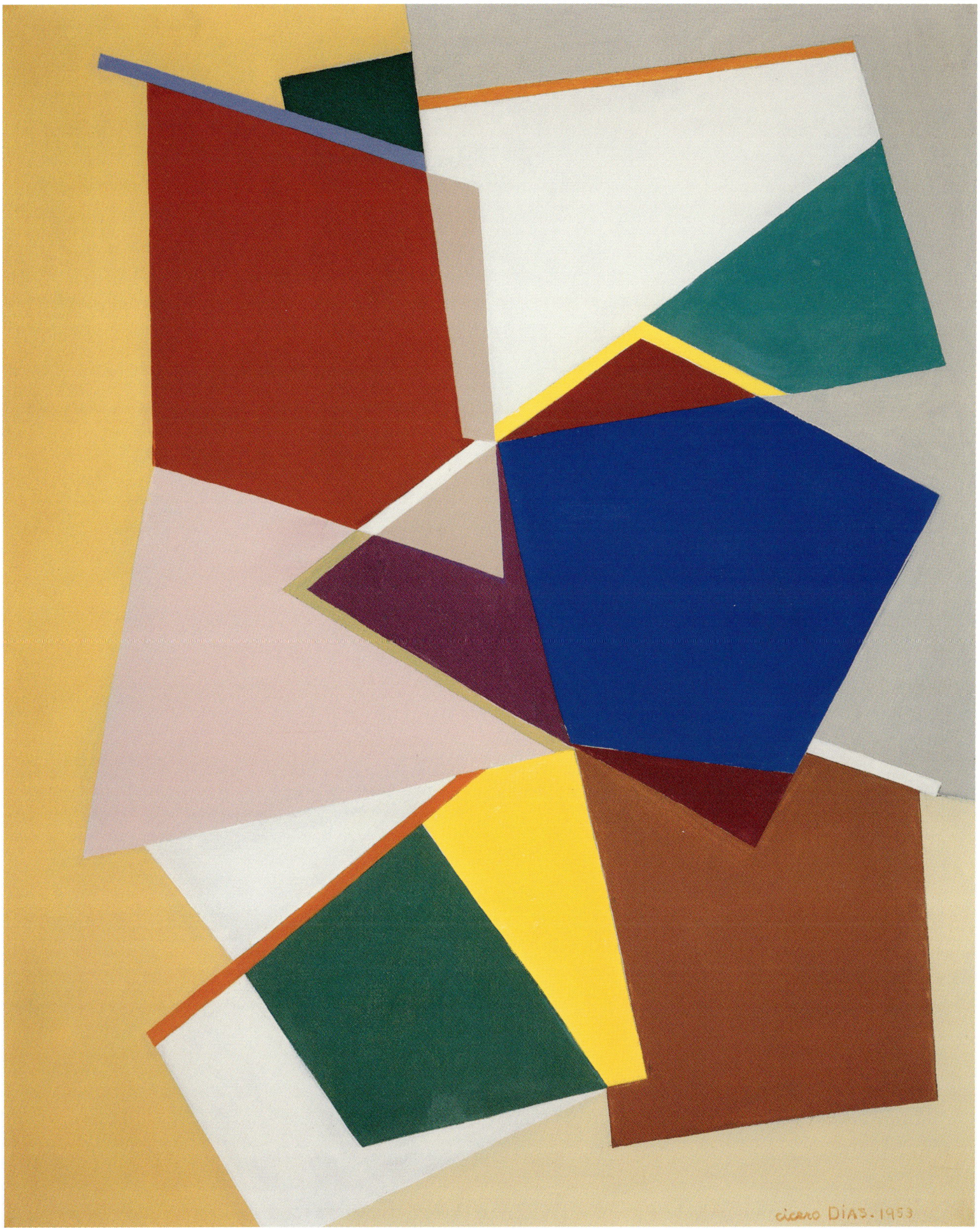
cicero DIAS. 1953

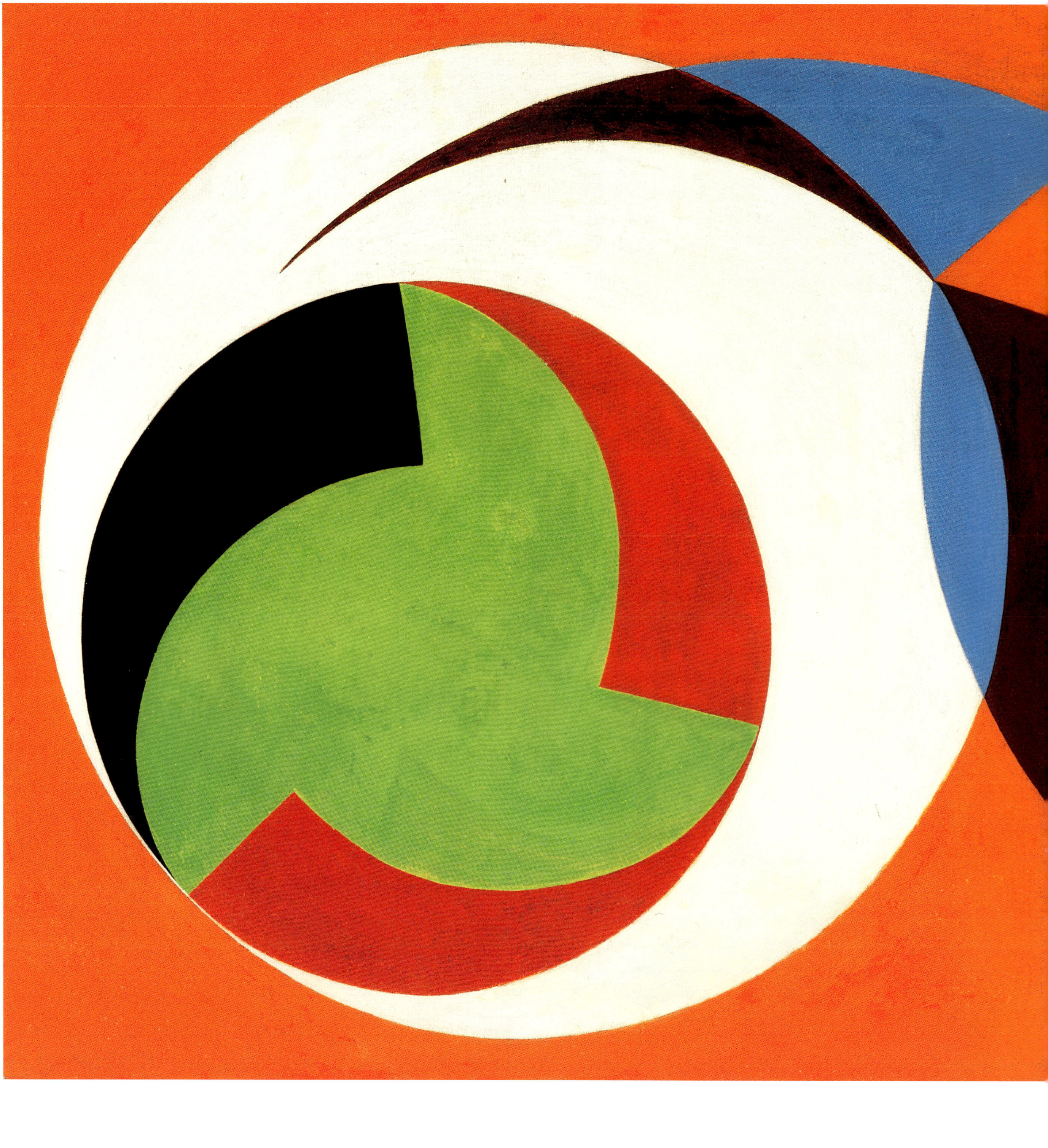

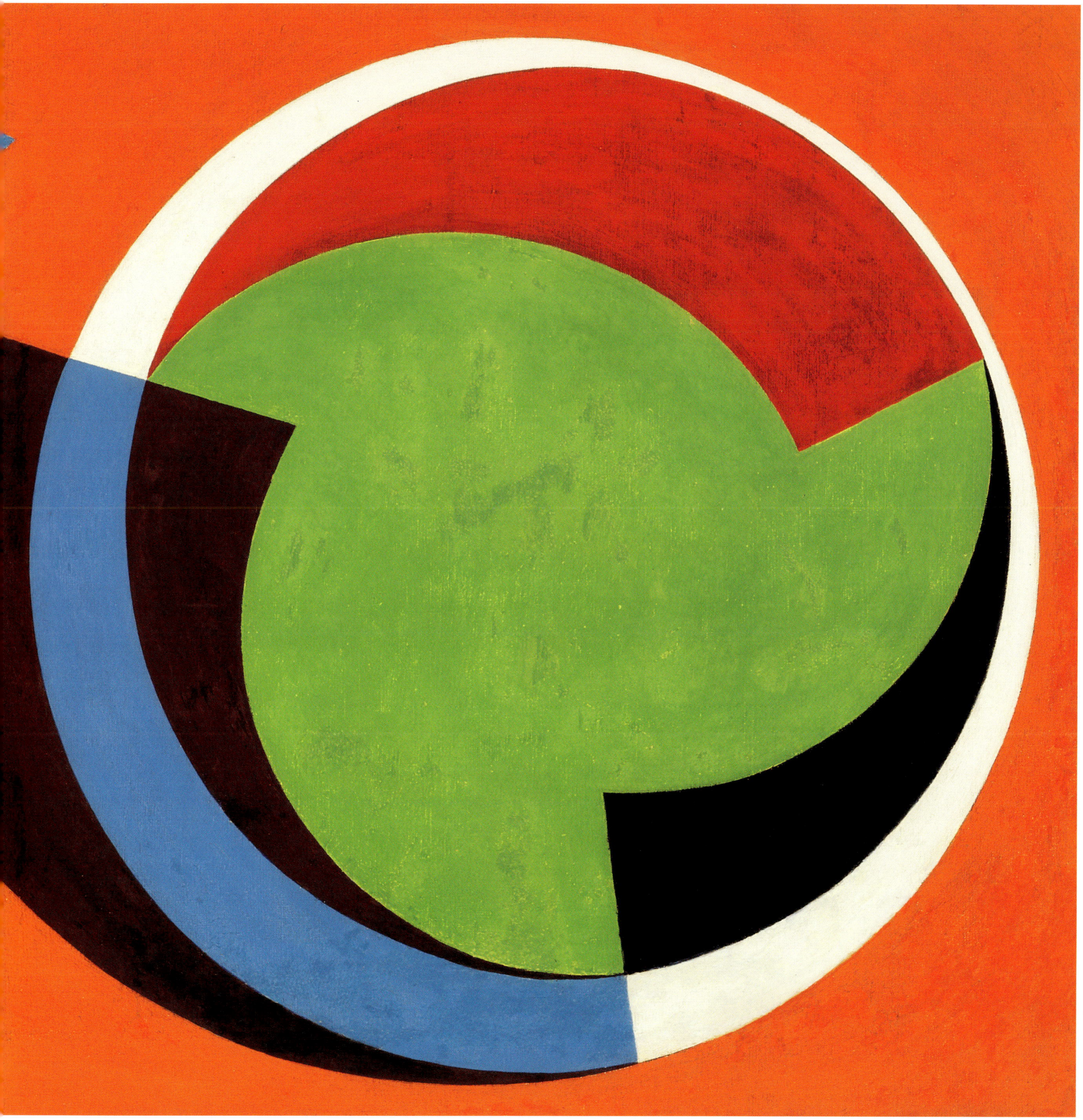

PREVIOUS PAGES
Ubi Bava
Sem título [*Untitled*], 1950s
Oil on canvas
24 1/2 x 49 1/2 inches
(62.2 x 125.7 cm)
The Adolpho Leirner Collection of Brazilian Constructive Art, gift of the Caroline Wiess Law Foundation
2005.983
PHOTO: Tom Jenkins

Mario Silésio
Estudo para mural da Faculdade de Direito de Belo Horizonte [*Study for a Mural for the Law School of Belo Horizonte*], 1958
Oil on canvas
21 1/8 x 25 1/2 inches
(53.6 x 64.8 cm)
The Adolpho Leirner Collection of Brazilian Constructive Art, museum purchase with funds provided by the Caroline Wiess Law Accessions Endowment Fund
2005.1030
PHOTO: Rômulo Fialdini

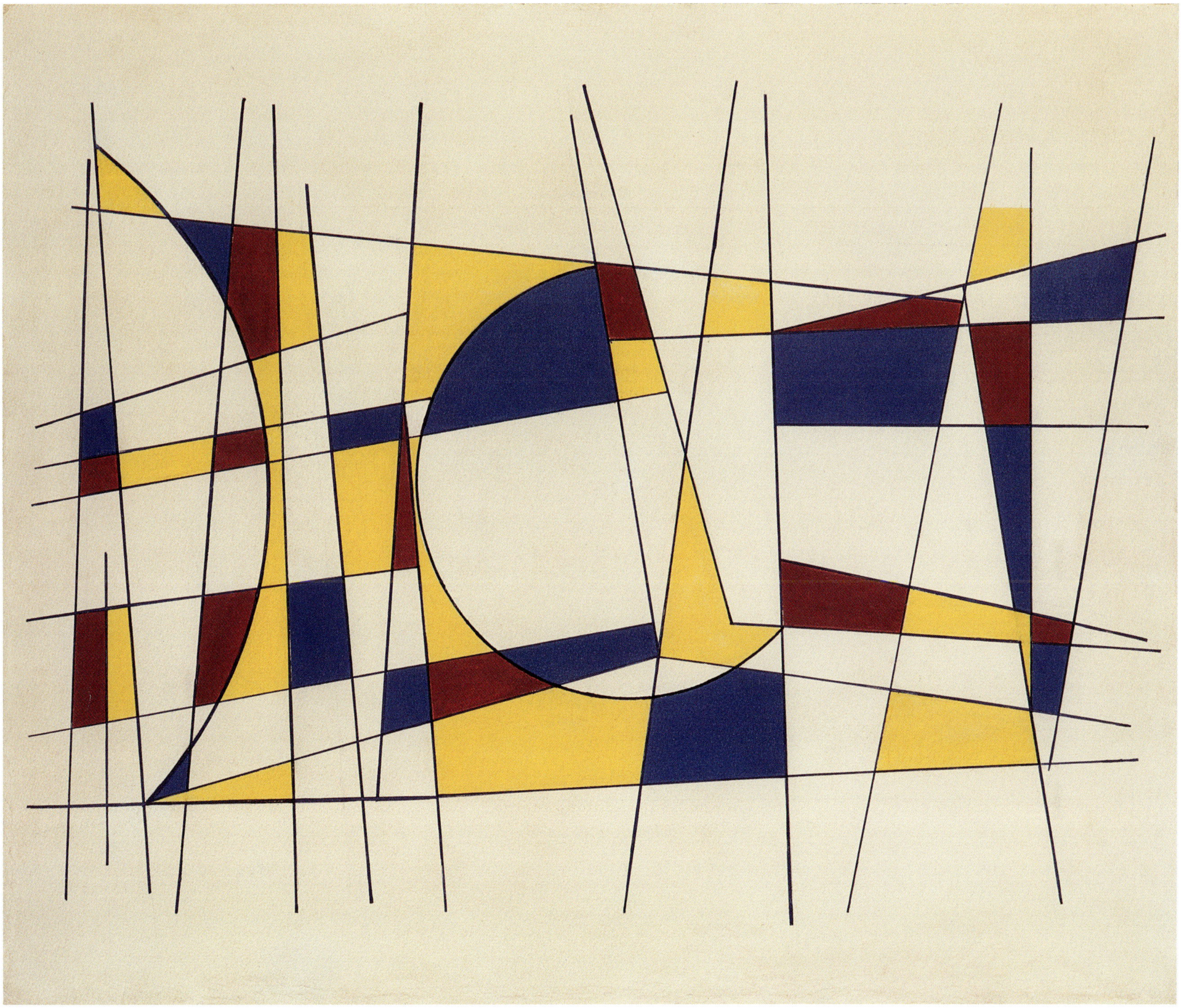

Dionísio del Santo
Estrutura [*Structure*], 1957
Oil on canvas
23 5/8 x 23 5/8 inches
(60 x 60 cm)
The Adolpho Leirner Collection
of Brazilian Constructive Art,
gift of the Caroline Wiess Law
Foundation
2005.1029
PHOTO: Rômulo Fialdini

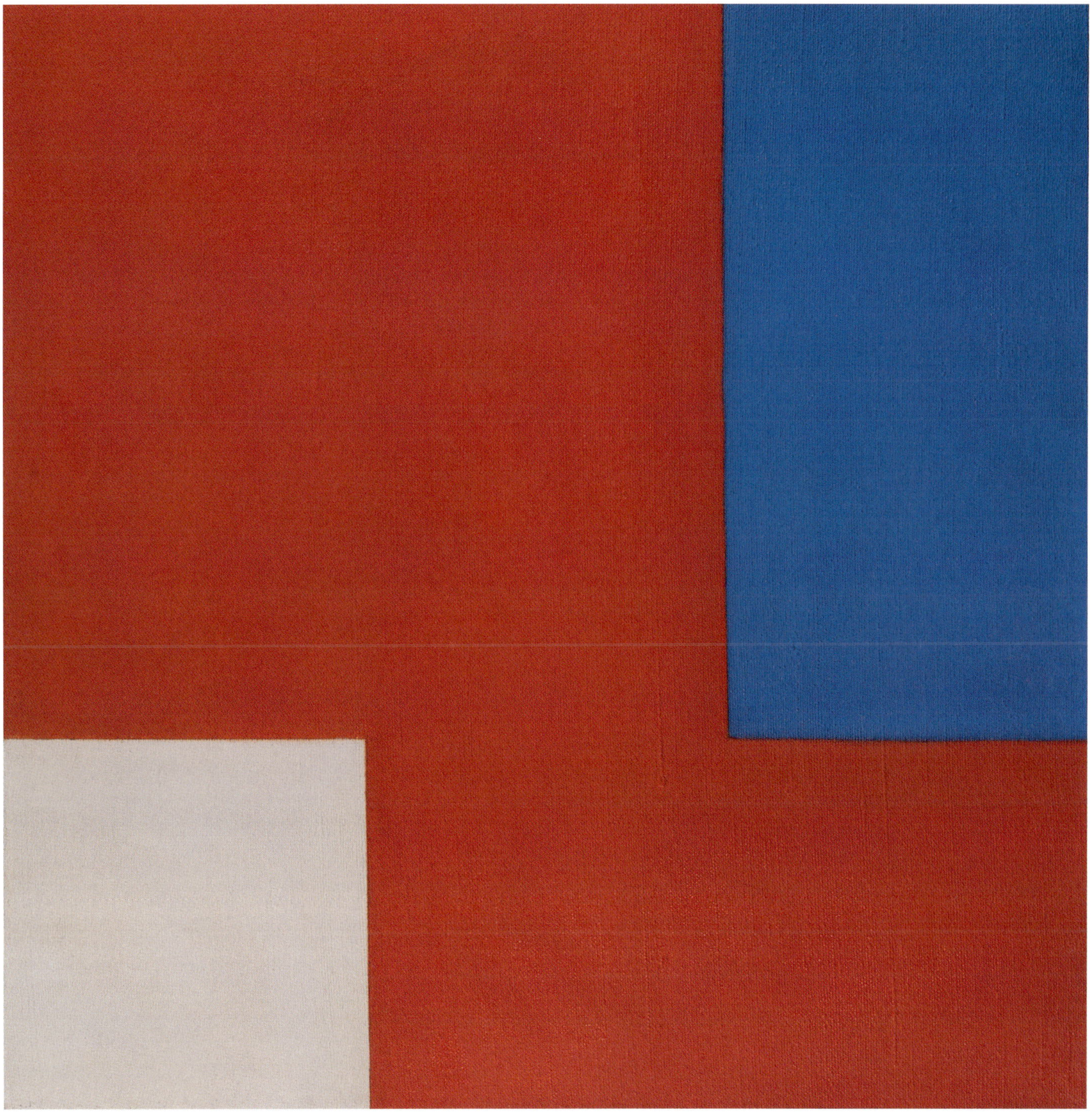

Ione Saldanha
Construção [*Construction*],
1959
Oil on canvas
24 5/8 x 35 1/8 inches
(62.5 x 89.2 cm)
The Adolpho Leirner Collection
of Brazilian Constructive Art,
gift of the Caroline Wiess Law
Foundation
2005.1028
PHOTO: Tom Jenkins

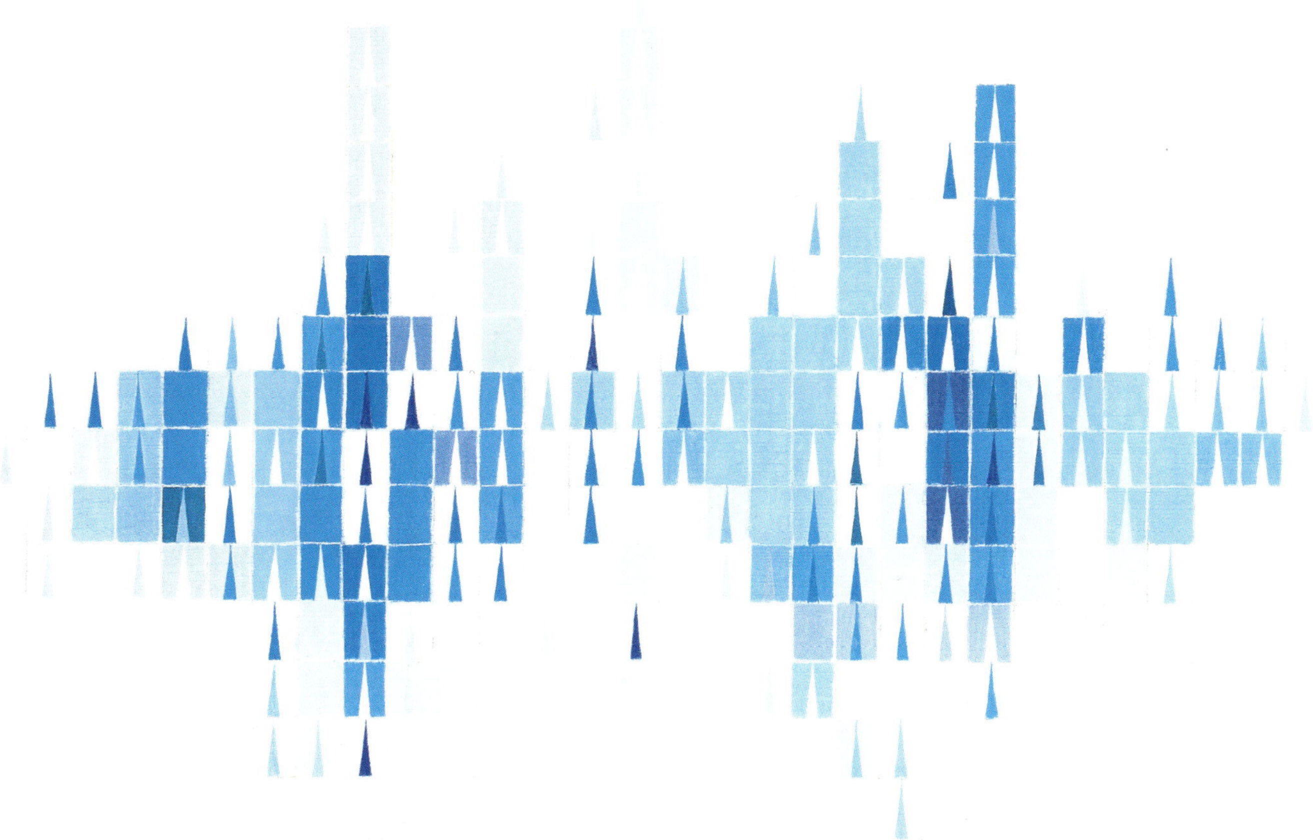

Maria Helena Andrés
Fantasia de ritmos
[*Rhythmic Fantasy*], 1958
Oil on canvas
19 5/8 x 27 1/2 inches
(49.8 x 69.9 cm)
The Adolpho Leirner Collection
of Brazilian Constructive Art,
gift of the Caroline Wiess Law
Foundation
2005.978
PHOTO: Tom Jenkins

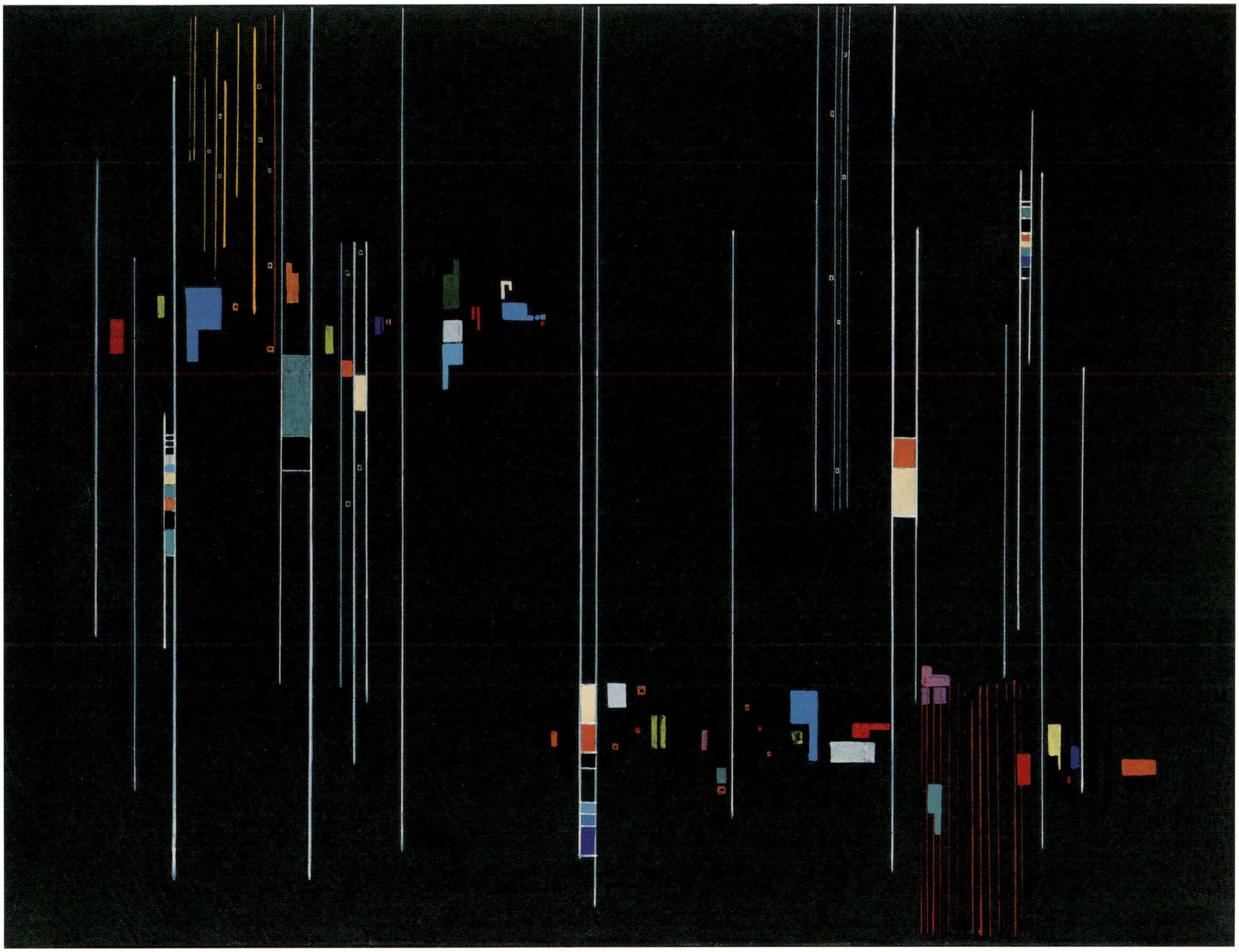

Aldo Bonadei
Sem titulo [*Untitled*],
1956
Oil on canvas
23 3/8 x 30 7/8 inches
(59.4 x 78.5 cm)
The Adolpho Leirner Collection
of Brazilian Constructive Art,
gift of the Caroline Wiess Law
Foundation
2005.984
PHOTO: Rômulo Fialdini

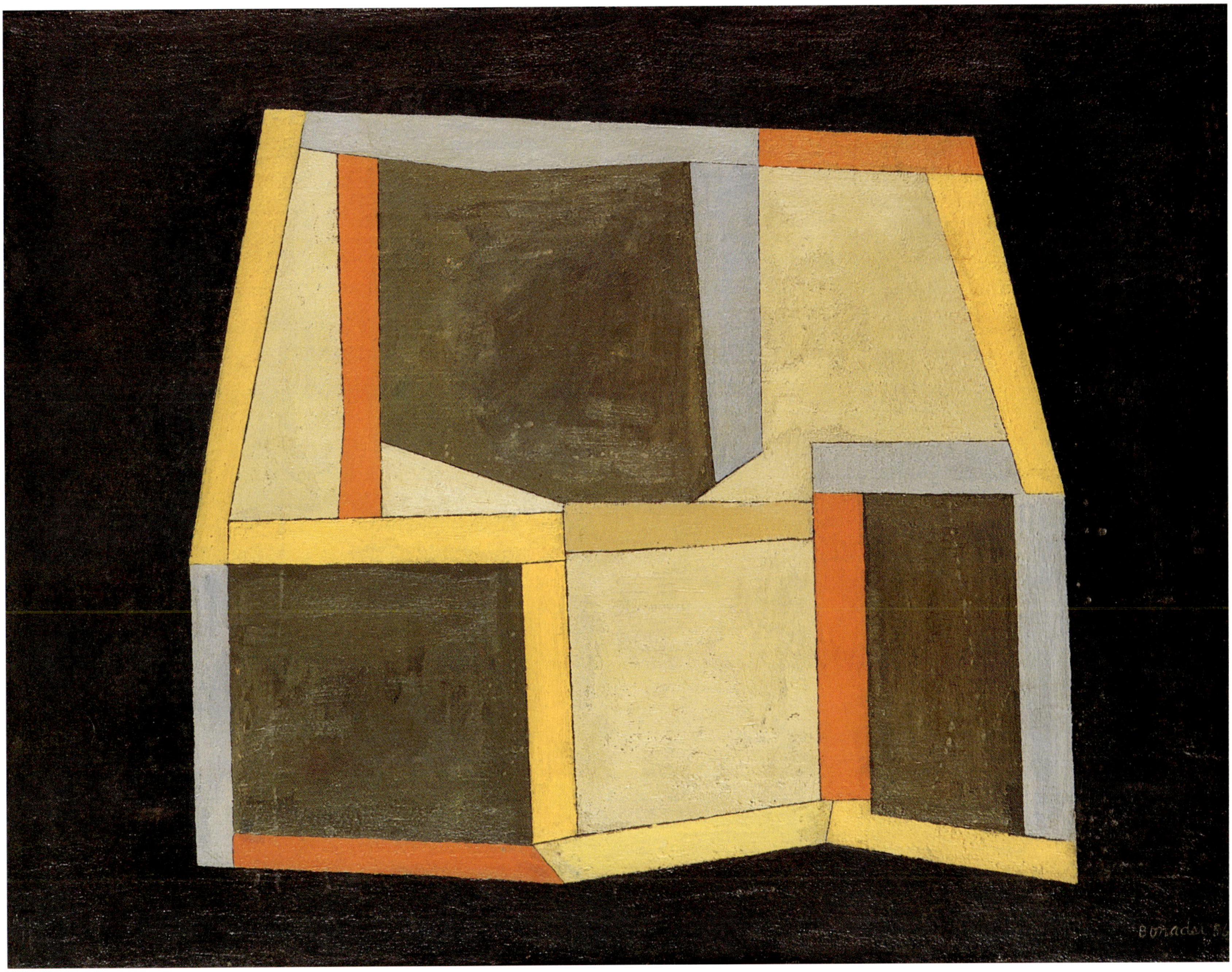

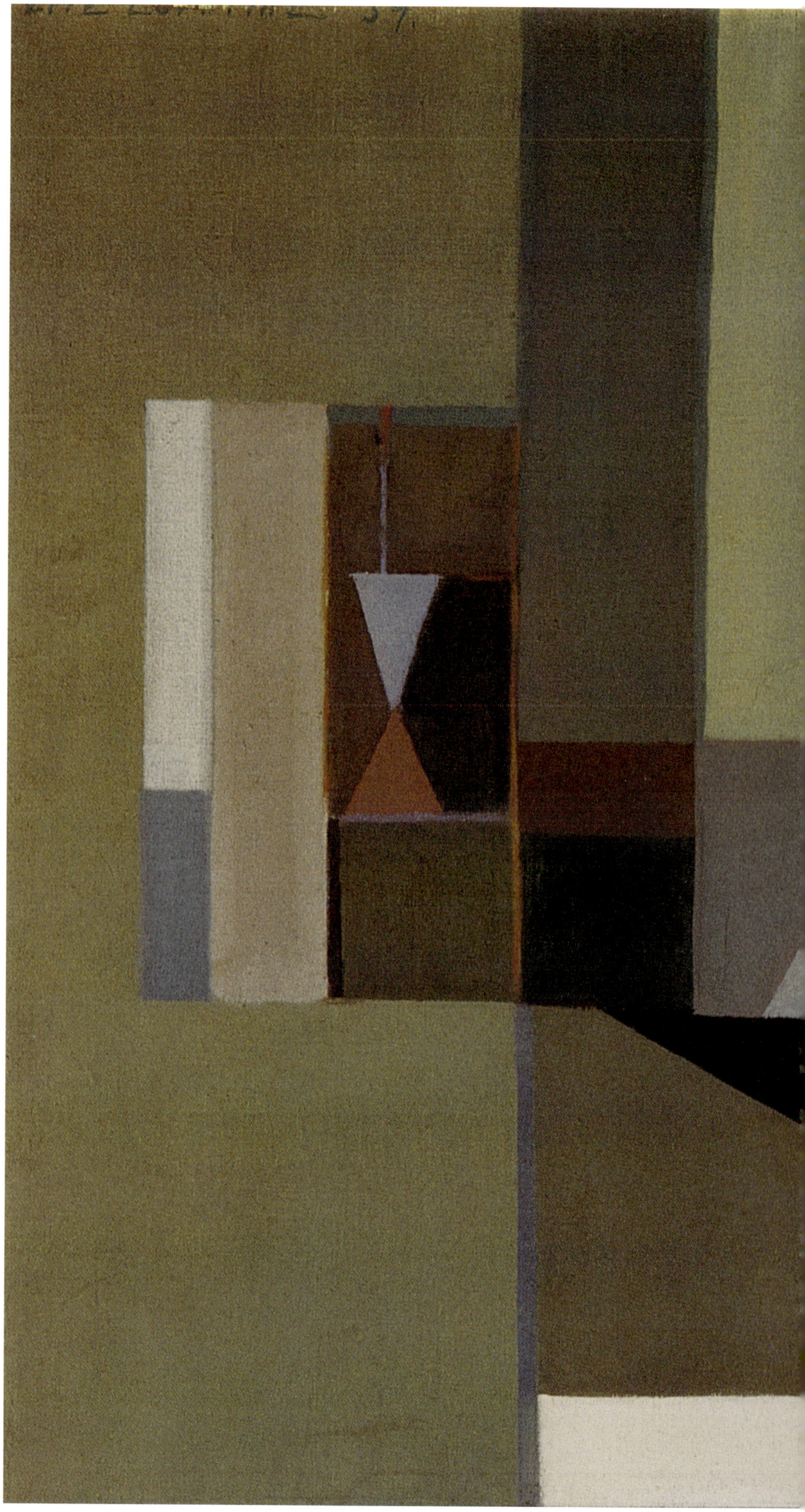

Maria Leontina
Os episódios II [*The Episodes no. 2*],
1959
Oil on canvas
23 1/2 x 36 1/4 inches
(59.7 x 92.1 cm)
The Adolpho Leirner Collection
of Brazilian Constructive Art,
gift of the Caroline Wiess Law
Foundation
2005.1011
PHOTO: Rômulo Fialdini

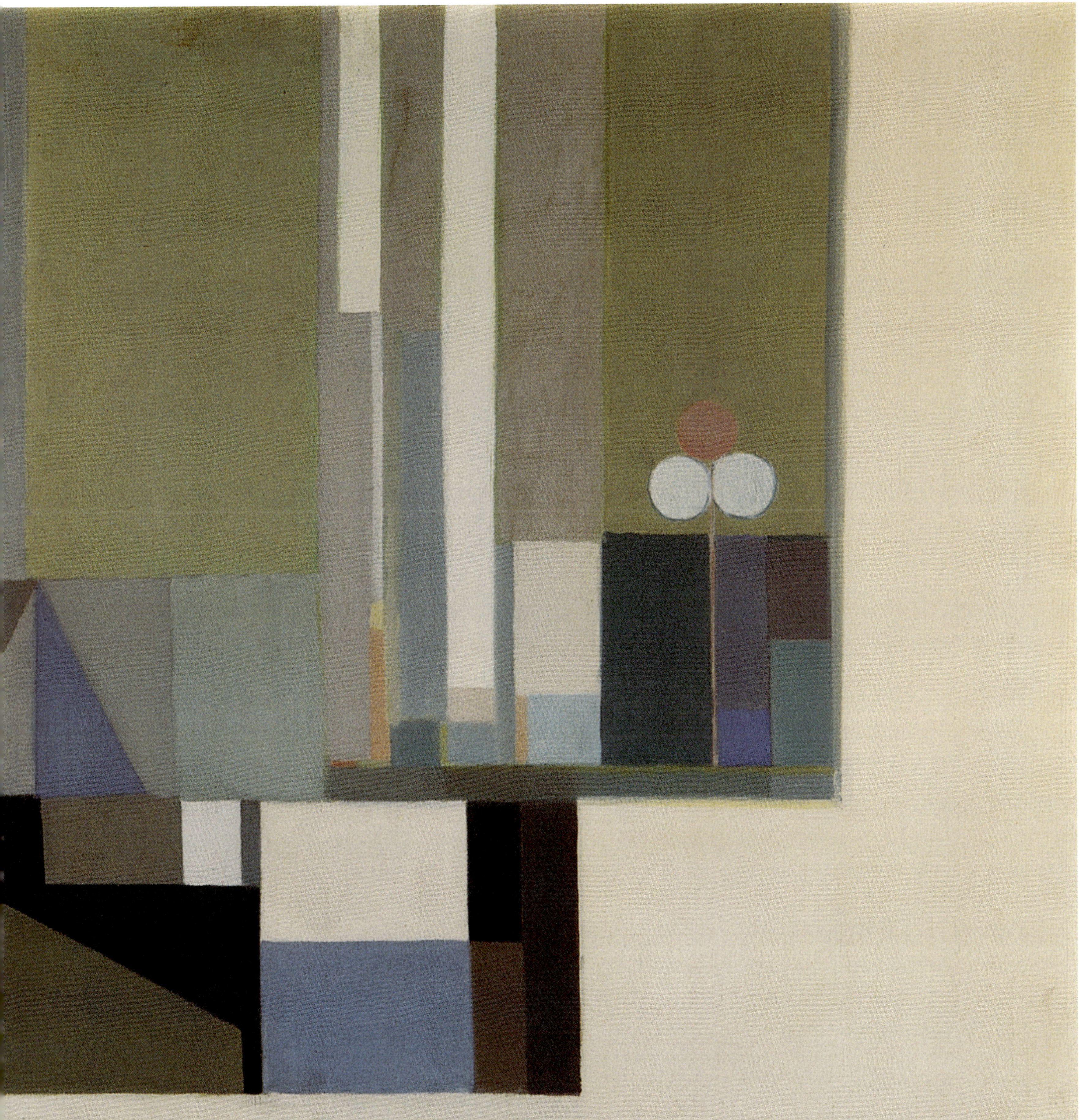

Heinz Kühn
Sem título [*Untitled*],
1963
Oil on canvas
31 1/2 x 27 1/4 inches
(80 x 69.2 cm)
The Adolpho Leirner Collection
of Brazilian Constructive Art,
gift of the Caroline Wiess Law
Foundation
2005.1009

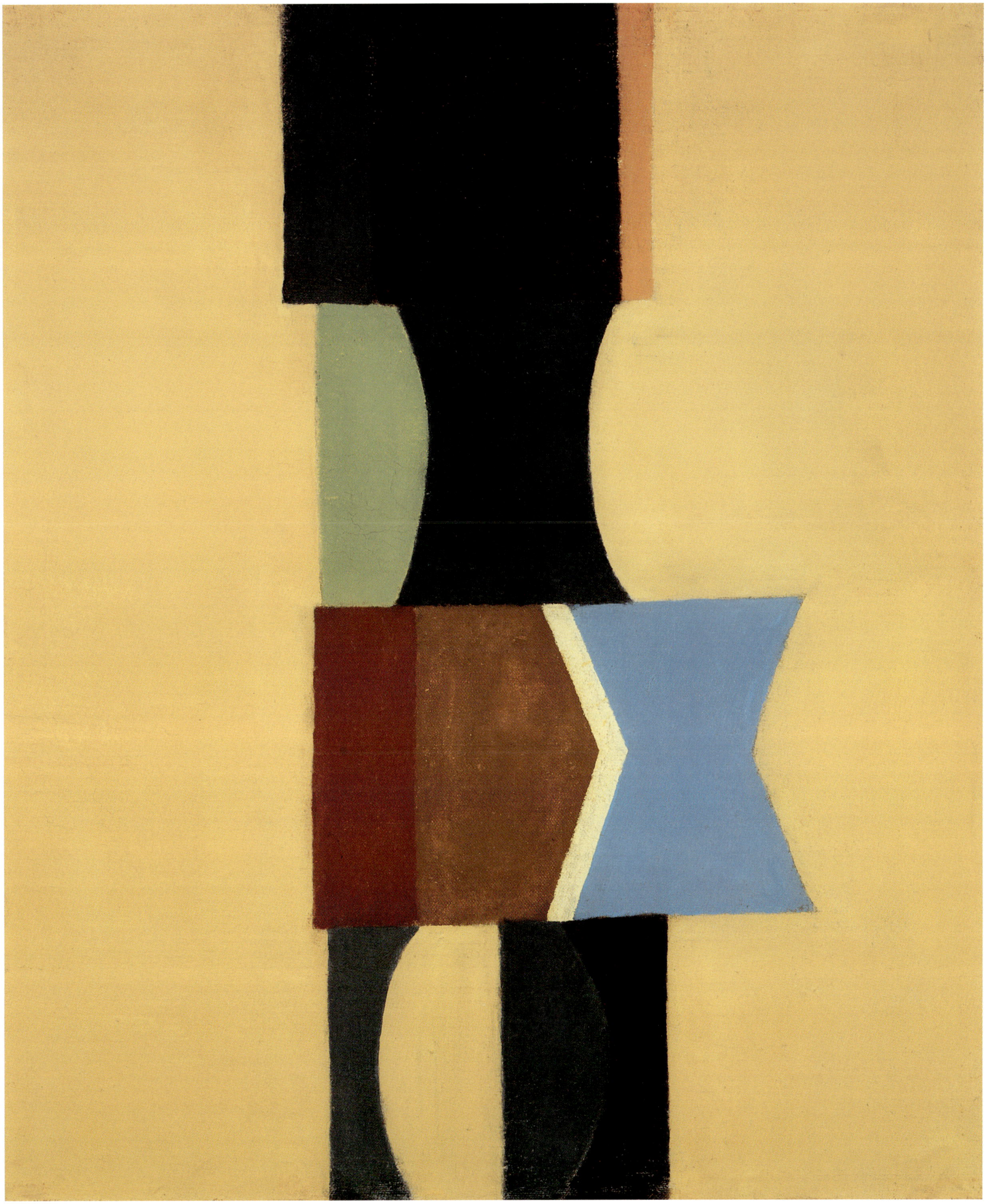

Rubem Valentim
Composição [*Composition*],
1960
Oil on canvas
17 3/4 x 11 3/4 inches
(45.1 x 29.8 cm)
The Adolpho Leirner Collection
of Brazilian Constructive Art,
museum purchase with funds
provided by the Caroline Wiess
Law Accessions Endowment
Fund
2005.1033
PHOTO: Rômulo Fialdini

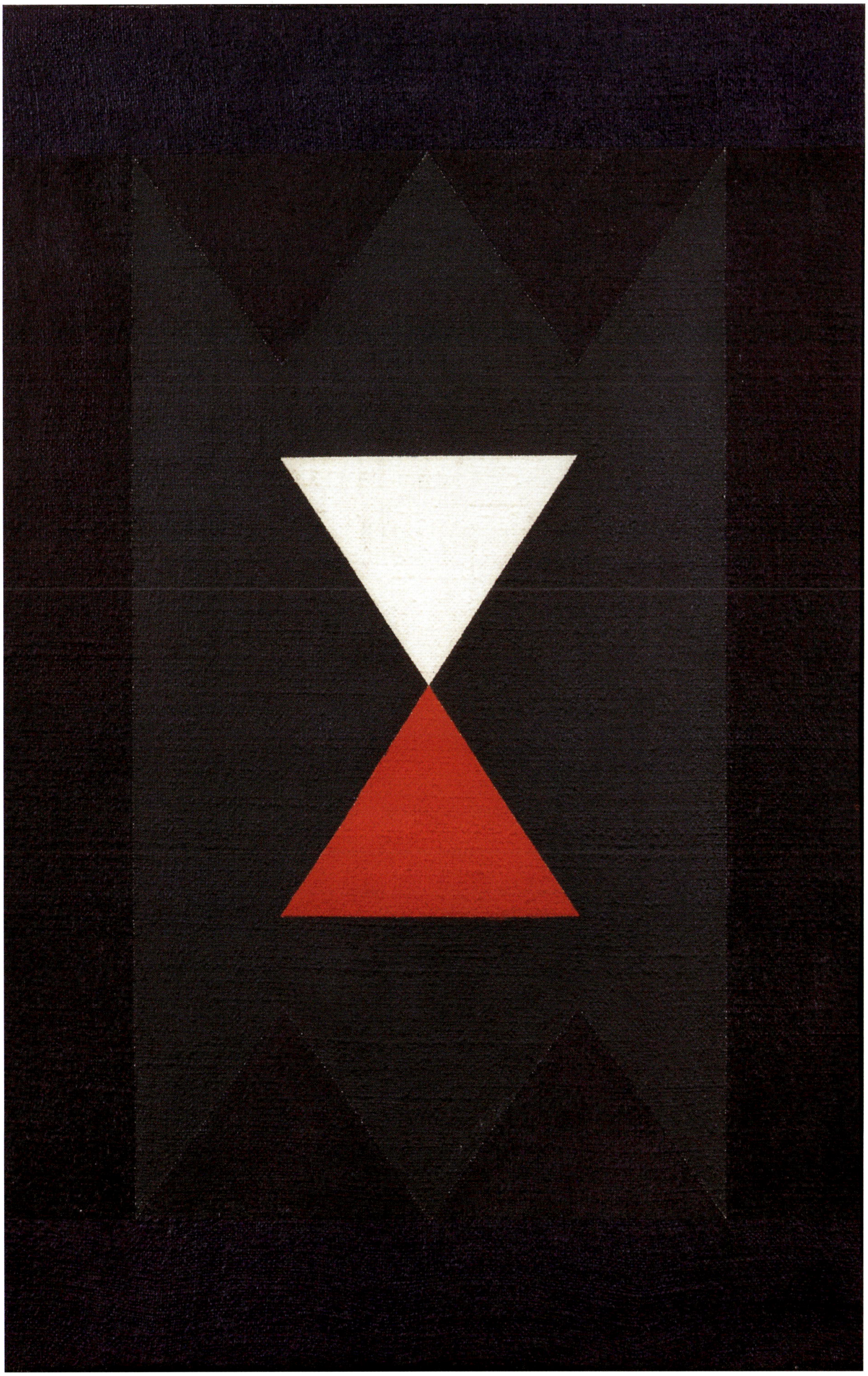

Waldemar da Costa
Estático semovente XXXV
[*Moving Stationary no. 35*],
1968
Oil on wood
33 1/4 x 25 5/16 inches
(84.5 x 64.3 cm)
The Adolpho Leirner Collection
of Brazilian Constructive Art,
gift of the Caroline Wiess Law
Foundation
2005.992
PHOTO: Tom Jenkins

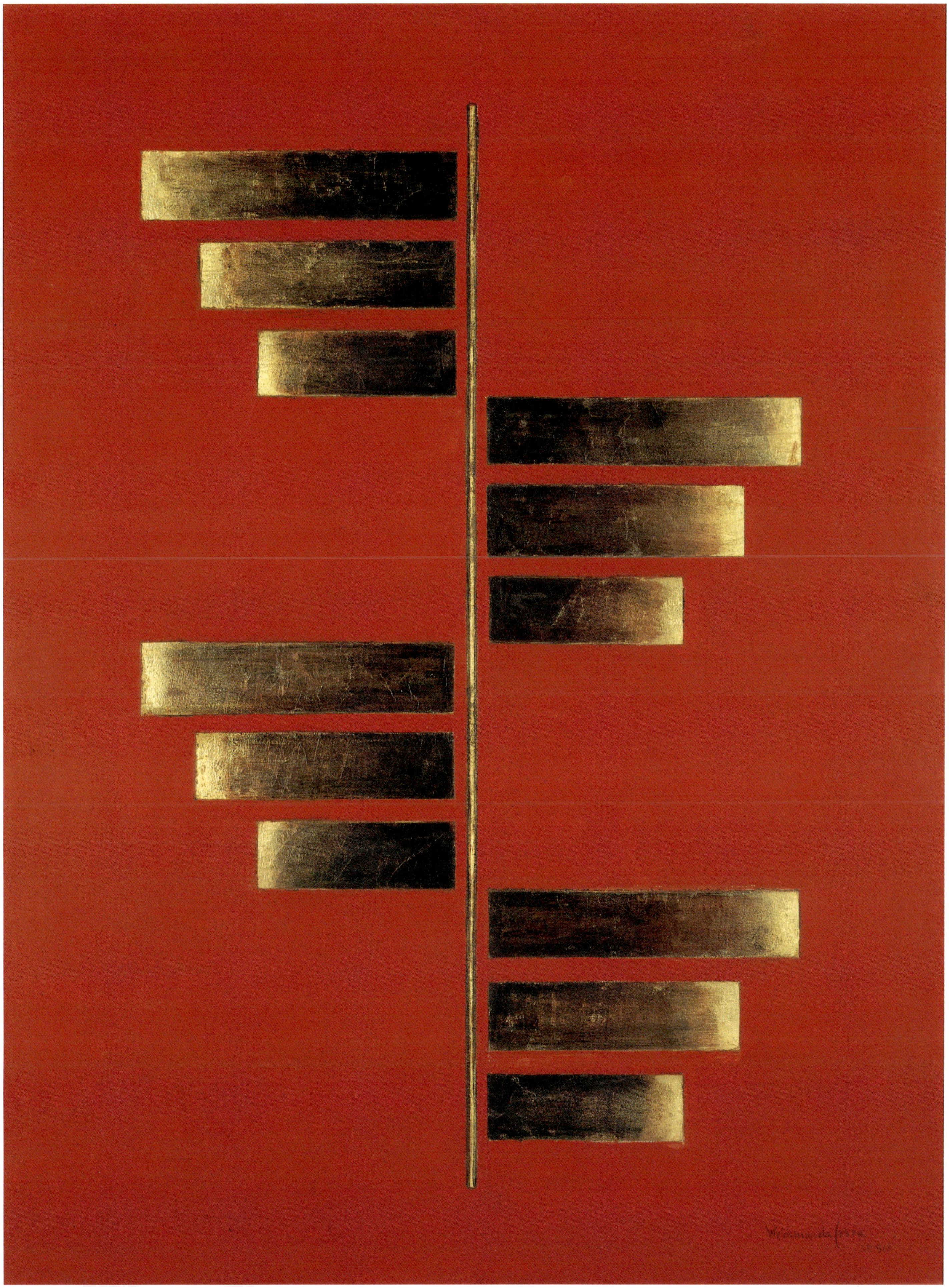

Arnaldo Ferrari
Composição vermelho-amarelo 51 [*Red and Yellow Composition no. 51*], 1960
Oil on canvas
30 x 24 inches (76.2 x 61 cm)
The Adolpho Leirner Collection of Brazilian Constructive Art, gift of the Caroline Wiess Law Foundation
2005.998
PHOTO: Tom Jenkins

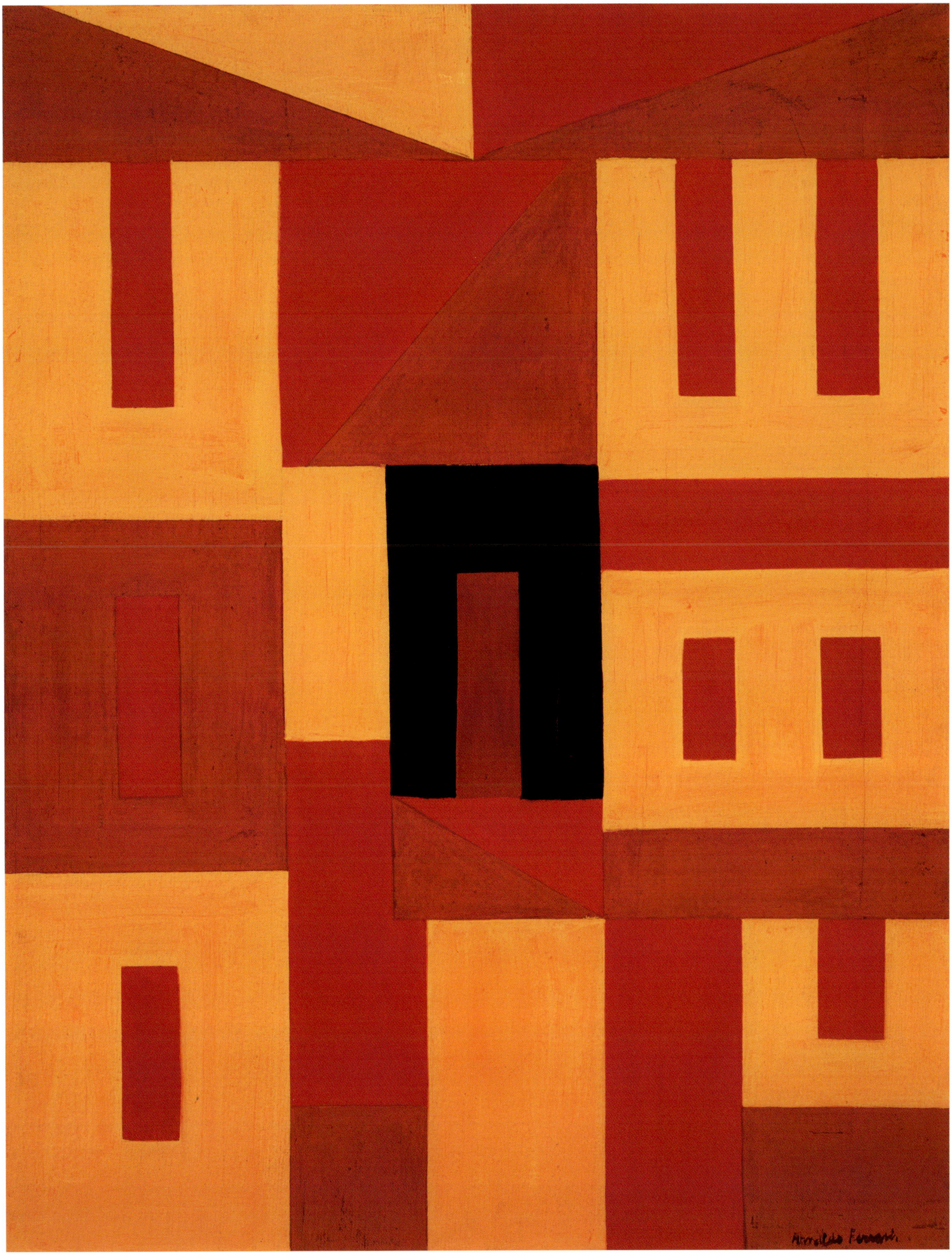

Joaquim Tenreiro
Sem título [*Untitled*],
late 1950s
Oil on canvas
21 11/16 x 18 1/8 inches
(55.1 x 46 cm)
The Adolpho Leirner Collection
of Brazilian Constructive Art,
museum purchase with funds
provided by the Caroline Wiess
Law Accessions Endowment
Fund
2005.1032
PHOTO: Rômulo Fialdini

Almir Mavignier
Durchdringung [*Seeping Through*],
1965
Screenprint
24 7/16 x 24 7/16 inches
(62.1 x 62.1 cm)
The Adolpho Leirner Collection
of Brazilian Constructive Art,
gift of the Caroline Wiess Law
Foundation
2005.1018
PHOTO: Tom Jenkins

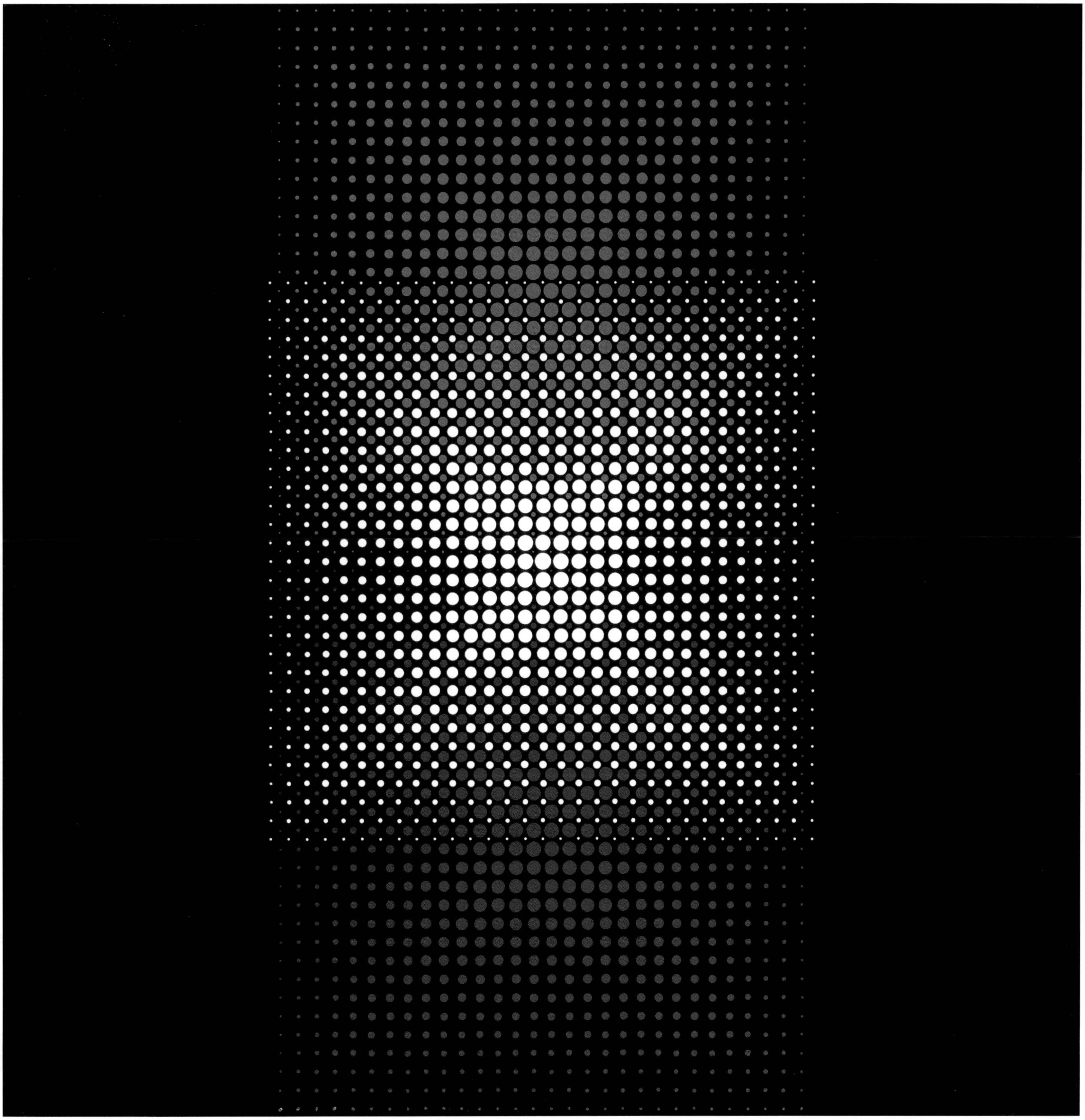

Sérgio Camargo
Relevo 326 [*Relief 326*], 1970
Painted wood
23 5/8 x 23 1/2 x 5 1/8 inches
(60 x 59.7 x 13 cm)
The Adolpho Leirner Collection of Brazilian Constructive Art, museum purchase with funds provided by the Caroline Wiess Law Accessions Endowment Fund
2007.12
PHOTO: Tom Jenkins

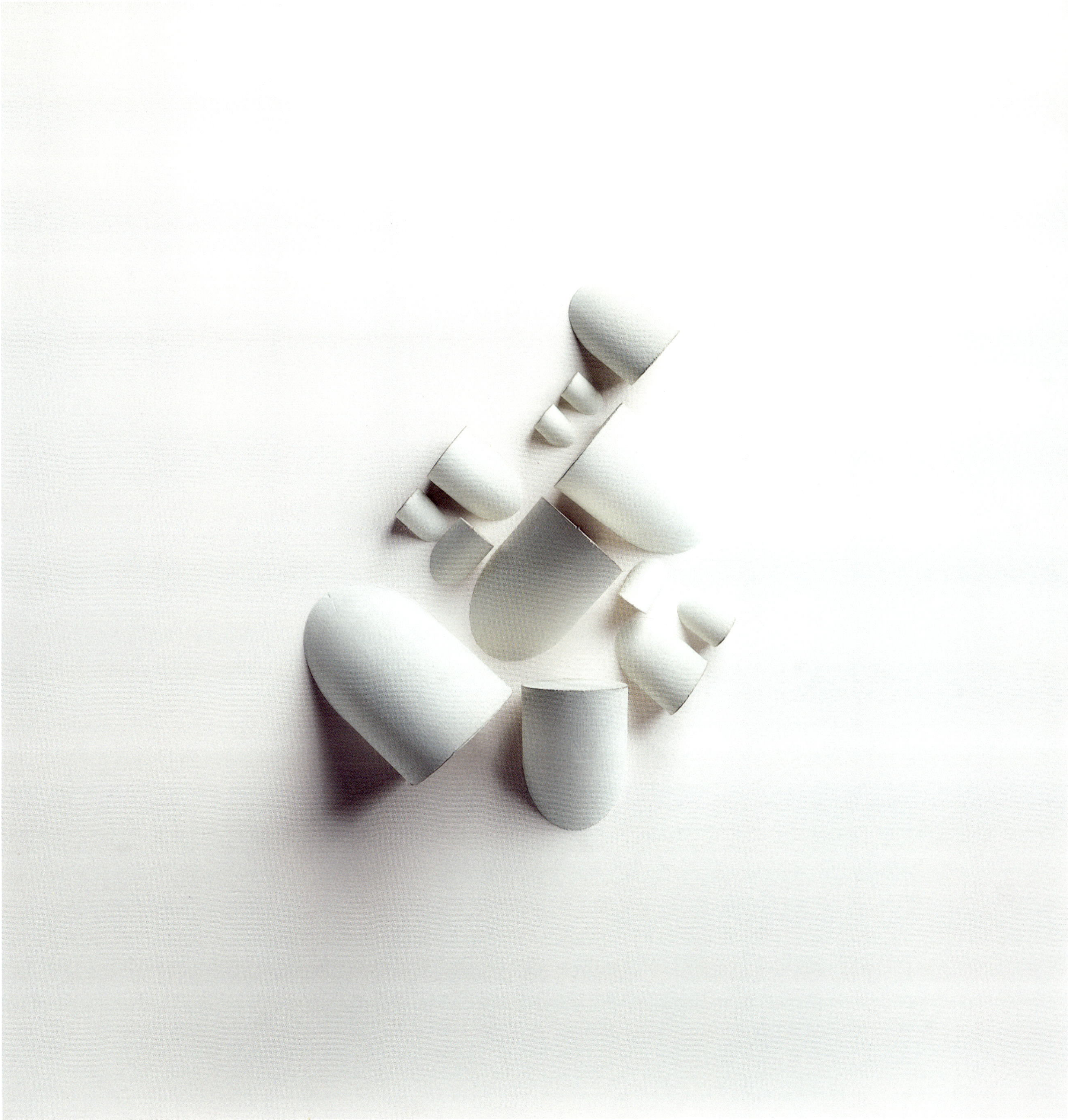

Danilo Di Prete
Sem título [*Untitled*],
early 1960s
Mixed-media relief on wood
14 x 13 3/4 x 4 3/4 inches
(35.5 x 35 x 12 cm)
The Adolpho Leirner Collection
of Brazilian Constructive Art,
gift of the Caroline Wiess Law
Foundation
2005.993
PHOTO: Rômulo Fialdini

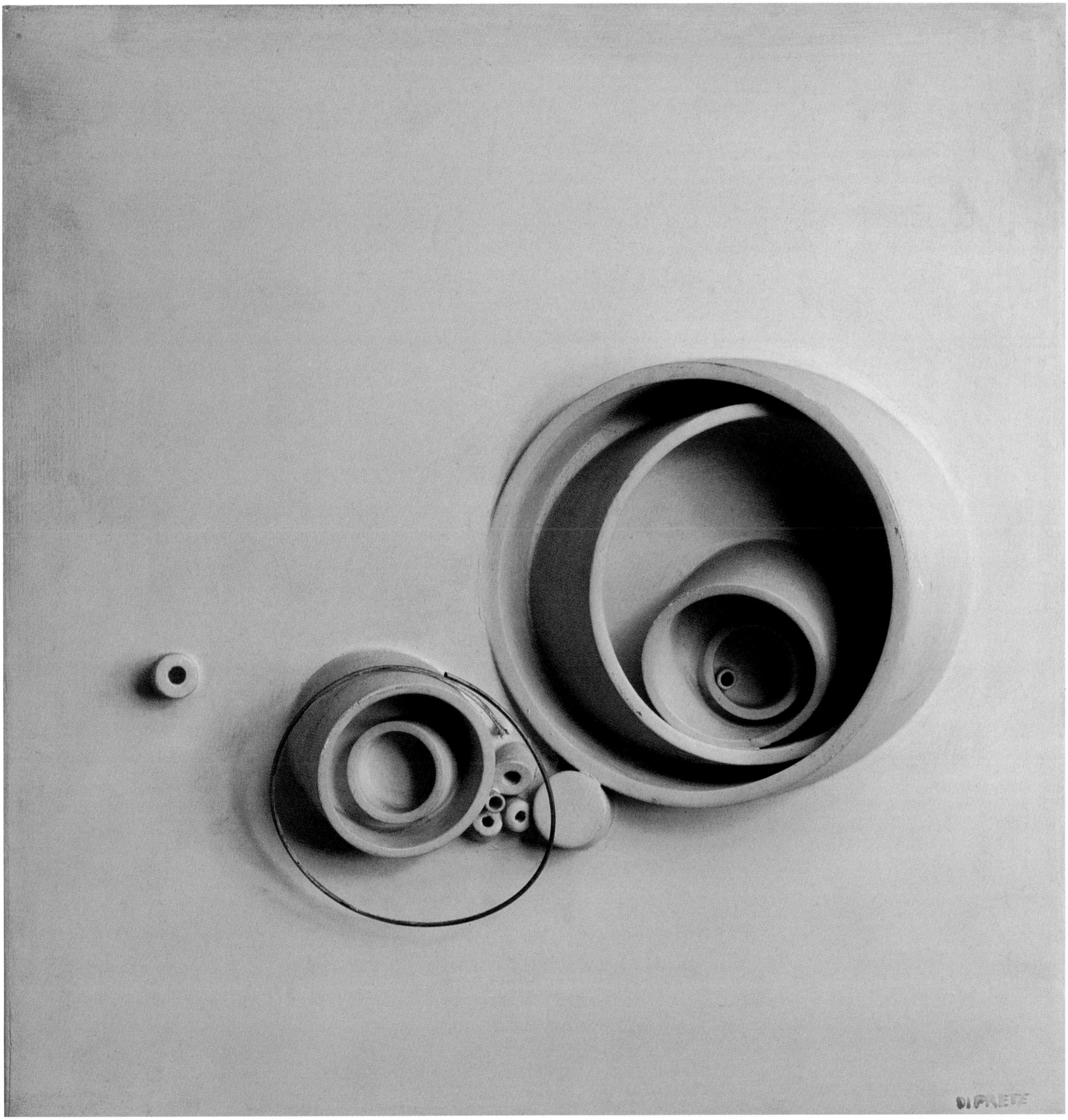
DI PRETE

Milton Dacosta
Em vermelho [*In Red*], 1958
Oil on canvas
28 5/8 x 36 1/8 inches
(72.6 x 91.7 cm)
The Adolpho Leirner Collection
of Brazilian Constructive Art,
museum purchase with funds
provided by the Caroline Wiess
Law Accessions Endowment
Fund
2006.48
PHOTO: Rômulo Fialdini

Mira Schendel
Sem título [*Untitled*], 1954
Mixed media on wood
20 1/8 x 26 inches
(51.1 x 66 cm)
The Adolpho Leirner Collection of Brazilian Constructive Art, museum purchase with funds provided by the Caroline Wiess Law Accessions Endowment Fund
2005.472
PHOTO: Tom Jenkins

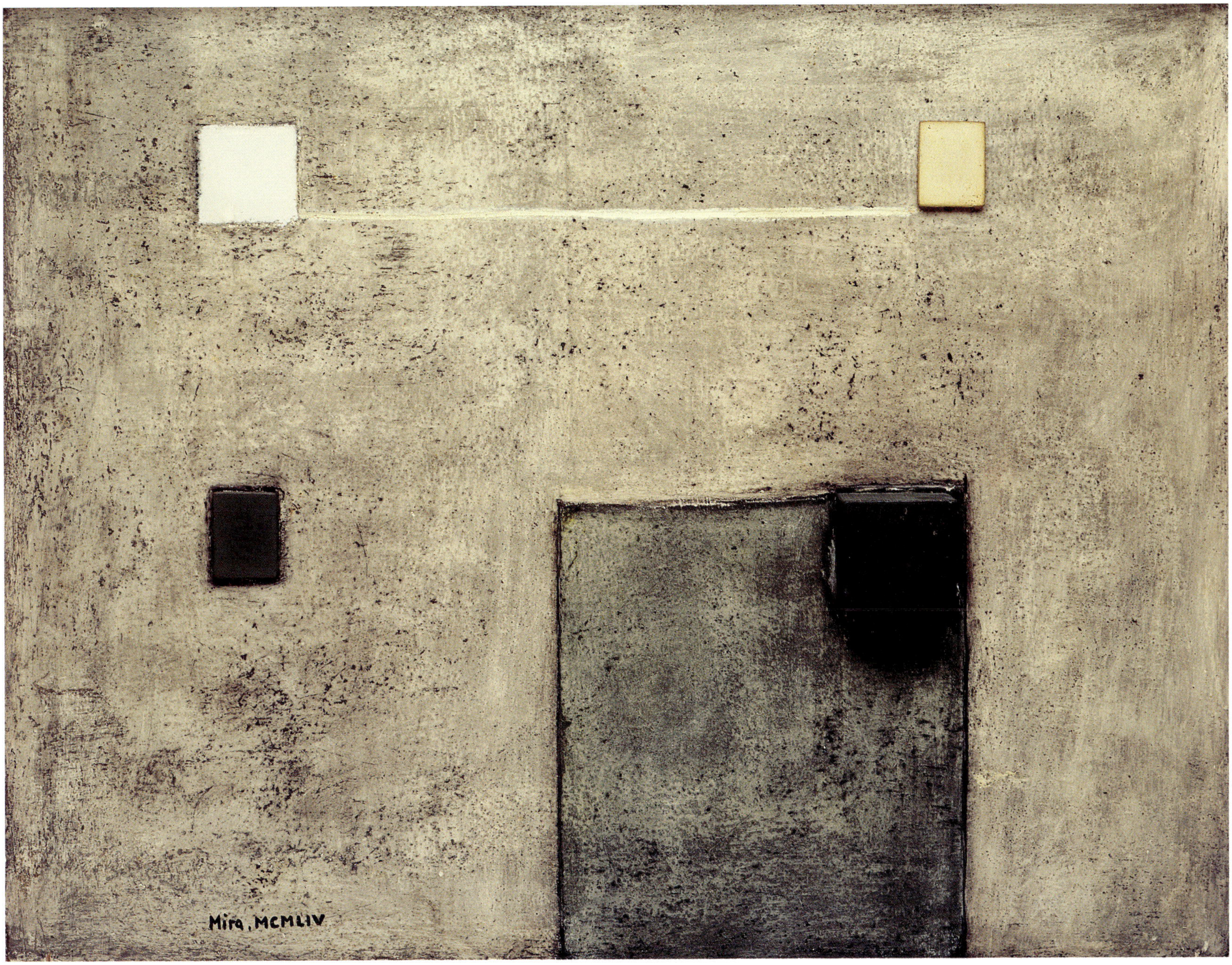
Mira, MCMLIV

Mira Schendel
Sem título [*Untitled*], 1962
Oil on canvas
29 1/2 x 29 3/8 inches
(74.9 x 74.7 cm)
The Adolpho Leirner Collection of Brazilian Constructive Art, museum purchase with funds provided by the Caroline Wiess Law Accessions Endowment Fund
2006.50
PHOTO: Rômulo Fialdini

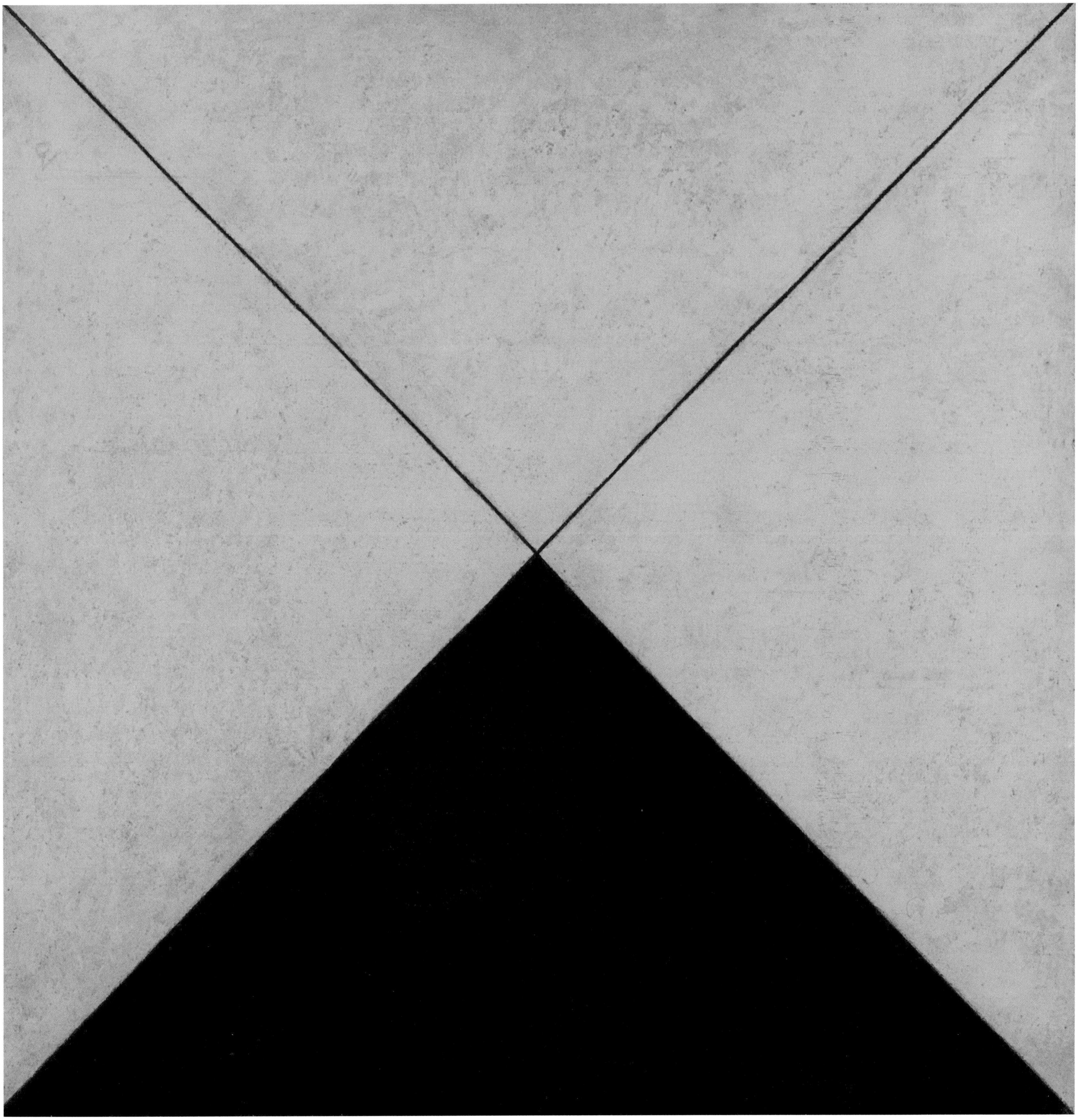

The following works in the Adolpho Leirner Collection of Brazilian Constructive Art are covered by claims to copyright that, as of the time of this publication, were not secured. As a result, these works were not reproduced in the preceding plate section.

Lygia Clark
Bicho (Máquina) [*Critter (Machine)*], 1962
Gilded metal with hinges
21 x 35 1/2 x 21 1/2 inches
(53.3 x 90.2 x 54.6 cm), variable
The Adolpho Leirner Collection of Brazilian Constructive Art, museum purchase with funds provided by the Caroline Wiess Law Accessions Endowment Fund
2005.470

Lygia Clark
Espaço modulado no. 2 [*Modulated Space no. 2*], 1958
Industrial paint on wood
35 3/8 x 11 3/4 inches
(89.9 x 29.8 cm)
The Adolpho Leirner Collection of Brazilian Constructive Art, museum purchase with funds provided by the Caroline Wiess Law Accessions Endowment Fund
2005.1048

Lygia Clark
Ovo [*Egg*], 1959
Industrial paint on wood
13 inches (33 cm) diameter
The Adolpho Leirner Collection of Brazilian Constructive Art, museum purchase with funds provided by the Caroline Wiess Law Accessions Endowment Fund
2007.13

Lygia Clark
Planos em superfície modulada no. 1 [*Planes on Modulated Surface no. 1*], 1957
Industrial paint on wood
34 1/4 x 23 5/8 inches
(87 x 60 cm)
The Adolpho Leirner Collection of Brazilian Constructive Art, museum purchase with funds provided by the Caroline Wiess Law Accessions Endowment Fund
2005.469

Lygia Clark
Planos em superfície modulada no. 5 [*Planes on Modulated Surface no. 5*], 1957
Industrial paint on wood
31 3/8 x 27 9/16 inches
(79.8 x 70 cm)
The Adolpho Leirner Collection of Brazilian Constructive Art, museum purchase with funds provided by the Caroline Wiess Law Accessions Endowment Fund
2007.14

Lygia Clark
Trepante [*Creeper*], 1965
Aluminum and wood
14 1/2 x 16 x 19 inches
(36.8 x 40.6 x 48.3 cm)
The Adolpho Leirner Collection of Brazilian Constructive Art, museum purchase with funds provided by the Caroline Wiess Law Accessions Endowment Fund
2006.47

César Oiticica
Sem título [*Untitled*], 1959
Gouache on cardboard
15 3/8 x 23 1/2 inches
(39.1 x 59.7 cm)
The Adolpho Leirner Collection of Brazilian Constructive Art, gift of the Caroline Wiess Law Foundation
2005.1022

Hélio Oiticica
Metaesquema 12, 1957
Gouache on cardboard
17 5/8 x 21 7/8 inches
(44.7 x 55.6 cm)
The Adolpho Leirner Collection of Brazilian Constructive Art, museum purchase with funds provided by the Caroline Wiess Law Accessions Endowment Fund
2007.19

Hélio Oiticica
Relevo espacial [*Spatial Relief*], c. 1960
Paint on cut-out wood
45 x 45 1/16 x 9 15/16 inches
(114.3 x 114.4 x 25.3 cm)
The Adolpho Leirner Collection of Brazilian Constructive Art, gift of the Caroline Wiess Law Foundation
2005.1023

Hélio Oiticica
Vermelho cortando o branco [*Red Going through White*], 1958
Oil on canvas
20 1/8 x 23 5/8 inches
(51.1 x 59.9 cm)
The Adolpho Leirner Collection of Brazilian Constructive Art, museum purchase with funds provided by the Caroline Wiess Law Accessions Endowment Fund
2007.20
ref.: 171

Alfredo Volpi
Bandeiras [*Flags*], 1960s
Tempera on canvas
28 1/4 x 21 1/4 inches
(71.8 x 54 cm)
The Adolpho Leirner Collection of Brazilian Constructive Art, museum purchase with funds provided by the Caroline Wiess Law Accessions Endowment Fund
2006.51

Alfredo Volpi
Bandeiras verdes sobre rosa [*Green Flags on Pink*], c. 1957
Tempera on canvas
19 11/16 x 28 3/4 inches
(50 x 73 cm)
The Adolpho Leirner Collection of Brazilian Constructive Art, museum purchase with funds provided by the Caroline Wiess Law Accessions Endowment Fund
2005.1039

Alfredo Volpi
Composição [*Composition*], c. 1958
Tempera on canvas
27 9/16 x 27 9/16 inches
(70 x 70 cm)
The Adolpho Leirner Collection of Brazilian Constructive Art, gift of the Caroline Wiess Law Foundation
2005.1035

Alfredo Volpi
Concreto [*Concrete*], 1950s
Tempera on canvas
45 3/4 x 28 7/8 inches
(116.2 x 73.4 cm)
The Adolpho Leirner Collection of Brazilian Constructive Art, gift of the Caroline Wiess Law Foundation
2005.1037

Alfredo Volpi
Estudo para bandeiras [*Study for Flags*], c. 1957
Collage on paper
6 1/4 x 9 3/8 inches
(15.9 x 23.9 cm)
The Adolpho Leirner Collection of Brazilian Constructive Art, museum purchase with funds provided by the Caroline Wiess Law Accessions Endowment Fund
2005.1038

Alfredo Volpi
Sem título [*Untitled*], 1950s
Screenprint
Image: 28 9/16 x 20 3/4 inches
(72.5 x 52.7 cm)
Sheet: 38 3/8 x 27 1/8 inches
(97.5 x 68.9 cm)
The Adolpho Leirner Collection of Brazilian Constructive Art, museum purchase with funds provided by the Caroline Wiess Law Accessions Endowment Fund
2005.1036

Copyright and Reproduction Credits